3/00

THE SABBATICAL MENTOR

D0145032

THE SABBATICAL MENTOR

A Practical Guide to Successful Sabbaticals

Kenneth J. Zahorski
St. Norbert College

ANKER PUBLISHING COMPANY, INC.
Bolton, MA

THE SABBATICAL MENTOR
A Practical Guide to Successful Sabbaticals

ISBN 1–882982–00–2

Composition by Deerfoot Studios.
Cover Design by Deerfoot Studios.

Anker Publishing Company, Inc.
176 Ballville Road
P.O. Box 249
Bolton, MA 01740–0249

DEDICATION

To Marijean, my lodestar

and safe harbor

About the Author

Kenneth J. Zahorski is Professor of English and Director of Faculty Development at St. Norbert College, De Pere, Wisconsin. He received his B.S. (1961) in English from the University of Wisconsin-River Falls, his M.A. (1963) from Arizona State University, and his Ph.D. (1967) from the University of Wisconsin-Madison. He has done post-graduate study at the University of Iowa under a National Endowment for the Humanities Scholarship.

Zahorski was appointed Director of Faculty Development at St. Norbert College in 1984, helping build a holistic Faculty Development Program comprised of over a dozen major components including a resource center, a new faculty orientation and mentor program, a summer grants program, a faculty development newsletter, and a faculty resource inventory. In 1988, Zahorski took a leadership role in creating a statewide faculty development network aimed at providing a vehicle for the sharing of expertise, ideas, and resources among liberal arts institutions. The St. Norbert College program has received national recognition through such works as Green and McDade's *Investing in Higher Education: A Handbook of Leadership Development* and Seldin's *Successful Use of Teaching Portfolios.*

Zahorski is the author of over fifty articles and reviews, and of ten books, one of which received the ALA Outstanding Reference Book Award in 1979. In addition, he has given presentations and led numerous workshops on the sabbatical and other faculty development topics at colleges and universities throughout the U.S. and Canada. He has received both the St. Norbert College Outstanding Teacher of the Year Award and the Donald B. King Distinguished Scholar Award. In 1991 he received the Sears-Roebuck Foundation's Teaching Excellence and Campus Leadership Award. Zahorski currently serves on *The Journal of Staff, Program, and Organization Development* Editorial Board, and in 1991 served as editor of *To Improve the Academy,* published by the Professional and Organizational Development Network in Higher Education.

Contents

Preface

The sabbatical leave is the most cherished of all professional growth opportunities—and it is not difficult to understand why. In a demanding profession which gobbles up our time as relentlessly as Chronus devoured his children, the unencumbered semester or two the sabbatical affords is truly a priceless gift. Perhaps "necessity" is the better word, since most ambitious, scholarly, pedagogical, and artistic projects stand little chance of being launched—let alone of being completed—without the boost of a sabbatical leave. Then, too, many teachers suffering the inevitable fatigue and stress of prolonged life in the academic trenches might succumb to burnout were it not for the rejuvenative potency of the sabbatical.

The concept of the sabbatical is fundamentally important to higher education. Most American universities and colleges either have, or have thought about, initiating sabbatical programs. Yet, for a practice so widespread, so jealously preserved, and so expensive, astonishingly little has been written about this cornerstone of faculty and instructional development, and what has appeared in print typically has taken the form of either data-oriented studies, or of personal reminiscences based upon sabbatical diaries or journals.

The Sabbatical Mentor takes a different tack, offering practical suggestions for making the entire sabbatical experience more productive, satisfying, enriching, and enjoyable. In addition, it aims at reducing the apprehensiveness some might have about applying for a sabbatical by removing the mystery from the application process. While there may be good reasons for not making a sabbatical application, doubt, apprehension, and uncertainty should not be among them.

We all appreciate having a friendly, dependable, and knowledgeable guide when exploring new territory. *The Sabbatical Mentor* is designed to be such a guide, offering helpful information and counsel to all those interested in the sabbatical. Working from the premise that a complex process can be demystified and better understood when broken down into discrete units, *Mentor* divides the sabbatical into five distinct stages: (1) pre-proposal reflection and planning; 2) the application process; (3) pre-sabbatical preparation; (4) the leave period; and (5) reentry and follow-through. The *Mentor* offers concrete and practical suggestions for moving through each stage with comfort and confidence.

The Sabbatical Mentor, then, is intended to offer guidance in an area where faculty seldom receive it. But its scope embraces other audiences as well. *Mentor* also speaks to chief academic administrators, providing specific strategies they can use to support, promote, administer, and evaluate leave programs. In addition, it should prove helpful to departmental and divisional chairs hoping to use the leave as a tool for faculty development while maintaining the integrity of curricular programs. Further, part of the text is aimed at faculty development agents, offering them some practical suggestions for making the sabbatical an even more effective vehicle for professional growth. Finally, much of what the *Mentor* says about the sabbatical in higher education also will be applicable to those in secondary education and the corporate world, where sabbatical systems of various types are becoming more commonplace.

My information about, and suggestions for enhancing, the sabbatical derive from a wide variety of personal and professional experiences, from key in-house and off-campus sources, and from intensive research. To begin with, during my twenty-five year college teaching career I have had the privilege of taking two sabbatical leaves; thus, I have personally explored the territory covered in this guide. Secondly, during my tenure on the St. Norbert College Faculty Personnel Committee I read, discussed, and evaluated many sabbatical proposals. Thirdly, as Director of Faculty Development I have helped dozens of colleagues through every stage of the sabbatical process—invariably learning as much from these pleasant experiences as my colleagues did from me. Further, my role as Director has helped me better understand how the sabbatical complements all the other threads in the broad tapestry of a holistic faculty development program. And, finally, I have done extensive research on the sabbatical: searching, collecting, and reading the literature; conducting interviews with faculty development directors throughout the nation; soliciting sabbatical policy statements and guidelines from chief academic officers at scores of colleges and universities; studying faculty responses to questionnaires I, and other researchers, have administered on the sabbatical experience; and reading hundreds of sabbatical proposals. Into this pool I cast down my bucket for the information contained in the following pages.

My hope is that all readers find something useful in *The Sabbatical Mentor.* My own experience has been that no matter how many times one goes through a rather complicated process, like that of planning and applying for a sabbatical, there is always something new to learn. At the very least, there is always something of which we need reminding, for the memory betrays us with frustrating regularity. Thus, even though the *Mentor* will probably be of greatest value to those new to the application process, sabbatical veterans should also find most of the sections helpful. To those familiar with some of the terrain described herein, I extend the same invitation Chaucer proffers in his *Canterbury Tales*— simply "turn over the page and choose another."

Kenneth J. Zahorski

ACKNOWLEDGMENTS

I could not have completed this project without the help of many kind and generous people from both within and without the St. Norbert College academic community. My sincere thanks to Bob Horn, Dean of the College, for his support and encouragement; to St. Norbert College research assistants Molly Michels, Karie Kazik, and Kimber Wendland—Molly for helping me get the project started, and Karie and Kimber for helping me bring it to closure; to Chris Utech and Alice Beard for sharing their secretarial expertise with unflagging congeniality; to Vivian Foss of the Institutional Advancement Office for guiding me through the bewildering realm of grant seeking and grant writing resources; to all my colleagues who filled out the Sabbatical Questionnaire, graciously submitted to my interviews, and contributed materials to *The Sabbatical Mentor*; and special thanks to Bob Boyer, Jim Hodgson, and Elizabeth King, for sharing ideas on the role of the division chair in the sabbatical process.

Thanks must also go to all those outside the college who contributed information and materials: Richard Abrams, Marquette University; Sally Atkins, Appalachian State University; Robert Boice, SUNY-Stony Brook; Kathleen T. Brinko, Appalachian State University; William E. Cashin, Kansas State University; Jonathan Collett, SUNY College at Westbury; Dan Cornfield, Vanderbilt University; David Deal, Whitman College; Robert M. Diamond, Syracuse University; Nancy A. Diamond, University of Illinois; Joan F. Dinan, Marquette University; James Eison, University of South Florida; Glenn R. Erickson, University of Rhode Island; Thomas Franklin, University of Wisconsin-Stout; Peter Frederick, Carleton College; Glenn Ross Johnson, Texas A&M University; Kenneth Klein, Valparaiso Univeristy; Karron G. Lewis, University of Texas-Austin; Janet Malone, University of Wisconsin-Stevens Point; Linda Milson, Marquette University; Linda B. Nilson, Vanderbilt University; Deborah Olsen, Indiana University; William L. Perry, Texas A&M University; Daniel R. Rice, University of North Dakota; Robert Rohm, University of Rhode Island; Leane Rutherford, University of Minnesota-Duluth; Peter Seldin, Pace University; Edwin L. Simpson, Northern Illinois University; Spelios Stamas, Ithaca College; Harold Taylor, Time Consultants, Inc.; Thomas Trebon, Sacred Heart University; Daniel W. Wheeler, University of Nebraska-Lincoln; Deborah Du Nann Winter, Whitman College; John Winter, Whitman College; and Brother John Wozniak, Clarke College. I also wish to acknowledge a special debt of gratitude to Victor J. Larson, Information Specialist, Office of Research and Sponsored Programs at University of Wisconsin-Milwaukee, for the generous assistance he gave me in compiling the lists of grant seeking and grant writing resources found in Appendix D.

Dr. Thomas Franklin once said, "the heaviest debt is that of gratitude when 'tis not in our power to repay it." While it may not be in my power to repay all the generous and good folk who helped bring this undertaking to fruition, I can at least express my heartfelt gratitude.

INTRODUCTION

1

The Sabbatical Leave:
An Overview

Every seven years faculty need to be repotted.
John Gardner

Professor Evans simply could not wait to reach his classroom. He hadn't felt so much energy and enthusiasm for a long, long time, and each day he genuinely looked forward to being with his students. "Come to think of it," he mused, walking briskly down the sunlit corridor, "I haven't had so much get-up-and-go since graduate school." Even the students had noticed his newfound dynamism, reflecting Evans' own enthusiasm through their alert questioning and lively discussions. Evans grinned as he moved into earshot of the cheerful buzz of students chatting in his classroom; it was still five minutes until the bell and all but one or two students enrolled in his Shakespearean Drama class were in their seats and eager to begin. He chuckled softly: "I guess things must be going well this semester. Seven fifty-five a.m., and everyone seems wide awake and raring to go. Wonder of wonders!"

Evans had prepared for his students a special treat: a slide presentation featuring some of the hundreds of photographs he had taken during his recent year-long sojourn in Stratford-upon-Avon: Anne Hathaway's charming thatched-roof cottage, the King Edward VI Grammar School where Shakespeare had learned his Greek and Latin, the lovely Church of the Holy Trinity where the Bard had been baptized and buried. It would be great fun sharing with his students what he had seen and learned.

Smiling mischievously, Evans began his class by promising not to become unbearably rhapsodic while commenting on the slides. Later, he planned to share insights about Shakespeare's poetic style gleaned from his close study of manuscripts at the British Museum. Why, he might even try some of the interactive classroom techniques he had always thought about using, but had never had the energy, or self-confidence, to employ. The time seemed right now to do what he had perennially put off for more years than he cared to remember.

Professor Evans remembered hearing from colleagues how the sabbatical leave had reenergized their personal and professional lives, but he had thought their glowing reports exaggerated. His own leave expectations had been modest. He had intended to pursue some long-delayed research—no more, no less. Little had he known his year's leave in England studying the life and works of Shakespeare would work such magic. He was already looking forward to his next sabbatical.

The scene just described is fictional, but grounded in fact. In thousands of colleges and universities throughout the nation, reinvigorated instructors return from extended leaves bringing with them fresh energy, new perspectives, and renewed self-confidence. They return to their students and colleagues with a new lease on both their professional and personal lives. They return having learned firsthand that the sabbatical leave is a remarkably potent antidote to stagnation, burnout, and mediocrity. And they return prepared to contribute even more mightily to their academic communities.

The Sabbatical Mentor is a book about the sabbatical leave. Forming its infrastructure are five basic premises: (1) the sabbatical constitutes one of academia's most important vehicles for professional renewal and development; (2) although well-established and cherished, sabbatical programs need careful monitoring and regular nurturing; (3) despite the intrinsic attractiveness of sabbatical leaves, faculty neither automatically apply for, nor always take full advantage of, them; (4) maintaining a dynamic sabbatical program requires a team effort, with both administrators and faculty working together to ensure a program's efficiency and productivity; and (5) while the sabbatical is rightly viewed as a vehicle for faculty development, its benefits extend beyond the faculty recipient to students and the institution as a whole.

The *Mentor* casts a broad net. Faculty will find plenty of practical advice on how to capitalize on the tremendous potential of the sabbatical leave; departmental and divisional chairs will find suggestions on how to use their positions to help faculty grow through extended leaves; deans, provosts, and presidents will be invited to reexamine their roles as stewards of sabbatical programs; and faculty development personnel will find a chapter delineating their role in the process. In short, while this text tries to be specific in its suggestions and recommendations, it attempts to be holistic in approach, placing the sabbatical in a broad institutional context and demonstrating how the entire academic community benefits from the restorative potency of the sabbatical leave.

DEFINITION

But what exactly is a "sabbatical leave"? Like so many popular terms, "sabbatical" sometimes means different things to different people. Toomey and Connor (1988), for example, write that "the term sabbatical means a break or change from normal routine" (p. 81), and Hayward M. Daugherty, Jr. (1979) defines the sabbatical as "a leave with pay which might be available to a faculty member or administrator" (p. 5). More specific is Carter V. Good's (1959) oft-quoted working definition: "[The sabbatical is] a plan for providing teachers with an opportunity for self-improvement through a leave of absence with full or partial compensation following a designated number of years of consecutive service (originally after six years)" (p. 424).

Good's definition is particularly useful in that it identifies the three defining elements that help us distinguish a sabbatical from other kinds of extended leaves of absence. First, the sabbatical has a clearly-defined *purpose* of providing opportunities for self-improvement; second, the sabbatical is a *paid leave*, with the awarding of full or partial salary a vital part of the arrangement between faculty and institution; and third, the prime determinant of eligibility is a designated period of *prior service* (usually six years). At least two other distinguishing traits need mentioning: most sabbatical policy statements also stipulate (1) a required return to service and (2) the filing of a sabbatical report. Add these to Carter's common-denominator features and we have a practicable working definition that will serve as a solid launching pad for our exploration of the realm of the sabbatical.

ORIGIN OF THE TERM

The concept of a sabbatical year has a long and colorful history laced with mythological and religious significance. As far back as the first century A.D., Pliny the Elder, in Book 31 of his *Natural History*, recounts a fascinating Jewish legend featuring an "ancient river in Media named Sabbation, which flowed for six days, but rested the seventh" (Eells and Hollis, 1962, p. 5). And in the Book of Leviticus (25: 1–4, Authorized King James Version) we hear God directing the Israelites to observe a "sabbath unto the Lord" by resting their land every seventh year, neither sowing their fields nor pruning their vineyards.

From this notion of resting on the seventh year for the purpose of rejuvenation and restoration the sabbatical takes both its current popular meaning and its mystique. A concept arising from such an abundant wellspring of mythical and religious origins is likely to assume an aura of attitudes, feelings, and associations reflecting those origins. Bruce A. Kimball (1978) is one of many commentators reflecting this historical influence, explaining that "it is these spiritual and intellectual needs which the sabbatical attempts to meet by providing—as the Sabbath has for centuries—the time for rest and renewal of the individual, a time to ask 'Who are we?' and 'Why does our work have meaning?'" (p. 313). The sabbatical, then, has come to be seen as supplying not only intellectual renewal, but spiritual and physical regeneration as well. In short, the concept of the sabbatical comes to us enveloped in a values-rich context, a context interwoven with rich religious and mythic threads.

BRIEF HISTORY OF THE SABBATICAL LEAVE

The "first definite system of sabbatical leave" can be traced to Harvard University (Eells, 1962) when in 1880 President Charles W. Eliot used the promise of every seventh year off to lure the noted philologist, Charles Lanman, from Johns Hopkins University to Harvard. Two other Eastern institutions, Cornell and Wellesley, followed Harvard's lead in the mid 1880s, and before the turn of the century seven more colleges and universities offered sabbatical leaves: Columbia, Brown, Amherst, Dartmouth, Stanford, and the Universities of California and Illinois. Thus, at least ten institutions of higher learning boasted sabbatical systems at the close of the nineteenth century.

The twentieth century witnessed significant growth of the concept. During its first two decades, forty other institutions joined the ranks of the nineteenth-century pioneers, bringing to fifty the number of institutions nurturing newly-inaugurated sabbatical systems (Eells). The sabbatical's popularity revealed itself not only in burgeoning numbers, but also through the attention it began receiving in the professional literature. In 1913, for instance, Monroe's *Cyclopedia of Education* featured a substantive article on the sabbatical leave, and in the twenty-year period following that notice three national organizations—the National Research Council, the Association of American Colleges, and the American Association of University Professors—sponsored and published the results of "detailed studies" of the sabbatical (Eells).

The spread of sabbatical systems slackened somewhat after 1920. Woodburne (1950) chronicles a slow but steady growth until World War II, when "leaves to provide free time were put aside as a luxury" (p. 132), primarily because of acute staff shortages suffered during the War years. In fact, the effects of tight budgets and overstretched staffs were felt for some years after the War. Administrators were slow to reinstate their sabbatical programs not only because of "continued pressure on the physical and intellectual resources" of their institutions, but also because of a perceived abuse of a system which had often granted leaves in too "automatic" a manner (p. 135).

When Walter Eells and Ernest Hollis conducted their national study of the sabbatical in 1962, they identified only 72 sabbatical programs. Since then, however, the numbers have increased dramatically, with a majority of U.S. colleges and universities now boasting sabbatical programs of one type or another. Hayward M. Daugherty (1979) in his study of 467 randomly selected two- and four-year institutions, found that 73.3% offered sabbatical leaves—up nearly 10% from the 64.2% reported by Thompson and Eberle in 1972. In their major national study of 1981, Anderson and Atelsek (1982) reported that nearly all universities had sabbatical systems, 84% of all four-year colleges had them, and 60% of all two-year colleges had instituted them. In other words, of the approximately 3,400 private and public two- and four-year institutions in the United States (*Digest of Education Statistics*, 1992), roughly 2,500 of them offer some type of sabbatical program—thirty-four times as many as in 1962.

However, even though most institutions have some type of sabbatical or extended leave program, the situation varies widely throughout the nation. Some state university systems like Wisconsin's and Pennsylvania's, for example, have strong, well-defined sabbatical programs, while those in North Carolina and Texas have no provision for traditional "sabbatical" leaves. Indeed, in some states it is illegal for public institutions to grant sabbatical leaves, while in others sabbatical leaves are either heartily encouraged or made compulsory.

The situation also seems to differ from region to region. Hugh Stickler's (1965) survey of major institutions of higher learning, for example, reveals that in five of six regions studied, about three-quarters or more of the schools offered sabbaticals, but in the region served by the Southern Association of Colleges and Schools only two institutions out of every five (39.1%) had sabbatical programs (p. 52). While no major study has been done to determine the reasons for these regional differences, we do encounter some interesting speculation in the sabbatical literature. Why, for instance, during the early years of the twentieth century were so many of the pioneering sabbatical programs found in public institutions of the Western region (e.g., University of Arizona, Montana State University, University of Wyoming, Utah State University, North Dakota State University, and the University of Utah)? In Appendix II of the Eels and Hollis report (1962) the University of Arizona's (then) President Babcock offers an explanation, through extension, pointing out that "the isolation of the University [of Arizona] both in distance and in expenses of travelling to centers of inspiring instruction and investigation made all the more significant the adoption of the principle that a [teacher] may expect…a leave of absence every seventh or eighth year…."

SABBATICAL LEAVE POLICIES AND PRACTICES

As might be expected, sabbatical leave policies and practices vary considerably from institution to institution. However, a study of the institutional literature reveals a number of common traits. The following profile is based upon the findings of the most significant sabbatical studies of the past thirty years (Stickler, 1958; Eells and Hollis, 1962; Ingraham and King, 1965; Eberle and Thompson, 1973; Daugherty, 1979; Anderson and Atelsek, 1982; Marker,

1983; and Franklin, 1993) along with the author's own informal five-year study of over 100 U.S. colleges and universities.

Purpose

Institutional sabbatical policy statements regularly identify the following four purposes of the sabbatical leave: (1) to provide opportunity for scholarly enrichment; (2) to improve teaching; (3) to promote course and curriculum development; and (4) to enhance artistic performance and creative growth. In sum, the overarching function of the sabbatical leave is to stimulate a faculty member's professional, personal, and intellectual growth. Further, most institutions insist on a mutuality of purpose, stating that the sabbatical leave project must show promise of benefitting *both* applicant and institution.

While most of these defining purposes have been a part of the sabbatical landscape for nearly a century, the terrain keeps changing. For example, in 1965, when Ingraham and King conducted their monumental study of 745 institutions of higher learning, they found that the "most frequent reason for leaves from most colleges [was] advanced graduate work often aimed at the attainment of the doctorate" (p. 72). Daugherty's (1979) study fourteen years later revealed that 74.2% of all institutions surveyed were still granting sabbaticals for the purpose of pursuing higher degrees. However, in the intervening years this situation has changed significantly, with many institutions now actually prohibiting the use of sabbatical leaves for graduate work.

Eligibility

Almost all colleges and universities require faculty to serve six years before becoming eligible for a sabbatical leave. In addition, most policies stipulate that candidates must be tenured and have attained the rank of assistant professor or higher. However, in a small, but growing, number of institutions faculty with the rank of instructor are also eligible to apply for sabbaticals. Further, during the past decade or so, some colleges and universities have begun offering the sabbatical opportunity to untenured junior faculty with as little as two to three years of service to the institution. This is a significant trend well worth watching.

Application and selection policies and procedures

For approximately the first half-century of the sabbatical's existence, faculty and administrators commonly viewed it as a faculty entitlement or right. Since World War II, however, there seems to have been an opposite trend, with the sabbatical being viewed not so much as a right but as a privilege, not so much an entitlement granted automatically as an award made on the basis of comparative merit. Most institutions now require sabbatical applicants to submit detailed proposals which are then carefully screened either by designated academic officers (often departmental chairs or academic deans) or by peer review committees. In their study, Anderson and Atelsek (1982) reported that nearly half the institutions offering sabbaticals awarded them competitively, and another third "semiautomatically."

While few institutions seem to employ actual "quota systems," many do set some limit on the number of sabbaticals awarded in a given year. These limits vary, but the general range seems to be from no set percentage to about six percent permitted on leave per year, with the average range from three to five percent (Cardozier, 1987). The most common reasons for imposing such limits appear to be financial constraints, staffing problems, and concern about maintaining the integrity of academic programs.

Compensation

By far the most common salary arrangement for sabbatical leave is half salary for a full year, or full salary for a half year. However, many institutions offer sabbatical recipients a variety of salary options. Some schools, for example, allow faculty to use as a leave period two consecutive summer sessions at full pay; others invite applicants to apply for in-house grants as a way of supplementing a full year's leave at half pay.

While most institutions encourage faculty to seek outside funding, few encourage remunerative employment. In fact, "many policies explicitly forbid a faculty member from engaging in gainful employment while on sabbatical leave" (Marker, 1983, p. 41). Even part-time teaching is discouraged unless it demonstrably helps the sabbatical recipient fulfill project goals. Limited employment may be possible under some systems, but usually only upon approval of the appropriate academic officer. In the case of outside funding, most institutions stipulate that the amount of a grant allocated to salary plus the amount of leave salary should not, in total, exceed the recipient's normal salary for the period of the sabbatical. Faculty are expected to return to the institution the amount in excess of the baseline salary.

In most cases, fringe benefits are unaffected by a sabbatical leave, with the individual and institution maintaining their schedule of contributions toward retirement, social security, and the broad spectrum of group insurance policies. A few institutions offer only a percentage of the amount normally contributed to benefit packages, but these exceptions appear to be rather rare.

Individual obligations

Although sabbatical policy statements contain a wide variety of specific faculty obligations, the following three appear most often in official institutional publications:

1. Sabbatical recipients must make every reasonable effort to fulfill the terms of the sabbatical agreement.

2. Recipients must return to the institution after leave for one to three years of service. Most frequently this is an explicitly stated contractual agreement,

but sometimes it is more of an implicit "moral obligation" (Ingraham & King, 1965). Faculty members failing to meet this requirement are usually required to pay back the salary received during the leave, or at least some specified percentage thereof.

3. And, finally, upon returning from leave recipients must submit a formal written report to a designated academic officer, or to the sabbatical review committee. This report, summarizing the activities and accomplishments of the recipient, is sometimes made available to the entire faculty, and in some institutions is even used in promotion and salary considerations. A growing number of schools also expect recipients to give public presentations reflecting the accomplishments, and challenges, of the leave.

In some institutions, the individual is also expected to help make staff "coverage" arrangements, with the understanding that the replacements will come from within the department rather than from outside the institution.

Institutional obligations

The most common institutional strictures and obligations have been identified already through the preceding overview of sabbatical leave policies and practices. Most sabbatical policies mention the following two institutional obligations: (1) the institution will allow sabbatical leave periods to count towards eligibility for promotion and tenure; and (2) the institution will maintain full fringe benefits for sabbatical leave recipients.

CONCLUSION

While there are many similarities in the way sabbatical systems are administered in U.S. colleges and universities, there is considerable variance in the shape of individual programs and even in the types and numbers of programs in particular regions. Further, the way sabbaticals are viewed and awarded also vary considerably. In some cases, sabbaticals are automatically granted to eligible faculty; in others, there is a largely proforma application process; and in still others the awards are highly competitive. Eberle and Thompson (1972) point out that sabbatical programs seem related to institutional age and to tradition in higher education, that "their availability appears to fluctuate in terms of faculty supply and demand and institutional finances" (p. 6), and that the percentage of institutions granting leaves rises steadily as enrollments increase (i.e., the larger the school, the more likelihood of a sabbatical program).

Something a bit troubling about the national picture is that while many schools tout the existence of sabbatical programs, not all back the programs with adequate financial resources. Then, too, in some institutions the major source of funds to cover the replacement costs of sabbatical recipients is the amount of salary dollars released by faculty on full-year leaves at half salary.

Thus, the fate of faculty who apply for one-semester sabbatical leaves at full pay is often determined by how many of their colleagues can afford to take off a full year on half salary. Clearly this is not an ideal situation. Further, in the mid-1960s Ingraham and King (1965) reported that "in some institutions over 75% [of the faculty did] not take leaves when they [were] eligible" (p. 77), a dismally low percentage more recently confirmed by Franklin (1993) in a statewide study of Wisconsin system institutions.

In short, the sabbatical landscape is varied and fascinating. More of its terrain will be explored in the ensuing chapters. But let us first concentrate on how faculty can best make use of this most important of professional development opportunities.

Works Cited

Anderson, C., & Atelsek, F. (1982). *Sabbatical and research leaves in colleges and universities* (Higher Education Panel Report No. 53). Washington, DC: American Council on Education.

Cardozier, V.R. (1987). *American higher education.* Brookfield, VT: Avebury.

Daugherty, H., Jr. (1979). *Sabbatical leaves in higher education, 1979.* Unpublished doctoral dissertation, Indiana University, Bloomington, IN.

Digest of education statistics (1992). Washington, DC: National Center for Educational Statistics.

Eberle, A., & Thompson, R. (1972). *Sabbatical leaves in higher education.* Bloomington, IN: Indiana University Student Association of Higher Education.

Eells, W.C. (1962). The origin and early history of sabbatical leave. *AAUP Bulletin, 48,* 253–255.

Eells, W.C., & Hollis, E. (1962). *Sabbatical leave in higher education: Origin, early history, and current practices* (Bulletin No. 17). Washington, DC: U.S. Office of Education.

Franklin, T. (1993). Planning successful sabbaticals. *The Department Chair,* Spring, 8–9.

Good, C. (Ed.). (1959). *Dictionary of education. (3rd ed.).* New York, NY: McGraw-Hill.

Ingraham, M., & King, F. (1965). *The outer fringe: Faculty benefits other than annuities and insurance.* Madison, WI: University of Wisconsin Press.

Kimball, B. (1978). The origin of the sabbath and its legacy to the modern sabbatical. *Journal of Higher Education, 49*(4), 303–315.

Marker, D. (1983). Faculty Leaves. In J.W. Fuller (Ed.), *Issues in faculty personnel policies*, 11, 37–46, New Directions for Higher Education. San Francisco, CA: Jossey-Bass.

Stickler, W.H. (1958). Sabbatical leave in the state universities and land-grant institutions 1957–58. *Higher Education*, 14, 118–119.

Toomey, E., & Connor, J. (1988). Employee sabbaticals: Who benefits and why? *Personnel*, 65,81-84.

Woodburne, L. (1950). *Faculty personnel policies in higher education.* New York, NY: Harper & Brothers.

THE FIVE STAGES
OF THE SABBATICAL
EXPERIENCE

Overview

At first glance, it seems futile to attempt breaking down into stages something as complex as the sabbatical enterprise. To begin with, trying to divide any organic process into discrete units is difficult. Furthermore, each sabbatical's uniqueness dictates its own particular emphases and timetable. Nonetheless, conversations with sabbatical veterans reveal they have undergone strikingly similar experiences, have followed similar timetables, and have moved through similar sequential patterns. These patterns provide evidence of five distinct stages in the sabbatical enterprise.

1. Pre-application reflection and planning

2. The application process

3. Pre-sabbatical preparation

4. The leave period

5. Reentry and follow-through

While it may be possible to have a satisfactory leave experience without expending much time and energy preparing for it, empirical evidence indicates that truly enriching and productive sabbaticals result from careful thought and planning. Further, the planning process appears to be significantly strengthened when faculty see the leave period not simply as an amorphous whole, but rather as a series of discrete, but integrally related stages. Each stage plays its own unique role in the sabbatical enterprise. This section looks closely at each of them, offering observations and suggestions along the way.

2

Pre-Application
Reflection and Planning

Invaluable is the perspective gained when for a short time one can substitute distance and reflection for active involvement and instant response.

Marianne G. Riely

At least a year, preferably two, in advance of making your application, set aside some time for seriously thinking about a sabbatical leave and how it might fit into your professional and personal life. Snatching a few minutes here and there will not suffice. Instead, you must build planning and reflection sessions into your weekly schedule, making sure these quiet periods are long enough (at least an hour) for you to move into a genuinely reflective mode. Reviewing your professional career and personal priorities is no small task. The process demands ample time, a clear head, and honesty. Don't give it short shrift. Surveys conducted with sabbatical recipients (e.g., Jarecky and Sandifer, 1986) reveal that presabbatical planning is the key to a productive and satisfying leave. A candid appraisal will not only help you make the right decisions in regard to your sabbatical, but will also provide you with a rare opportunity for getting to know yourself better.

Successful sabbaticals rest on solid foundations. The following activities constitute the primary building blocks of a strong and durable foundation for your sabbatical.

CLARIFYING GOALS AND OBJECTIVES

Deciding whether to apply for a sabbatical is serious business. A leave, whether for a semester or year, can profoundly affect you and those around you. Departmental peers, students, academic administrators, and family members will feel the consequences of your decision. Your own professional and personal life will never be the same.

Begin this important decision-making process by thoughtfully reexamining your personal and professional goals and objectives. But be sure to ask yourself tough questions that will generate genuine introspection:

- Is this the right time for me to take a sabbatical? Will it help me carry through, or will it interrupt, an important ongoing teaching, scholarly, or administrative project?

- Are there any personal, financial, or family matters that may prevent me from carrying out my sabbatical plans?

- What do I really hope to gain from the sabbatical experience? How will it promote my growth as a teacher? a scholar? a collegial citizen? a human being?

- How does a sabbatical fit into my short- and long-term career goals and objectives? My short- and long-term personal goals and objectives?

- What kind of project will best help me achieve my goals?

- Have I been trying to avoid applying for a sabbatical? If so, why?

The first step, then, is to make your sabbatical decision in the context of *both* your career and personal goals. A caveat: Don't rely upon your memory as a storehouse for your musings and reflective conclusions. Rather, keep a journal record of your thoughts and reflections. Heed the old Chinese proverb: *The palest ink is better than the most retentive memory.*

DEFINING YOUR PROJECT

In some cases, a topic already born and nurtured will serve as motivation for a sabbatical application. In others, notice of eligibility may prompt a search for suitable sabbatical topics. No matter what the genesis, now is the time to explore the terrain and set the boundaries of your project. It takes months to design a solid research, artistic, or pedagogical project. Begin the task by asking yourself the following questions:

1. *Am I choosing a topic that truly interests me?* A sabbatical proposal should reflect a sincere interest in, ideally even a passion about, a subject. Choose a project that genuinely challenges and engages you. Don't do what you think you should do, and don't let others set your agenda. Rather, pick a topic

that will stretch your intellectual horizons and foster professional growth. Further, be bold and willing to take some risks. Now is the time to transform your dream project into reality.

2. *Am I choosing a project that warrants a sabbatical leave?* Ask yourself the following three questions when trying to determine if the scope of your proposed sabbatical project is sufficiently grand to justify a sabbatical leave: (a) Could I complete my project without the large block of uninterrupted time offered by a sabbatical leave? (b) Could I carry out my proposed sabbatical project while concomitantly discharging my usual faculty responsibilities? (c) Could I accomplish what I propose by simply working harder or by managing my time better during the course of a regular academic year? If the answer is yes to any of these questions you may not have chosen a topic of sufficient scope to justify a sabbatical leave.

   Just as important as choosing a project of adequate scope and depth, however, is choosing one that is achievable during the proposed time frame. Members of review committees are rightly suspicious of overly-ambitious proposals. You must seek the *via media*: a project of considerable scope, but one possible to complete in the time allotted. Seek counsel from colleagues in trying to find this balance. An outside reader may be able to spot potential difficulties you may miss because of your closeness to the project. Sabbatical veterans who have undertaken similar projects are particularly helpful guides.

3. *Am I choosing a topic that will promote my personal and professional growth at this stage of my career?* Let Hamlet's dictum, "readiness is all," serve as your guide. The question of *fit* and *timing* are of vital importance. Some projects work better in certain phases of your professional career. Teaching-enhancement projects may be more important than research, for example, when your classroom performance is in the doldrums. On the other hand, a retooling leave may be in order if you are a member of a rapidly-changing field (e.g., biotechnology, aeronautical engineering, computer science, chemistry) and you feel that your knowledge base, skills, and techniques need updating. Or, perhaps your own academic community seems to be losing some of its color and excitement and you feel that spending some time in a new academic culture will provide a refreshing change of scene. Only you can determine what is best for you, so spend plenty of time carefully analyzing your needs.

DETERMINING FEASIBILITY

Once you have decided to apply for a sabbatical, conduct a feasibility study. Avoid the sharp disappointment of beginning work on a proposal only to discover later that irresolvable conflicts will make it impossible for you to apply. The following steps should help you determine the feasibility of your plan.

Step One: Meet with your departmental or divisional chair.

Set up an appointment with your departmental or divisional chair to discuss your sabbatical plans. Your chair knows better than anyone your department's staffing and programmatic needs, and thus will be able to point out potential difficulties resulting from your absence. Further, if more than one departmental member intends to apply for a sabbatical in a given year, the chair will be the key to solving the logistical problems. Similarly, if replacement staff must be recruited, your chair will be central to the process. Finally, because the chair is familiar with your teaching and research aspirations, he/she will be able to provide helpful guidance.

Step Two: Meet with departmental colleagues.

Next, discuss your sabbatical plans with departmental colleagues. This will be a crucial meeting, since staffing needs are almost always a key to feasibility. Indeed, you will probably need your colleagues' help in covering courses during your absence. But your colleagues can also help in other ways. Because of their expertise in your discipline, for example, they may be able to offer considerable help in exploring and refining your topic. Invite and take full advantage of their counsel.

These initial discussions with your departmental colleagues are very important. Bring your colleagues into the process early and take the time to explore the possible effects of your absence from the department. As James B. Reuler (1989) points out, clear and open communication is of the utmost importance:

> Because most academic units don't have financial resources available to hire a replacement faculty member, many of the responsibilities of the departing member must be borne by those remaining. Being saddled with additional work can breed resentment in colleagues who perceive that their abilities to be productive academically are already severely impaired by an unreasonable work load. Therefore, open communication and planning are important for maintenance of esprit de corps,...(p. 409).

Back communication with deeds. For example, make a list of your ongoing departmental responsibilities and then try to complete as many as possible before you leave. Further, if your chair must find a temporary replacement for you, offer to aid in the search and to help train your replacement. In a large research university you might be able to find a graduate teaching assistant with the requisite expertise and skills to serve as a temporary replacement.

Further, you might explore the possibility of a faculty exchange arrangement. Later in this chapter you will find information about the National Faculty

Exchange, the Clearinghouse for International Faculty & Staff Exchange, and the Faculty Exchange Center. Each of these organizations provides access to a pool of individuals for short-term hiring needs. In addition, you might want to look into the Academic Resource Network's Emeriti Placement Program, which provides access to retired higher education professionals for institutions with short-term or emergency personnel needs.

Finally, try to identify potential problems resulting from your leave and do your best to provide solutions for them. In short, make your planning a team project and try to build a foundation of support within your own department. But most importantly, do your fair share in solving logistical problems. One final caution: remember that despite your best efforts and the quality of your plan, external factors—especially staffing factors—may require you to defer your application until a later date. Preparing yourself psychologically for the possibility of such temporary delays may save you from undue disappointment.

Step Three: Conduct a preliminary study of your budgetary needs.

Some projects, especially those involving travel abroad, can be quite expensive. Now is the time to determine just how financially draining your sabbatical might be and how much supplemental funding you are likely to need. Estimate as closely as possible the primary expenses: transportation, lodging, food, equipment, and materials. Be realistic in your appraisal, but generous in your estimates. Most costs are higher than you anticipate. Your preliminary study should help determine if you will need to apply for external funding to carry out your project. The budget-making process will be treated more thoroughly in Chapter 3.

Step Four: Study institutional compensation and benefit stipulations.

Each institution has a different set of policies pertaining to compensation and benefits for faculty on leave. Find these policy statements and study them. Here are some important questions to ask:

- How will my health and disability plans be affected? Will I have coverage if I leave the area while on sabbatical? What procedures do I follow for getting reimbursed for health-related expenses incurred while traveling abroad?

- Will my time on sabbatical count toward promotion and retirement eligibility?

- Will my retirement allotments be affected?

- At what rate of my normal base salary will I be compensated? How will the percentage differ from a one-semester to a full-year's leave?

- Does my institution allow me to earn income beyond my sabbatical compensation? How much? Are certain kinds of employment prohibited?

The answers to these questions will constitute an important part of your feasibility study.

Step Five: Examine your personal circumstances.

If your sabbatical is to be successful it must be in harmony with *both* your professional and personal life. Your health, your emotional condition, your financial state, your relationships—all should be carefully considered before you apply for a sabbatical.

Sabbatical returnees stress that gaining the understanding, approval, and support of spouse and family are vital factors in the formula for a successful sabbatical. Be as conscientious in consulting with family members, relatives, and friends as you have been with your departmental chair and colleagues. If you have a spouse, for example, you should discuss the following kinds of issues: If your leave involves travel, or perhaps an extended stay away from home, will your spouse accompany you? If not, will there be any difficulty in maintaining your home while you are away? Will your spouse have to give up any professional and/or community service commitments if forced to shoulder additional responsibilities on the homefront? Will the potential benefits of study abroad outweigh the potential hardships involved?

Do not underestimate the profound effect your sabbatical may have upon your own lifestyle and on your personal relationships. At this juncture in your planning you may find it helpful to read about how the sabbatical has influenced the lives of others. For starters, I recommend Sophie Freud Loewenstein's *Last Sabbatical: A Midlife Journey* (1983), a poignant and thought-provoking monograph which should give you greater insight into your own situation. Much shorter, but also revealing, is Frank Laycock's "*...And One to Grow On*" (1955), a fascinating description of the author's stay at the University of Chicago in 1952–53 under a Ford Fellowship Program. Also instructive are John R. Coleman's *Blue-Collar Journal: A College President's Sabbatical* (1974), Bonnie Miller Rubin's *Time Out* (1987), and Charles E. Frank's *Six Franks Abroad: One Man's Sabbatical* (1967).

DETERMINING THE LENGTH OF YOUR SABBATICAL

How long should your sabbatical be? A year? A semester? Your choice will profoundly affect your sabbatical experience. Unfortunately, the decision will not be an easy one, perhaps not even yours to make, since a number of factors—both institutional and personal—will come into play.

Semester or year's leave?

First, there is the matter of financial constraints. Few institutions provide a year's leave at full salary. The more common policy provides half salary for full-year leaves and full salary for semester leaves. Some institutions have less generous policies, providing only a set percentage of the salary you would normally draw for the time period on leave, no matter if for a semester or year. Thus, your institution's policy, and not how much time you actually need for completing your project, may determine whether you take a semester or year's leave. No matter how attractive the prospect of a year's leave, you may discover that your budget simply cannot stand the strain of a year at half salary.

In many instances, the answers to questions pertaining to programmatic and staffing needs will dictate your choice. For example, are your courses central to an area of the general education program? to your department's major program? Will it be possible to cover the courses you typically teach in your department's major program? If you are a teacher in a small liberal arts college *you* may constitute an entire department. In this case, it will be impossible to find a departmental colleague to cover your courses, and finding a temporary replacement may also be difficult because of the wide range of courses you teach and the responsibilities you assume as *de facto* head of your department. Solving these problems for a semester's duration may be very difficult, but perhaps possible; solving them for a year may be virtually impossible.

Even if institutional policy poses no difficulty in opting for a year's leave, however, there are still personal factors to be considered. These factors become even more crucial if you intend to spend your sabbatical away from home. And still more crucial if you have school-age children. Again, many questions must be asked and answered: What do I do with my apartment or house? Do I arrange to have my spouse (or my family) stay with me? What about my spouse's job? My children's education? If I leave my spouse and family behind how will they fare? How often will I be able to see them? Will my loneliness be a distraction? Perhaps you should even consider how difficult it will be to reacclimate yourself once you return home after a year's leave. A recent study (Franklin, 1993) of the sabbatical leave indicates that "faculty who took full-year and those who spent their leaves off-campus indicate they were significantly more likely to suffer post-sabbatical depression on returning to their work after sabbatical leaves" (p. 8).

Having stressed some of the potential difficulties of a full year's leave, it is only fair to say that its advantages almost always outweigh the disadvantages. Faculty who have experienced the bounty of a year's sabbatical are rhapsodic in their praise of the experience, volunteering glowing testimonials on the benefits of a year-long experience. Indeed, they often wonder aloud about how any truly demanding scholarly project can be accomplished during as brief a time as a semester.

But a multitude of faculty have proved that a semester's leave, although perhaps not ideal, can be long enough to get the job done. Indeed, the majority of sabbaticals taken are of a semester's duration. But here, too, some important decisions must be made. For example, if programmatic and staffing needs do not dictate your choice, should you take your sabbatical in the fall or spring semester? Is there really any difference? Here are some things you may wish to consider.

Fall or spring semester?

First, a look at the potential benefits and drawbacks of a fall semester sabbatical. Perhaps the greatest benefit of a fall term leave is being able to use the summer months as a launching pad for your project. Assuming that commencement occurs in mid-May, you will have three-and-a-half months to gain momentum. Or, looked at in an even more sanguine fashion, by combining the summer vacation with the four months of the fall semester you will have arranged for nearly a nine-month leave.

There are at least two drawbacks, however. First, many faculty need more than the two to four weeks of the semester break to prepare for returning to a full schedule of teaching and collegial responsibilities. Secondly, given the demands and distractions of the holiday seasons, the weeks from Thanksgiving through Christmas may not be conducive to the kind of concentration you will need when reaching this climactic point in your research. In effect, your fall semester leave may be significantly shorter in reality than in theory.

And what about scheduling a spring semester sabbatical? If you are the kind of person who needs plenty of adjustment time, seriously consider scheduling your leave for the spring term so you can use the summer as a buffer between your leave and a return to full-time collegial responsibilities. Further, the summer can serve as your "safety net"—a grace period during which you can put the finishing touches on tasks left unfinished at the end of your leave.

BENEFITS AND DRAWBACKS OF AN OFF-CAMPUS PROJECT

Now that you have decided on the duration of your sabbatical, you must come to grips with location. In some cases, the very nature of the project will determine your choice. For example, a research project requiring a more sophisticated laboratory than your home institution possesses will force you to find an institution with the requisite facilities. Similarly, a project dependent upon the intensive study of relatively inaccessible primary sources will point you in the direction of an archival or museum library. On the other hand, a project depending heavily upon the work of your own research assistants may require you to maintain a home-based operation.

However, many situations offer choice. For instance, while you may be able to complete a project through the use of interlibrary loan, it might be much more convenient and less time consuming to take up residence near a large library offering immediate access to all the materials you need to examine.

Given the choice between a home-based or away-from-home sabbatical, which path should you take? The prevailing wisdom of sabbatical veterans is to spend at least part of a sabbatical leave away from home. Faculty who move off-campus report being more productive. Further, they comment on how much they appreciate the enrichment opportunities afforded by travel, especially the privilege of learning about another culture. Others comment upon the benefits derived from effecting a change of scene, pace, and routine. Franklin (1993) reports that "those faculty who assumed greater risk by taking sabbaticals off-campus…viewed their leaves as significantly more important, major career events than those who spent their sabbaticals locally." Further, those spending their leaves on campus had the "lowest success ratings," while faculty with "off-campus leaves, particularly those in Europe, had the highest overall ratings" (p. 8).

However, you shouldn't feel obliged to take a certain type of sabbatical because of the experiences of others. Nor should you have to apologize for deciding on a home, or close-to-home, site. But do make sure you are staying close to home for the right reasons. Irresolvable logistical problems may constitute a compelling reason for staying closer to home, but you should not allow mild feelings of apprehension to deter you from packing your bags and embarking on what may turn out to be one of the best experiences of your life.

This is not to say that you can take the prospect of studying away from home lightly. Alice Kuramoto (1990), who spent the fall of 1988 in Bergen, Norway, states that while studying and living abroad can be one of the most memorable and enriching experiences of one's life, it can also be one of the "worst." Cautioning that "it is not for everyone," Kuramoto points out that you must consider many factors, but most especially "timing" in terms of your work and family. Before making your decision about studying abroad try to read some of the literature on the subject (see Chapter 4 for a list of books) and to talk with colleagues who have lived abroad so that you can get a clearer idea of the benefits, challenges, and potential problems of such a sojourn.

REVIEWING THE REPORT ON YOUR LAST SABBATICAL

If you are a sabbatical veteran, carefully review your last sabbatical report. Such a review will serve to remind you of some things you should have done but did not do on your last sabbatical, or of some things you did do, but should not have. In short, thoughtful study of a sabbatical report or journal can help keep you from repeating the errors of the past. If sabbatical reports are kept on open file be sure to read the reports of your colleagues as well.

CONSULTING WITH FACULTY DEVELOPMENT PERSONNEL

Your institution's faculty development director should be able to provide you with answers to questions you might have about sabbatical policy and guidelines, the application process, and sources of in-house and external funding. Should your director not have answers to your questions, he/she will probably be able to direct you to someone who does. Because of their special training in pedagogical and curricular matters, faculty development personnel can be especially helpful to faculty embarking on sabbaticals aimed either at enhancing teaching or developing new courses.

EXPLORING FUNDING POSSIBILITIES

All sabbatical projects cost money, but the expenses are often modest enough to be covered by in-house grants, or by a combination of personal resources and in-house grant monies. If the price tag is unusually high, however, you may have to seek external funding. Although challenging, this task need not be daunting. Two institutional agencies—faculty development and institutional advancement—have resources, both human and material, to help you in your search.

Office of faculty development

Many faculty development resource centers have informational files on foundations and granting agencies, helpful reference and "how-to" texts, and videotapes on grant writing. In addition, most faculty development personnel are prepared to help in the search for grant funding. (Please see Chapter 7 for more information on how the office of faculty development can help in your search for funding.)

Office of institutional advancement

Your college or university's office of institutional advancement is also prepared to help you seek funding for your sabbatical project. Perhaps most importantly, this office has the tools and expertise to conduct comprehensive searches for external funding sources, including government, foundation, and corporate agencies. Through the use of extensive data bases such as the IRIS Data Base of Sponsored Opportunities (U. of Illinois at Urbana-Champaign: Research Services Office), the staff of an institutional advancement office can do in a day what it might take you several weeks to accomplish. Further, through its information networks this office monitors not only funding patterns throughout the nation, but also state and federal legislation influencing granting agencies. In addition, the staff of this office can (a) provide you with contact information for the various agencies; (b) help you understand and follow the often complicated and stringent granting guidelines; (c) help you conceptualize your project by brainstorming the idea with you; (d) set up conference calls; (e) serve as a good source of critical reaction, providing you with an informed (and objective) critique it would be difficult to get from a less experienced source; and (f) provide you with valuable editorial assistance in reading proposal drafts. Some institutional advancement offices will even write the final draft for you, but this depends upon such factors as the size of the staff, the workload, and the institutional impact of your project.

Besides these valuable services, most institutional advancement offices house scores of newsletters, bulletins, application kits, periodicals, foundation reports, agency guidelines, and "how to" texts. (Please see Chapter 7 and Appendix D for a listing of key sources.) Grantwriting is a very competitive enterprise, with the prizes going to those with up-to-date information and a good command of the requisite skills of grant writing.

Since many institutions stipulate that all applications for external funding must be processed by the office of institutional advancement, faculty should meet with someone from that office *early* in the planning for a sabbatical project. Inherent in most grant applications is considerable "lag time"—that is, the period of time from application to notification. In fact, most external grants take at *least* a year to process from application to funding, and more often two. Also, keep in mind that you will improve your chances for getting your sabbatical proposal approved if you send with it the promise of external funding, thereby providing evidence that one kind of screening committee has already given your project a strong vote of confidence.

EXPLORING THE POSSIBILITY OF A FACULTY EXCHANGE

One way of enhancing the feasibility of sabbatical projects is through some type of faculty exchange. Semester or year long exchanges may be difficult for an individual to arrange, but not so difficult through one of the major national exchanges. (The following descriptions use the wording and information from the most recent brochures available).

National Faculty Exchange (NFE)

Founded in 1983, the National Faculty Exchange negotiates or brokers faculty and staff exchanges. These exchanges—conducted among a group of member colleges and universities, education associations, and federal agencies—are primarily within the U.S., with the availability of some international sites. Further, the exchanges may (1) be unilateral, bilateral, or multilateral; (2) cross disciplines; and (3) be home or host funded.

Members receive a handbook, directory of campus coordinators, monthly newsletter, and support from NFE staff. Both the applicants and the institutions are informed of progress at each step in the exchange process. Following placement, NFE staff members work with home and host campuses to complete negotiations through exchange agreements.

Member institutions must appoint a coordinator to serve as an administrative link with other member campuses and the NFE office. In addition, institutional representatives are responsible for processing both outgoing and incoming applications. According to the most recent brochure, "NFE has placed hundreds of faculty and administrators for periods of a few weeks to two years."

There is a $650 annual membership fee. However, the fee for institutions with fewer than 100 full-time faculty is $325.

For more information contact: Academic Resource Network
4656 W. Jefferson Blvd., Suite 140
Fort Wayne, IN 46804
219/436-2634 phone
219/436-5676 fax

Clearinghouse for International Faculty & Staff Exchange (CIFSE)

The CIFSE provides world-wide exchange opportunities, thereby expanding the NFE's mission. Developed in conjunction with the International Student Exchange Program (ISEP), based at Georgetown University, CIFSE assists faculty and staff in identifying potential exchange counterparts at exchange sites being developed in 35 countries around the world. Unlike NFE's negotiated exchanges, responsibility for arranging and finalizing exchanges rests with individuals and institutions. Individual participants initiate the exchange process.

Provided to campuses at no cost are: (1) guidelines and materials for promoting the opportunity; (2) registration forms for faculty and staff; (3) guidelines for negotiating exchange agreements; and (4) CIFSE directories to use as a resource for hiring individuals with international expertise.

Registrants receive a CIFSE directory upon registration and their names are included in the next two semi-annual directories. The directories include basic personal information, institutional affiliation, rank, field of specialization, language expertise, and interest in exchanging domiciles. Registrants are also provided with guidelines for negotiating an exchange.

There is no institutional subscription fee. Individuals pay a $35 registration fee for listings in two semi-annual directories identifying others interested in exchange.

Both the NFE and CIFSE are part of the larger Academic Resource Network (ARN), which also administers the Emeriti Placement Program.

For more information contact: Academic Resource Network
4656 W. Jefferson Blvd., Suite 140
Fort Wayne, IN 46804
219/436-2634 phone
219/436-5676 fax

Faculty Exchange Center (FEC)

Established in 1973, the Faculty Exchange Center makes it possible for college and university teachers to exchange positions with colleagues from institutions both on this continent and overseas. Each September, the FEC publishes a

Directory containing each participating instructor's name, rank, field of specialization, and home institution. The *Directory* also identifies the regions where the registrant prefers to teach, and indicates if he or she is willing to exchange homes.

Upon receiving the *Directory*, members match themselves with one or more colleagues in their fields and initiate correspondence with them to discuss the details of exchange. Then, in consultation with the appropriate administrative officers, the prospective exchange participants work out an agreement satisfactory to all parties.

In order to facilitate housing exchanges during summers, holidays, and sabbatical leaves, the FEC prepares a house-exchange supplement that, like the *Membership Directory*, is published and distributed early in the fall.

According to the most recent *Directory*, over 200 American and foreign institutions currently participate in the Faculty Exchange Center. Representing all the major disciplines, the registrants come from throughout the United States as well as from many other countries.

The annual membership fee is $150. However, it is the policy of the FEC to renew an institutional membership *gratis* in cases where there have been no participants despite campus-wide distribution of informational materials.

For more information contact: Faculty Exchange Center (FEC)
952 Virginia Avenue
Lancaster, PA 17603
717/393-1130

CONSIDERING APPLICATION FOR SCHOLAR-IN-RESIDENCE STATUS

This is also the right time to begin looking into the possibility of applying for scholar-in-residence status at another college or university. Arranging for this type of position is often surprisingly easy. In most cases all you need do is send a curriculum vitae and cover letter describing your sabbatical project to the appropriate departmental chair of the institution in which you'd like to work, explaining why you would like to study there. Write a concrete letter, detailing your needs and expectations. Follow up this correspondence with a telephone call, during which you can iron out the details of your stay.

There are exceptions to this *pro forma* application. You may find, for example, that before approval is gained the host department must vote on your application. Again, the key to success is to take the time to write a meaningful letter of application, accompanied by materials demonstrating your scholarly track record.

Most colleges and universities are happy to grant scholar-in-residence status to worthy candidates, but it will be up to you to request specific privileges and amenities. Determine what your particular requirements are and discuss them with your host-institution contact. Be as modest in your requests as possible, but don't make the mistake of failing to arrange for resources and facilities absolutely necessary to the successful completion of your project. Following are some of the most commonly requested privileges:

- temporary faculty status with attendant rights and privileges
- library privileges
- a suitable study area, including office space with a telephone
- laboratory privileges
- use of a departmental or laboratory research assistant
- after hours access to key buildings
- course audit privileges
- access to office staff (for typing letters, etc.)
- access to computers with on-line capabilities
- access to departmental copy and fax machines
- departmental mail box
- parking permit

Your letter should also specify what you intend to do for your sponsoring institution. For example, you might offer to serve as an occasional guest lecturer in your research area. Or, you might volunteer to share some of your research findings with interested faculty through a seminar scheduled near the end of your residency. If your field is in the natural sciences and you are using the laboratory facilities and equipment of your sponsoring institution you might explore the possibility of collaborating on a research article with the laboratory director. In short, your request for a scholar-in-residence position will be viewed more positively if your host institution realizes it will also benefit from the relationship.

A final word. Although setting up a scholar-in-residence position is relatively simple, do not become too blasé about the arrangements. As one faculty member put it, "Make sure you make adequate contact with your host institution so that there's a clear understanding on both sides." As a researcher, you will have your own set of expectations, but so will your host institution. Clearly understanding and agreeing to these expectations is part of the formula for mutual satisfaction and success. Rose A. Bast, in an article in *BioScience* (1992), is even more specific, providing this caveat for science faculty:

> Whether you have been invited to spend your sabbatical with a particular research group or are making an application, do not commit yourself until you have investigated the laboratory....Visit the laboratory for several days so that you can assess its safety practices, observe its

general functioning, and evaluate the personal interactions in the workplace" (p. 547).

FORMING A LEARNING PARTNERSHIP

Neither teaching nor scholarship should be done in absolute seclusion. Scholars who have formed learning partnerships extol the pleasures and fruitfulness of the collaborative approach. Not all scholarly, pedagogical, curricular, or artistic sabbatical projects lend themselves to collaboration, of course, but if your project—or even some discrete component of it—does, be willing to expend the added effort to set up the partnership. Sabbatical veterans who have worked collaboratively tell of being "doubly productive," of having someone to "spur [you] on" when the "going gets tough," of having "someone to pull in the slack when you're busy," and of having someone to talk to about ongoing research. A partner may serve as catalyst, as confidant, or as a resource for ensuring quality control: whatever the function, you are sure to find it of substantial value.

SOME *DOs* AND *DON'Ts*

1. *Do* start the reflection and planning process early—at least one year before applying for your sabbatical.

2. *Do* give the reflection and planning process serious attention.

3. *Do* engage in some genuine soul searching.

4. *Do* read a book or two on the sabbatical experience.

5. *Do* keep everything in perspective and don't try to do too much.

6. *Don't* let the reflective process become a solitary exercise. Talk over your plans and concerns with colleagues, academic administrators, friends, and family members. Use these people as sounding boards for your ideas.

WORKS CITED

Bast, R. (1992). A sabbatical? Do it! *BioScience*, 42(7), 546–547.

Coleman, J. (1974). *Blue-collar journal: A college president's sabbatical*. New York, NY: Lippincott.

Frank, C. (1967). *Six Franks abroad: One man's sabbatical*. Cleveland, OH: World Publishing Co.

Franklin, T. (1993). Planning successful sabbaticals. *The Department Chair*, Spring, 8–9.

Jarecky, R., & Sandifer, M. (1986). Faculty members' evaluations of sabbaticals. *Journal of Medical Education*, 61(10), 803–807.

Kuramoto, A. (1990). A sabbatical abroad: Planning the trip, enjoying your stay. *Adult Learning*, 2, 29.

Laycock, F. (1955). ...And one to grow on. *AAUP Bulletin*, 41, 733–741.

Loewenstein, S.F. (1983). *Last sabbatical: A midlife journey*. Grand Forks, ND: University of North Dakota Office of Instructional Development.

Reuler, J. (1989). Sabbatical. *JAMA*, 261(3), 408–410.

Riely, M. (1971). Sabbatical leave: The teacher's R and R. *The Independent School Bulletin*, 30(3), 68–70.

Rubin, B.M. (1987). *Time out: How to take a year (or more or less) off without jeopardizing your job, your family, or your bank account*. New York, NY: W.W. Norton.

3

The Application Process

*Careful advance planning, balanced by a flexibility and a willing-
ness to do different—at times unplanned—things will result in an
exciting, successful sabbatical.*

Anonymous sabbatical recipient

Sabbatical application procedures differ considerably from institution to
institution. For some faculty, the process is as simple as filling out a one or
two page form which is then forwarded to the departmental chair or academic
dean for approval. For others, the application process is fully as demanding as
developing a proposal for a prestigious external grant. Generally speaking, however, the brief *pro forma* application seems to be the exception rather than the
norm.

Most sabbatical programs demand thorough and detailed proposals which
are then judged on comparative merit. Thus, one of the first things to remember
about applying for sabbatical is that it takes considerable time and should not be
postponed until the eleventh hour. Sabbatical veterans suggest beginning the preliminary draft no later than early summer, thereby leaving sufficient time for
revising and polishing before the typical fall submission deadline.

REQUEST LETTERS OF REFERENCE WELL IN ADVANCE
OF THE APPLICATION DEADLINE

In-house letters

Requests for reference letters should be made early in the application
process. Begin contacting your colleagues about three months ahead of the
application deadline—before they become preoccupied with preparing courses
for the fall semester. Think back to the times you were asked to write a letter of

recommendation on the very eve of an application deadline. Do you remember being forced by time constraints to write a letter not quite as detailed and thorough as you might have drafted under more congenial circumstances? The more lead time you give your colleagues, the more concrete, substantive, and thorough their letters of support are likely to be.

Off-campus letters

Asking for support letters well ahead of time is especially important when the recommenders are off-campus, and doubly important if they are prominent educators or scholars since their in-baskets are probably heavy with such petitions. Request off-campus letters of support at the beginning of summer; even with this seemingly comfortable time line you may still find yourself sending reminder letters at the beginning of the fall semester.

Give plenty of time and thought to securing on- and off-campus colleague and/or community support. There is no surer way of giving your application credibility than through testimonials from colleagues who know your work and who, ideally, are recognized authorities in your proposed area of study. Off-campus recommendations are particularly important for establishing the validity and value of research projects in that such statements are likely to be viewed as more objective than those from campus colleagues.

Whether from on- or off-campus, the concreteness of a reference letter determines its value. To help ensure specificity provide your recommender with a detailed description of your project. The more your recommenders know about your proposed study, the better they will be able to address meaningfully its strengths and challenges, as well as to comment on its feasibility. If possible, give recommenders a draft of your application, thereby enabling them to critique not only the concept, but also the proposed strategy for accomplishing the sabbatical study.

STUDY INSTITUTIONAL SABBATICAL LEAVE GUIDELINES AND CLOSELY FOLLOW THEM

Suggesting careful study of your institution's sabbatical guidelines and policy might seem unnecessary, but the many sad tales of applications being denied because of inattention to institutional guidelines suggest the need for this gentle reminder. We can learn much from the following observation made by a member of a sabbatical review committee in response to a questionnaire on sabbatical practices:

> How painful it is to reject an application that is basically sound and apparently good for the institution and the faculty member, but that is poorly thought out, poorly organized, and that fails to address the guidelines for preparing sabbatical applications. Frequently, the culprit

is not a disinterested applicant, but rather one who too hastily prepares a proposal and assumes the members of the Personnel Committee will read between the lines. *Not so.* Every candidate should know that the quickest route to certain rejection is poor execution of the application (SNC Sabbatical Survey, 1989).

Drafting an application without fully understanding institutional policies can have disastrous consequences. However, a few simple steps can be taken to ensure a happy ending. First, obtain a copy of your institution's sabbatical policy. Next, carefully study it. And, finally, if you have questions about either the policy or the guidelines do not hesitate to call someone who has the answers: your academic dean, your departmental or divisional chair, the director of faculty development, a member of the sabbatical review committee, or perhaps a colleague who recently has gone through the application process.

PREPARE YOUR PROPOSAL WITH CARE

A good sabbatical proposal is like a good syllabus. Both contain a list of goals and objectives to provide motivation and direction, along with a timetable to help keep you on track. Further, both contain philosophical overviews, lists of basic resources, and descriptions of evaluative procedures. In short, both are invaluable guides, steering you along your journey in dependable fashion. While each takes considerable time to complete, a generous investment of time and energy yields rich dividends. Just as a solid syllabus will help you create a well organized, comfortably-paced course, a solid sabbatical proposal will help you achieve a productive and enriching sabbatical leave.

Here are some specific steps to follow when preparing your proposal:

1. *Consult with colleagues who have been on sabbatical.*

   Colleagues who have recently taken sabbaticals constitute a particularly valuable human resource upon which to draw. Seek their good counsel. They will not only be able to provide answers to many of your questions, but will appreciate being given an opportunity to share their knowledge and experience. However, before making your visit, compose a list of questions that address your primary concerns. Your colleagues will appreciate your thoughtfulness, and you will be more likely to obtain information and advice specific enough to be of genuine value.

2. *Attend informational sessions and workshops on the sabbatical.*

   In some institutions the academic dean, or sabbatical review committee, sponsors informational sessions for prospective sabbatical applicants. These sessions not only provide a forum for asking questions and clarifying misconceptions, but also help remove some of the uncertainty and apprehension applicants may feel about the application process. Even if you don't have specific questions about sabbatical guidelines and policy, attending these sessions is a good idea. You may gain valuable insight into the sabbatical application process just by listening to the concerns of others. In addition, if your office of faculty development offers sabbatical workshops be sure to attend. Sabbatical workshops can provide you with procedural tips and information that will save you a great deal of time in the long run.

3. *Study copies of successful sabbatical proposals.*

If possible, obtain and study a successful sabbatical proposal. Nothing can adequately substitute for this helpful resource. Examining a complete application provides you with invaluable information about the requisite length, format, specificity, and tone of a successful proposal. In addition, you will be able to see, firsthand, the kinds of supporting materials that make a proposal more meaningful to sabbatical review committee members.

If your institution does not keep an open file of sabbatical applications ask your faculty development director, departmental chair, or appropriate academic officer to start one. If you do not have access to an open file, ask a colleague who has been on sabbatical for a copy of her or his proposal. In addition, you may find helpful the sample applications contained in Appendix E of this volume.

4. *Address all the items in your institution's sabbatical guidelines, being sure to follow the suggested application format.*

In the event your institution has not provided you with an outline of application components, the following compilation, based upon information gleaned from dozens of institutional policy statements, may help guide you through the proposal drafting process. Help make your sabbatical proposal concrete and thorough by including the following elements:

- A title page containing such information as your (1) name, (2) academic rank, (3) department, (4) home address, (5) home and office telephone number, and (6) the proposed duration of the sabbatical leave with year or semester specified;

- A project abstract outlining your intended research;

- A statement of rationale for your project;

- A narrative describing why you are proposing the project, what you hope to accomplish, and by what means you intend to achieve the stated objectives;

- A statement on the impact of the leave on your department's programs and staffing, including a description of any known or foreseeable contingencies which may affect the project;

- A statement on the project's value to you, your department, your students, and your institution;

- A list of projected outcomes (be as specific as possible: for example, if you are undertaking a teaching enhancement project indicate the kind of classroom materials that will result and the kinds of teaching skills you will gain or have enhanced; if you are working on a book, include a proposed table of contents);

- A timetable for accomplishing each outcome with dates and locations (identify such things as host institutions and specific arrangements for library facilities, as well as for office, laboratory, and studio space);

- An itemized budget, with supporting rationale;

- A statement of anticipated sources (e.g., grants, fellowships, part-time teaching) and amounts of financial support for the sabbatical project;

- A curriculum vitae that concretely documents your skills and accomplishments, particularly those pertinent to the proposed sabbatical leave activity.

It is difficult to overemphasize the importance of this step in the process. Remember that you are writing your proposal not only as your own personal guide, but also as a document to be judged by peers and academic administrators. One of the things an evaluator will be especially interested in is your past performance, especially your track record on similar kinds of projects as well as on obtaining research grants and fellowships. Thus, be sure to comment concretely on past accomplishments, even to the extent of including evaluations of, and reports on, those projects.

In addition, a review committee will be eager to learn not only where you will be studying, but *why* you have chosen the designated location. Will it best serve the needs and purposes of your leave? Are there special facilities there? What sort of study arrangements have you made? Would another location serve you better?

Finally, try to get a good sense of just how much information you ought to include by talking with sabbatical review committee members and sabbatical recipients, as well as by studying other sabbatical applications. Review committees want plenty of detail, but they don't want a voluminous tome filled with irrelevant, or only tangentially related, information. In short, be thorough and concrete, but don't pad.

5. *Provide evidence of your planning through supporting documents.*

Supporting documents make your proposal more meaningful, give it credibility, and provide compelling evidence of your careful planning. They can be of immense value to a review committee in the application screening process. Although the kinds of supporting documents you should include will depend upon the nature of your project, the following materials are almost always helpful and appropriate:

- a bibliography relevant to your sabbatical project;
- letters of recommendation, both from in-house and off-campus sources;
- letters from collaborators in research, teaching, and artistic endeavors;
- documents confirming scholar-in-residence status;
- grant awards, or copies of applications for research support from both in-house and external agencies;
- evaluations and testimonials from authorities in the subject area of the project;
- letters from editors testifying to the publication potential of your sabbatical study, or, if you are so fortunate, a copy of the publishing contract for the book on which you will be working;
- travel itineraries;
- samples of previously published work, especially works related to the proposed sabbatical project;
- diagrams, charts, graphs, and illustrations that help describe your project;
- newspaper or journal articles attesting to the importance or timeliness of your sabbatical topic.

6. *Provide evidence of your project's value to the institution.*

Sabbatical applicants generally do a good job of identifying the benefits they anticipate receiving from their proposed project, but they sometimes forget to describe the project's potential benefits to the institution. This omission may seriously weaken an application.

Most sabbatical policies either explicitly state, or at least imply, that the institution and its students should also benefit from the sabbatical system. Thus, it is important that you take the time to identify the sabbatical outcomes that will have an impact on your institution as a whole. For example, will you be able to strengthen existing courses by incorporating your sabbatical research findings? Will you be able to develop some new courses as a result of your sabbatical research? How will departmental and general education programs be strengthened as a result of your studies? Will you share your learning and cultural enrichment with students and faculty through presentations? While studying abroad will you be willing to help set up contacts for your institution's international study programs? These are the kinds of questions a review committee might ask about the outcomes of a sabbatical project. Anticipating such questions and incorporating answers into your application constitute a good investment of time.

7. *Develop a detailed and realistic budget.*

Using your preliminary budget estimates as a base, you should now more closely research the costs of your sabbatical. Inaccurate budget projections may result in some serious problems during the leave itself—a time when you can least afford distractions and setbacks. For example, underestimating the cost of travel, lodging, equipment, supplies, and the like may either put you in debt, or make it impossible for you to complete certain parts of your project—or both. One sabbatical returnee reported that because he underestimated apartment rental rates he was forced to cut short his projected stay by two weeks, thus jeopardizing the successful completion of his project.

Careful investigation is the key. Once you have thought through your project, review each stage of it, identifying activities that will probably cost you money. Make a list of these activities with an eye toward ferreting out "hidden" costs. Most of us remember to figure in the cost of typical relocation expenses such as travel, lodging, and food, for example, but sometimes forget things like utilities, postage, telephone and fax expenses, commuting costs, and parking fees—the latter a considerable expense in large cities.

We also sometimes forget that the everyday services we enjoy at low cost at our home institutions can be quite expensive in other settings. For instance, making copies on your departmental photocopying machine may cost as little as five cents a page or less, but as much as twenty-five cents per copy, or more, in such places as museums and archival libraries. Further, you may accrue considerable expense from online and interlibrary loan searches at fee-charging libraries. In addition, since much research, laboratory work, and writing is now computer driven, you should carefully estimate possible computer equipment and software expenses.

Make direct inquiries about costs. Sometimes only through personal contacts can you get an accurate estimate of the cost of living at your sabbatical home away from home. It might also be helpful to spend some time talking with colleagues who have undertaken similar projects and made similar travel arrangements. If you have applied for scholar-in-residence status, a good person to call is the departmental chair at your host institution. Whenever possible, use a variety of sources in estimating basic expenses such as lodging and public transportation. For example, compare estimates received from the local Chamber of Commerce with figures you glean from reading the classified ads for a week or two.

The budget shown in Figure A is taken from a successful sabbatical proposal (Peterson, 1985) and should give you a better idea of the kinds of items you ought to include.

Figure A

FUNDING REQUEST — FACULTY IMPROVEMENT FUND

A. Research Supplies and Equipment

1. Purchase of Delrin and UHMW (ultra-high molecular weight) polyethylene stock for tool and die fabrication — $275

2. Purchase of components for construction of spray photo-etching equipment (poly tanks, acid resistant nozzles, acid resistant pumps, mordants, etc.) — $400

3. Purchase of sheet metal stock for forming and etching — $250

4. Purchase of photographic supplies (Kodalith film, photo resists, chemistry, etc.) — $200

    SUBTOTAL $ 1,125

B. Travel

Estimated expenses for one-week conference and subsequent research in Arizona

1. Transportation (4200 miles @ 20¢) — $ 840[1]

2. Lodging ($23/day x 33 days) — $ 759[2]

3. Meals ($10/day x 33 days) — $ 330

4. Conference Registration — $ 50

    SUBTOTAL $1,979

    TOTAL ANTICIPATED COSTS $3,104

Requested from Faculty Improvement Fund, a minimum of $1,750[3]

---

[1] Necessity of travel to several sites (NAU, U of A, ASU, Ft. Defiance) by bus, plane, or rental car plus air fare to Arizona make commercial transportation both more costly and less flexible than use of private automobile.

[2] Budget motel rates with taxes currently average $23-$27/day during August and September in locations to be visited. As a visiting scholar, some less costly on-campus lodging may be available. Also, as an Army Reserve Officer (Col.) I may be able to use Visiting Officer's quarters on a space-available basis at Davis Monthan AFB near Tucson.

[3] Approval of a lesser amount will necessitate a reduction in scope of research and time away from research.

8. *Include a pre-sabbatical leave timetable.*

Don't overlook the pre-sabbatical period when drafting your proposal timetable. The months between award notification and the leave proper constitute an important period of foundation building. For your own planning purposes, as well as for the edification of the sabbatical review committee, clearly identify the steps you intend to take in preparing for the leave. The following "Time Frame" (Figure B) taken from a successful sabbatical application for a fall semester leave (Peterson, 1985) illustrates not only a pre-sabbatical, but also a post-sabbatical, schedule of activities.

Figure B
TIME FRAME

A. Spring and Summer, 1985

   1. Attended brief workshop on photo-etching techniques at Midwest Metals Symposium, UW-LaCrosse.

   2. Began dialogue with metalsmiths doing research in photo-etching techniques and identified potential sites for research on non-traditional metal forming techniques while attending the Society of North American Goldsmiths Conference in Toronto in July.

B. Academic Year, 1985–86

   1. Identify and review technical papers on industrial, commercial, and aesthetic applications of the photo-etching process and photo-milling as an industrial production technique.

   2. Visit some commercial firms using photo-etching and photo-milling as industrial production techniques. (Green Bay Engraving and Erffmeyer & Sons in Milwaukee, or others).

   3. Develop specifications for adapting industrial equipment for my anticipated needs.

C. Summer, 1986

   1. Continue research and small-scale technical experiments using area commercial firms' facilities when possible.

   2. Remodel my metals studio in Oneida to provide for space and

safety considerations prior to fabrication and installation of spray photo-etching and metal forming equipment.

3. Attend one-week Society of North American Goldsmiths Conference in Flagstaff in late August.

D. Fall, 1986

1. Research on aspects of the total process involved in the project at the Center for Creative Photography, Arizona State Museum, at U. of A., Tucson, and ASU in Tempe (September).

2. Possible study with a Navajo metalsmith, Elmer Milford, vicinity of Ft. Defiance on the Navajo Indian Reservation. I was invited to visit the Ft. Defiance area by Mr. Milford while at a metals conference in 1983. I intend to correspond with him later if it seems feasible in terms of total time commitments in August and September, 1986.

3. Work in my studio in Oneida integrating experimental metal-forming techniques with video-computer generated images applied through spray photo-etching. (October, 1986–January, 1987).

4. Produce a body of work, metal sculpture, in which both technical and aesthetic problems are resolved.

E. Spring, 1987

1. Exhibition of finished works and/or presentation for interested colleagues on results of my sabbatical leave.

---

9. *Enlist a trustworthy proofreader.*

Prior to submitting their work for publication, most professional writers—no matter how skilled at their craft—place their manuscripts in the hands of trusted copy editors. Authors of sabbatical proposals should follow their lead. Once you have written a complete draft of your sabbatical application, ask someone to check it over for such things as organization, clarity, coherence, concreteness, and tone. But be sure to ask someone whose judgment you respect, someone who is a trustworthy proofreader, and someone who will give you an honest critique of your work. Have a designated reader check over your draft at least a month before the application deadline so you will have time to make suggested revisions.

In particular, fight the temptation to describe your project in technical, discipline-specific jargon. Your goal should be to describe what you intend to do in clear, succinct, non-technical terms. Before submitting your application for review ask a colleague *outside* your discipline to read it. If he or she has difficulty understanding your description, work on it until it exhibits the requisite clarity.

WHAT TO DO IF YOUR APPLICATION IS NOT APPROVED

Having your sabbatical application denied can be very disappointing, even demoralizing. However, it need be nothing more than a temporary setback if you adopt the right attitude and assume a proactive stance. Here are a few suggestions for constructively dealing with a failed application:

1. Listen carefully to what the review committee or academic administrator has to say about your proposal's weaknesses. Try to determine just how serious those weaknesses are. If your project seems fatally flawed you may have to abandon it in favor of another. On the other hand, you may decide that some relatively minor modifications will make your present proposal strong enough for resubmission. In addition, you may wish to consult with the dean of the college, your departmental/divisional chair, or faculty development agent. Take full advantage of your institution's human resources and support system.

2. Don't delay reapplying. If at all possible, submit either a modified or new proposal before the next submission deadline. Be certain, however, to discuss programmatic and staff concerns with your departmental chair and colleagues before reopening the application process. Each year brings new staffing and programmatic needs. Further, other departmental colleagues may be planning to apply for sabbatical leave this time around. In short, you cannot proceed on the assumption that the arrangements agreed upon for your initial application still hold true.

3. Maintain a sanguine attitude. The resubmission process may result in a much stronger proposal with even greater potential for productivity and enrichment.

CONCLUSION

A thoughtful, thorough, well organized, and concrete sabbatical proposal will take considerable time to complete. The substantial dividends, however, justify a generous investment of time and energy. The proposal, after all, is more than a requirement in the sabbatical application process. It also serves as your roadmap throughout the sabbatical journey. The clearer, more detailed, and dependable your map the greater your chance for reaching your destination, as well as for enjoying and benefitting from all the stops along the way.

SOME *DOs* AND *DON'Ts*

1. *Do* give yourself plenty of time for drafting the application; you should begin the process no later than early summer.

2. *Do* request letters of recommendation well before the application deadline.

3. *Do* carefully study the policies and guidelines pertaining to sabbaticals and complete your application in strict accordance with those policies and guidelines.

4. *Do* prepare the proposal with care.

5. *Do* attend sabbatical informational sessions.

6. *Do* find a sabbatical advisor.

7. *Don't* let the application process become a solitary exercise; seek the help and counsel of colleagues.

8. *Don't* despair if your sabbatical request is denied; adopt a sanguine attitude and resubmit another application as soon as possible. Above all, maintain your sense of humor.

WORKS CITED

Anonymous response (1989). St.Norbert College Sabbatical Survey. De Pere, WI: St.Norbert College Office of Faculty Development.

Peterson, C. (1985). Sabbatical proposal. De Pere, WI: St. Norbert College.

4

Pre-Sabbatical Preparation

Breaking the pattern was central to my sabbatical. I could have dug ditches and it would have been as big a success as if I had written a book. Teaching requires a periodic break—if it is to remain good, enjoyable teaching.

Anonymous sabbatical recipient

Once your sabbatical application has been approved, you enter an even more earnest preparatory stage. Although the time-consuming regimen of teaching, advising, and committee work may prevent you from doing all you would like to do in preparing for your sabbatical leave, through careful time management you still should be able to get a good start on your project. The key is to set a realistic and manageable pre-sabbatical work schedule—one which will not exhaust you or compromise your teaching and collegial duties—and stick to it. In particular, you should try to accomplish two important goals: (1) work toward clearing your professional life of distractions and impediments; and (2) get as much foundation work done as possible so you can build up some momentum before your leave.

REASSESS YOUR PERSONAL AND PROFESSIONAL LIFE

A sabbatical leave provides you with a rare opportunity to engage in some truly meaningful personal house cleaning—that is, to take a careful, and honest, look at your life and to discard the excess baggage you may have accumulated over the years. While you may not be able to cast off all your time- and energy-draining commitments, a careful reprioritizing should enable you to remove a great many of them—at least enough to make a difference in your life style.

Sabbatical returnees deem this opportunity to undertake a thorough inventory and reordering of their lives to be one of the greatest benefits of the sabbatical experience. This is the way one faculty member summed up this dimension of her sabbatical leave:

> The sabbatical, by virtue of its disruption of the regular schedule, is an ideal moment to take stock of one's professional and personal commitments, and the daily routine that shapes them. After a number of years of saying yes to various causes, committees, and organizations, one's life can become incredibly cluttered with time consuming (although not necessarily important) responsibilities. This is a golden opportunity to inventory, prioritize, and clean house! The lean operating mode which is unleashed by this process is, in my opinion, critical to the long term continuation of growth and development initiated during the leave....[The sabbatical] provides an opportunity to step back and measure one's accomplishments, redefine professional and personal goals, and reflect upon the mundane and deeper aspects of life (Odorzynski, 1988, pp. 4–5).

SET UP A CONGENIAL WORK ENVIRONMENT

Your work environment constitutes one of your most important sabbatical leave support systems. Thus, it is essential to select—or create—a comfortable, convenient, quiet, congenial living/studying space.

The importance of your sabbatical "cocoon" cannot be overstated, even if your stay in it will be shorter than a year. Howard Good (1992), in a delightfully evocative description of the "frustrations and satisfactions" of a one-semester sabbatical, makes the point nicely: "I describe my study in some detail because it was the center—and the top, bottom, and sides—of my world for four months....I typically would remain in my study from 9 or 10 in the morning until midnight or later, coming out only to reheat my coffee in the microwave, find matches for my pipe, and eat dinner with people I vaguely recognized as my family" (p. B2).

If you intend to do most of your work on campus, try to find a location affording maximum privacy and quiet. Avoid your office like the plague. Even if you plan to work there only at night, or on weekends, you will still be discovered. And with discovery will come conversation resulting in a commitment of one kind or another. Minimize this probability by ferreting out a study area in the library stacks or in some other campus building not regularly frequented by close associates. Better yet, find an office at a nearby campus or in some professional building in the city. I know of one colleague who cloistered himself in a nearby abbey, thus ensuring a suitable academic retreat. In short, find a place where the odds are against chance meetings with social or professional acquaintances.

If you plan to conduct your research at home establish a *sanctum sanctorum* that is off-limits to all family members (at least to those old enough to know the meaning of "No Trespassing!"). Furnish this room with a desk or table large enough to spread out your research materials, make sure the shelves are stocked with the books (and snacks) you need, set up your computer, and lay in plenty of provisions. Nothing gobbles up research time as voraciously, or proves so disruptive, as frequent forays for writing supplies, articles and books, diskettes, and the like.

Spend some time during the pre-sabbatical period making a list of all the things you will need in your work area, asking advice of colleagues who have recently gone through the same process. Then fit out your room with everything on your list. This may very well turn out to be one of your best investments of time. Now is also the appropriate juncture to have a heart-to-heart talk with your family, or housemate, about quiet hours, those precious and crucial blocks of time during which you are not to be disturbed except for real emergencies. Not easy, all this, but essential to a productive sabbatical.

The ideal arrangement, of course, is to do all, or at least a large part, of your sabbatical work away from home. Just getting away from home and campus, however, does not guarantee a good living/studying environment. You must choose your location carefully. Make sure requisite equipment, supplies, library holdings, and key human resources are readily available. Perhaps most importantly, seek out quiet lodging that will afford quality study time and a good night's sleep. Inspect, or at least investigate through direct personal inquiry, your prospective home-away-from home before signing a rental agreement. A dormitory room or university guest house may be easy on the budget, but hard on the nerves. Being quartered next to one of the world's finest libraries will do you little good if you are too tired and stressed out to take full advantage of its resources.

Studying abroad

Travel and study abroad offer special challenges. You must attend to such things as applying for a passport or visa, making rather complex travel arrangements, studying your host country's culture and language as well as its monetary system and exchange rates, shipping books and materials, and arranging for housing. And if you take your family, you have the additional responsibility of arranging for your children's schooling and perhaps helping your spouse find work or study opportunities. Most sabbatical applicants planning to study and travel abroad are concerned about the potential stress placed upon familial relationships. If you have these concerns, you can take heart from Jarecky and Sandifer's (1986) survey of medical school faculty, which revealed that sabbatical recipients thought travel resulted in "increased family companionship," as well as from Mulrow's (1989) sanguine conclusion that "when you enter a strange environment, the family becomes very close as a group and does many activities together. A sabbatical has a very positive effect on family life" (p. 538).

Fortunately, some helpful handbooks have been written on the subject of study abroad. Before setting out on your sabbatical odyssey, you may want to read one or two of the following books:

> *Faculty Handbook for Sabbaticals Abroad* (1984)
> Sally Ann Klitz
> The University of Connecticut
> Storrs, CT 06268

> *The Sabbatical Book* (1987)
> Jayne and Tony Ralston
> The Roylott Press
> 129 Chatham Avenue
> Buffalo, NY 14216

> *Time Out: How to Take a Year (or More or Less) Off Without Jeopardizing Your Job, Your Family, or Your Bank Account* (1987)
> Bonnie Miller Rubin
> W.W. Norton & Company
> 500 Fifth Ave.
> New York, NY 10110

> *Educator's Passport to International Jobs* (1984)
> Rebecca Anthony and Gerald Roe
> Peterson's Guides
> P.O. Box 2123
> Princeton, NJ 08543–2123

GATHER MATERIALS AND DO BACKGROUND READING

Because you will want to spend precious leave time on study and not busy work, you should make every attempt to gather the necessary materials or laboratory supplies *before* the leave begins. Selecting, locating, and ordering texts and supplies/equipment, requesting articles via interlibrary loan, conducting database searches, and other such activities take considerable time and often involve unexpected delays. Don't fall into the trap of beginning the search too late, or of being too sanguine in your estimate of the time it will take for the search to be completed and the materials received.

Your literature search will probably take longer than you anticipate. To begin with, you will usually discover more pertinent articles than you anticipated.

In addition, an interlibrary loan request takes considerable time to complete, even if ordered through an efficient system. And finally, you are likely to run into interminable cul de sacs, sometimes finding after two or three months of following leads from one source to another that the final result is a microfilm copy nearly impossible to read.

In brief, do as much spade work as you can before the leave, thereby ensuring that your actual research, rather than the preliminary gathering of materials, will be the primary focus of your sabbatical. A final point. This is an excellent time to take advantage of your institutional resources. Student research assistants, for example, on both the graduate and undergraduate levels, are often capable of performing even the most sophisticated literature searches. Utilizing them for this task will not only be of immeasurable help to you, but will provide them with a fine learning opportunity.

FIND A SABBATICAL ADVISOR/MENTOR

When asked the question "In retrospect, what could you have done to have made your sabbatical even more enriching and productive?" many sabbatical recipients indicated they would have benefitted from the counsel of some type of sabbatical "advisor," "coach," or "guide." Some suggested an "expert in the field" or an "editor" would have made the ideal advisor, but most thought along more general lines, simply hoping to find someone who would provide regular feedback during the course of the sabbatical study and who could be trusted to be honest in his/her appraisal of their work.

Why then, don't more sabbatical recipients arrange to have an advisor? Many returnees report being apprehensive about compromising their sabbatical seclusion through such an arrangement. Unfortunately, the attempt to find a kind of sabbatical Shangri-la can result in unhealthy isolation. The following rather typical account of the consequences of cloistering oneself is instructive:

> I was not psychologically prepared for the isolation. There was no opportunity for feedback, so my ideas developed in a vacuum. When I had completed the reports and articles that were the tangible outcome of the project, I should have expected them to be returned for revision (which they were) because this was the first time that anyone else had evaluated my conclusions. Instead I assumed that the sabbatical was complete and that I could now turn my full attention to my previous position (Reynolds, 1990, p. 93).

Sabbatical recipients who work with advisors report feeling less isolated, more likely to meet their deadlines and stay on track, and more satisfied with their project in general. Those who don't often vow to seek the counsel of advisors the next time around, having found that most scholarly and pedagogical projects bloom earlier and more profusely when cultivated and nurtured by professional dialogue.

Leave recipients might consider going a step beyond the single advisor format, enlisting the help of a group of colleagues (perhaps three to five) serving as a kind of advisory board. This group would meet periodically with the recipient from start to finish of the project. The first meeting would take place during the pre-leave period for the purpose of furnishing the recipient with feedback on the project proposal and helping fine-tune research strategies. In preparation for this meeting, the recipient would send the advisory group copies of the complete proposal, asking them to focus on such things as: (1) appropriateness of the methodological approach for this kind of research, (2) the reliability of the data collection system, (3) the soundness of the planned statistical analyses, and (4) the reasonableness of the projected timeline.

The recipient's needs would dictate the number of meetings scheduled during the leave period. Probably no more than one or two would have to be scheduled: perhaps a mid-point meeting to talk about problems and concerns and to assess the progress of the project, and probably a debriefing session at leave's end. In addition to spurring the returnee to reflect upon the benefits and possible shortcomings of the leave, the debriefing meeting would prove valuable in helping the returnee prepare a formal sabbatical report.

The advisory group approach has the potential to deliver some significant benefits. First, it allows the recipient to take advantage of valuable human resources near at hand. In fact, the teaching staff of any given campus constitutes a veritable cornucopia of expertise and talent, but one all too seldom tapped. Second, this approach helps recipients monitor their progress and prevent the kind of mistakes sometimes made when we pursue scholarship in isolation. And, finally, such an approach fosters collegiality and nurtures the spirit of community.

MAKE NECESSARY SPECIAL ARRANGEMENTS

To avoid having to make disruptive trips and telephone calls during the leave period, make necessary special arrangements while you are still around the office. Reporting on a survey of seventy medical school faculty who had taken sabbaticals, Jarecky and Sandifer (1986) point out that sabbatical recipients frequently lost time "because needed equipment and technical assistance had not been identified and planned for, sometimes needing two to three months to resolve these organizational details"...(p. 805).

The following checklist identifies some of the most important arrangements that usually have to be made before you depart on extended leave.

✓ Ask your secretary to send your mail to your office, your home address, or your temporary leave address.

✓ Ask your secretary to regularly check voice mail and E-mail, and to retrieve and deliver fax messages.

✓ Notify the chairs of in-house, professional, and community committees on which you serve.

✓ See departmental and divisional chairs about reassigning your advisement responsibilities.

✓ Talk to your advisees about your anticipated absence, explaining how their needs will be met during the leave period.

✓ Make necessary arrangements with personnel services.

✓ Discuss with your secretary the kinds of calls you consider top priority and of which you would like to be immediately apprised.

✓ Designate a colleague who will help deal with emergency matters in your absence.

✓ Send a memo to your disciplinary colleagues reminding them of your departure date and thanking them for helping make your leave possible.

✓ Notify your security office that you will be off campus and that your office will be vacant.

✓ Place a notice on your office door indicating inclusive dates of absence.

✓ Leave a detailed itinerary with your secretary and departmental/divisional chair.

STUDY INCOME TAX LAWS

Learn all you can about income tax laws pertaining to leave expenses *before* you embark on your sabbatical so you can take full advantage of potential tax breaks. One of the best investments you can make is to purchase the most recent edition of Allen Bernstein's annual *Tax Guide for College Teachers and Other College Personnel* (Academic Information Services, Inc.: Washington, DC). This handy guide, designed to keep academics informed about the latest tax laws and rulings applying to them, has several sections pertaining to leaves and the tax system, including such topics as "books, supplies, and equipment," "home office," "educational travel," "tax-free grants," and "research expenses of college teachers." Still another practical resource is *The Tax Guide for U.S. Citizens and Resident Aliens Abroad* (U.S. Government pub. 54, cat. No. 14999E). An essential resource for sabbatical recipients traveling and studying abroad, the *Tax Guide* covers a broad range of topics, including: filing requirements, foreign earned income exclusion, foreign housing exclusion or deductions, moving expenses, credit for foreign income taxes, and taxpayer appeal rights and assistance. The aforementioned guides and your tax accountant should provide you with the specifics needed to take advantage of any tax breaks accorded a leave recipient.

One directive appears so often in the literature on the topic it deserves special mention: document all your activities and expenses concretely and meticulously. Matoney and Weston (1985), for example, identify documentation as the key factor in establishing deductibility of any travel expenses, pointing out that "in order to document properly the deductibility of…travel expenses, the taxpayer must be able to demonstrate the business purpose of the trips" (p. 11). They add that "an easy way to do this is to include detailed discussion of it in both the sabbatical proposal and the final sabbatical report. In fact, it is an excellent idea to write both these documents knowing that they may be needed as documentation for business travel in the event of a tax audit" (p. 11). In addition to keeping a careful running account of all activities, the leave recipient must assiduously collect all expense account artifacts (e.g., canceled checks, invoices, credit card receipts, and the like). In addition, Matoney and Weston suggest "keeping a diary on a timely basis," emphasizing that the key is "daily" and that the author must "remember to note dates and times" (p. 11). Finally, they recommend seeking "the advice of competent tax counsel…both before and after the fact" (p. 13).

PREPARE YOURSELF FOR FEELINGS OF DOUBT AND APPREHENSION

The months preceding your sabbatical are full of anticipatory delight. Nevertheless, you should not be surprised if twinges of doubt, uncertainty, and perhaps even anxiety invade your idyllic world. At this juncture the full weight of the enterprise settles on your shoulders. It is natural to feel a sense of awe at the magnitude of a sabbatical project, natural to find yourself asking "Can I really do what I plan to do?" The phenomenon is not unlike the "butterflies" speakers feel in their stomachs before making a presentation. As one sabbatical recipient so aptly put it: "Suddenly, you can do all the things you've put on the back burner over the years, and the burden of expectation is terrific!" Howard Good (1992), sharing his recollections in a *Chronicle of Higher Education* article, speaks for most recipients: "The more time you have to write, the more pressure you feel to produce something. A sabbatical isn't a chance to rest, but finally to work on a cherished project without classes, students, papers, and committees to distract and delay you. You sure don't want to blow it" (pp. B2–B3). View any anxiousness you may feel as a natural part of the territory, savor the piquancy it adds to the situation, and proceed apace.

PREPARE IN ADVANCE FOR A SMOOTH RETURN

It may seem a bit odd to suggest preparing for a smooth return from sabbatical before you actually begin it. However, the old saw about an ounce of prevention being worth a pound of cure seems particularly relevant here. As one sabbatical veteran succinctly put it: "You need to spend as much time planning to come back as planning to go. And if you don't, you're going to have problems" (Phythyon, 1993). Wheeler gives good advice in *A Prospectus on Sabbatical Leaves* when he suggests "discussion with the unit administrator before you go on leave about your responsibilities when you return to the unit. This discussion needs to include some thoughts about how you will use your new learning and what role(s) you will fulfill when you return" (p. 6). Especially important is protecting your time upon return by arranging for a reasonable class schedule and by trying to avoid being recruited for major new task forces or similar undertakings.

Conclusion

While very important, the pre-sabbatical stage is, nonetheless, only the prologue to the text. The actual leave period, with its large block of uninterrupted time, holds the key to sabbatical success...or failure. Chapter five will look at some things you can do to ensure a productive and enriching sabbatical leave.

Some *dos* and *don'ts*

1. *Do* take advantage of this precious opportunity to reassess your personal and professional life.

2. *Do* try to stick to your pre-sabbatical schedule of activities.

3. *Do* take the requisite time and care to select and set up a congenial working environment.

4. *Do* gather materials and equipment necessary for completing your sabbatical project.

5. *Don't* overdo it: get done what has to be done, but don't exhaust yourself before the sabbatical leave begins.

Works cited

Good, H. (1992, June). The frustrations and satisfactions of a sabbatical. *The Chronicle of Higher Education*, 24, pp. B2–3.

Jarecky, R., & Sandifer, M. (1986). Faculty members' evaluations of sabbaticals. *Journal of Medical Education*,61(10), 803–807.

Matoney, J., Jr., & Weston, M. (1985). Planning a sabbatical? These tips can save taxes. *AAHE Bulletin*, 38, 11–13.

Mulrow, P. (1989). Sabbatical leave: An important mechanism for revitalizing faculty. *The Journal of Laboratory and Clinical Medicine*, 113, 537–540.

Odorzynski, S. (1988). A case of slow growth: Economist takes a decade to develop seven year sabbatical itch. In K.J. Zahorski (Ed.), *The Beacon*, 3(2), 4–5.

Phythyon, J. (1993). Unpublished interview. De Pere, WI: St. Norbert College, June 1993.

Reynolds, S.J. (1990). Sabbatical: The pause that refreshes. *The Journal of Academic Librarianship*, 16(2), 90–93.

Wheeler, D. (undated publication). *A prospectus on faculty leaves: Opportunities for renewal and growth*. University of Nebraska, Lincoln, NE: IANR Office of Professional and Organizational Development.

5

The Leave Period

Open your mind and close the door behind.
Anonymous sabbatical recipient

Because each sabbatical is unique, generating a list of universally applicable suggestions for enhancing the leave experience is difficult—but not impossible. When asked to identify the key ingredients of a successful sabbatical leave, faculty respond in remarkably similar fashion. These common-denominator responses can be translated into a helpful list of recommendations.

CONSTRUCT A REASONABLE TIMETABLE AND FOLLOW IT

Sabbatical veterans emphasize the importance of faithfully following a pre-planned schedule. Most suggest that the schedule be challenging, even demanding. But while sabbatical veterans stress the importance of practicing self-discipline and of steadfastly adhering to a set schedule, they also recognize the wisdom of building *reasonable* schedules with adequate flex time. Those not doing so admit to suffering from self-imposed pressure, often feeling stressed-out by leave's end. They agree that the next time around they will try to "relax a bit more" and give themselves a "little more resting and breathing time," thus avoiding sabbatical burnout.

Faculty veterans also warn about losing control over the research process, about falling into the trap of spending too much time on the initial research phase. Few scholars have not felt the sirens' call of "definitiveness," continually expanding database searches, investigating side issues and tangentially-related topics, taking voluminous and precise notes on *everything* that might pertain to the topic being researched. Once you have succumbed to this compelling drive toward definitiveness, the three weeks you might have scheduled for a search expands into six, then eight, and so on. In brief, following a set timetable might sound easy to do, but there are potential pitfalls aplenty. Take the necessary precautions: carefully monitor your progress, enlist the aid of a sabbatical advisor to help you in the monitoring, and seriously question the need for extending the preplanned time on any particular project component—especially the initial literature search.

REMAIN FLEXIBLE

In an ideal world, all the careful planning that went into your sabbatical proposal would come to rich fruition: timetables would be followed, deadlines would be met, projects would be completed. In short, everything would happen just as planned. However, we do not live in an ideal world, and the research road, rather than being straight and direct, is typically full of hairpin curves, detours, and *cul de sacs*. In fact, most projects do not proceed as projected. There are almost always at least a few glitches in the process, necessitating modifications— often even radical modifications—in approach, methodology, and strategy.

Sometimes the very success of your project will depend upon your willingness to bend, to be flexible. If you find, for example, that your topic is too broad, you may have to narrow the focus of your project significantly, even if the new scholarly or pedagogical product you now envision bears little resemblance to the original. If your project involves considerable work with as yet unexamined archival materials you will more than likely be faced with the challenge of unexpected research problems. Historians and others working with primary materials, for example, cannot be certain about what they're going to find when they start digging through the archives. While they may find more materials than they anticipated, they may just as readily discover a paucity that necessitates a whole new line of research, thus throwing off the project's entire schedule. One sabbatical recipient reports planning carefully for the study of archival materials only to find that some of them were written in a rare language requiring a special translator. The weeks she had originally planned for this phase of the project turned into months. Uncertainty, then, is part of the sabbatical territory and you must prepare yourself psychologically for the change in plans it is likely to necessitate.

BREAK AWAY FROM YOUR REGULAR ROUTINE AND DUTIES

Faculty who have been on sabbatical seem to agree on one point: *It is essential to remove yourself as completely as possible not only from your regular routine and duties, but also from your "home territory."* This includes staying away from campus and colleagues, extricating yourself from all but the most vital domestic duties, excusing yourself from social and fraternal obligations, and leaving behind as many of your caretaking and caregiving responsibilities as possible.

Whether you believe it or not, your institution and professional colleagues *can* get along without you for a semester, or even a year. And while it may be more difficult for a spouse and children to get along without you, most families are resourceful enough to accommodate an extended leave.

Sabbatical veterans point out that learning to say *no* was central to their success while on leave. But perhaps just as important is avoiding situations likely to compromise the integrity of your sabbatical. One sabbatical returnee reports that when he absolutely had to be on campus he traveled "incognito," making certain no one else knew he was there. No matter what tack you take, however, the key is never wavering from your resolve to decline *all* invitations to deliver presentations, to serve on panels, to handle "pressing" departmental business, and the like.

Many sabbatical veterans strongly recommend travel, pointing out that only by using physical distance as an insulator can someone on leave truly hope to break free from the headlock of routine and responsibility. When living and studying hundreds, or even thousands, of miles away from home there is less likelihood of being asked to serve on a special task force, to fix a broken lawn-mower, to take a child to the dentist. Further, a sojourn in a new cultural setting is in itself refreshing and enriching. Not surprisingly, sabbatical veterans report that living in a new environment constitutes one of the most important parts of a sabbatical learning experience. Even faculty who at the outset are anxious and doubtful about leaving home for an extended period retrospectively deem the travel component the high point of their sabbatical leaves.

KEEP A SABBATICAL DIARY OR JOURNAL

Perhaps the strongest argument for keeping a sabbatical journal is the undependability of memory. Unfortunately, much of what we learn and experience we soon forget. For this reason alone, keeping a sabbatical diary is prudent. But there are several other good reasons for using this device.

- To begin with, the sabbatical journal serves as an excellent monitoring device, providing a detailed record of achievement. Those who have kept sabbatical journals point out that writing their journal entries helped keep them on schedule because in so doing they were continuously reminded of what they had planned to accomplish by certain dates.

- Second, a journal can become a valuable classroom tool if you make a point of recording information of potential use in your courses. The key is to highlight journal passages with classroom potential so that you can easily find this information when you're ready to use it.

- Third, the journal can provide you with concrete information for your sabbatical report. Discoveries, events, conversations, contacts which seem unforgettable at the time, soon become vague memories, or even fade into obscurity. By recording pertinent information while it is still clear in your mind you can construct the foundation for a concrete and meaningful sabbatical report.

- Fourth, the journal can serve as a kind of verbal photo album, enabling you to relive some of your experiences and adventures many years after your leave. Those who have kept a travel log will attest to the power this instrument has for coaxing activities, places, people, scenes, images, and experiences back to the forefront of the memory. The sabbatical diary can serve the same purpose, providing a fine vehicle for helping you retrospectively reflect upon the leave experience.

- Fifth, the journal can serve as a practical tool for documenting potential income tax deductions. James Reuler (1989) sums up the journal's practical value: "In addition to establishing a mechanism for recording sabbatical-related expenditures, a log of professional activities, including interviews, research work, presentations, and manuscript preparations, should be kept. This itemizes tax benefits and grant expenditures, as well as serving as a reference when preparing a summary of the sabbatical for submission to the parent institution on return" (p. 410).

- Sixth, the very act of writing reinforces learning. One of the reasons we assign student papers is because we know that writing enhances the process of critical thinking. The journal provides us with an opportunity to follow our own good counsel. In order to understand and appreciate fully all the things happening to us during a rich and stimulating sabbatical leave, we must reflect upon the process. Writing can prove invaluable to this reflective process, ultimately helping us become "reflective practitioners" (Schön, 1983).

- Seventh, writing can be marvelously therapeutic, helping reduce stress you might experience during the more challenging periods of your leave.

A caveat: If you try the journal or diary approach, use it for at least a month before deciding whether to continue or stop. You will need this period of time to give the process a fair trial. If you don't like the idea of keeping a handwritten journal, try taping your thoughts. Or, if you regularly use a computer, set up an electronic journal. What mode you choose is not particularly important. What is important, though, is avoiding the trap of relying wholly on your memory as a repository of sabbatical experiences. To do so is to invite disappointment and frustration. A final point. You may find it helpful to begin your journal *before* the leave period begins. Faculty trying to sort out their feelings about such things as leaving families behind for extended periods of time while they study abroad, for example, have found the journal to be both self-revealing and cathartic.

SAVOR THE FULL RANGE OF SABBATICAL POSSIBILITIES

Take full advantage of the various opportunities afforded by your sabbatical leave. Do follow your timetable, but don't forget to enjoy yourself. Sabbatical benefits should transcend the purely academic. If you're staying in a different region or in a foreign country, for example, take the time to explore your new locale, to learn about the people, to soak up the culture.

Scholars intent on completing their research projects sometimes isolate themselves, thus losing a splendid opportunity to enrich their sabbaticals, and lives, through interacting with those from different cultures. The most poignant moments of your sabbatical may result from the one-on-one contacts you establish on your travels. These contacts may even prove helpful to a future project. One sabbatical recipient, for example, recounts the following anecdote. While on a sabbatical in Spain in 1983 he sought out the history department offices at the University of Seville to ask for help with an elusive problem. Without realizing it, he ended up talking to the "Catedradico" of the Department of Medieval Spanish History, a prestigious scholar with an international reputation. Ten years later, when applying for another sabbatical in Spain, the faculty member wrote to the professor asking for his help in obtaining a scholar-in-residence position at the University of Cordoba. The professor graciously offered his full assistance, writing an eloquent letter of reference on behalf of the requester (Boyer, 1993).

Further, don't miss the opportunity of getting to know yourself a little better. Sabbaticals afford large blocks of uninterrupted time to think, to philosophize, to meditate. Exploit that luxury to the fullest extent.

In conclusion, do the kinds of things that will not only bring your project to completion, but that will also rejuvenate, refresh, and revitalize you. Go to museums and art galleries; attend concerts; spend time in sidewalk cafes; go out of your way to meet people; attend seminars and lectures. Be as conscientious about scheduling your personal time as you are your professional time. Strike a balance that will help you fully mine the riches of your sabbatical experience.

And, above all else, open yourself to the unexpected. Faculty returning from sabbatical frequently report personal epiphanies leading to new directions in their professional lives. It is impossible to predict what may come of a semester or year off. This delicious uncertainty, this chance for discovery and self-revelation, constitutes the beauty and excitement of the sabbatical.

SOME *DOs* AND *DON'Ts*

1. *Do* follow your sabbatical timetable closely, but make certain your schedule is not unreasonably demanding.

2. *Do* remove yourself as completely as possible from your regular routine and duties.

3. *Do* try to build travel into your leave.

4. *Do* learn to say "no" to non-emergency requests.

5. *Do* keep a sabbatical diary or journal.

6. *Do* schedule some recreational time into your schedule.

7. *Don't* follow a regimen so demanding that you're exhausted before the leave is over.

8. *Don't* rely solely upon your memory as a repository of the sabbatical experience.

WORKS CITED

Boyer, R. (1993). Unpublished interview. De Pere, WI: St. Norbert College, August 1993.

Reuler, J. (1989). Sabbatical. *JAMA*, 261(3), 408–410.

Schön, D. (1983). *The reflective practitioner: How professionals think in action.* New York, NY: Basic Books.

6

Reentry and Follow-Through

Returning to work was difficult. I had not realized how different the pace would seem. I was bothered by the loss of control over my schedule, by the inability to complete one task before being interrupted by something else, and by what seemed to be an enormous amount of wasted time. When I worked at home, I could rise at 6 a.m. and be working by 6:05; at the end of the day I had tangible evidence of my efforts in sheets of notes or writing. Now that I am back...much of my day is consumed by supervision, communication, and workflow management.

Sally Jo Reynolds

Not everyone coming off a sabbatical leave experiences reentry problems. Many faculty, however, do suffer varying degrees of reentry shock (Jarecky and Sandifer, 1986). Some find difficulty in returning to a regular routine after the exhilarating variety of leave activities. Others miss the heightened intellectual stimulation of focused research. Still others find it depressing to lose the freedom to control their schedules as well as the time to pursue areas of interest for uninterrupted periods. For others, colleagues' disinterest in their sabbatical projects creates feelings of disappointment. And still others find difficulty in readjusting to the demands of a full teaching load. In addition, some faculty return with concerns about recouping financial losses as well as continuity in their professional trajectories (Franklin, 1993). And as Jarecky and Sandifer (1986) point out, there are even occasions when those returning become aware not only of "jealousy and envy" in their colleagues, but even of some "resentment" on the part of those "who felt they had been required to absorb the...responsibilities [of their colleagues] while they were away on 'vacation'"(p. 805).

A certain amount of mild depression at the end of a sabbatical leave can be expected. It is as natural as the feeling of letdown we suffer practically every Monday morning—especially after a particularly invigorating, or relaxing, weekend. However, many faculty experience not mild depression, but a far more dramatic letdown. Fortunately, these more pronounced encounters with reentry shock may be prevented by applying antidotes to conditions over which we have some control.

A common denominator in faculty responses to questions about reentry shock is the feeling they could have made their reentry considerably smoother if only they had spent a little more time planning the time period following the sabbatical leave. One sabbatical returnee, after describing his reentry semester as a case of "perpetual jet lag," stressed that next time around he would try to anticipate potential reentry problems and seek appropriate solutions beforehand. Although the search for a panacea for reentry shock has been about as successful as the medieval alchemist's search for the philosopher's stone, some action steps can be taken to ease the shock of reentry.

ARRANGE FOR A "REENTRY FRIENDLY" RETURN SEMESTER

Most faculty returning from a sabbatical leave find themselves faced with a daunting backlog of work: stacks of mail and memos must be sorted through and read, letters must be written, questions from advisees must be answered, syllabi must be constructed, and the list goes on. While many of the collegial duties and responsibilities to which you will return are not negotiable, there are some things you can do ahead of time to make your reentry semester more congenial:

- First, try to avoid taking on new course preparations during the first semester after your return. Consult with your departmental chair about the possibility of setting up a teaching schedule consisting only of courses you've already taught. Further, try to arrange a schedule with as few different preparations as possible—for example, a schedule of one upper-division course and two sections of a multiple section introductory course.

- Second, try to arrange a course schedule providing substantial blocks of time for continuing work on your sabbatical research. For instance, you might try to construct a schedule that frees you from classes one day a week, or that keeps two or three mornings (or afternoons) a week open for research.

- Third, do not volunteer for any ad hoc committee or task force projects, and if at all possible arrange to be freed from your regular committee duties for an entire year.

- And, finally, explore the possibility of getting a one-course release for the return semester. Although this may seem like a "blue sky" recommendation, you will lose nothing by inquiring about the possibility.

BUILD A PSYCHOLOGICAL ADJUSTMENT PERIOD INTO THE LEAVE

Some sabbatical veterans prepare themselves for reentry by slowly working back into their regular professional lives during the last few weeks of the leave. This does not mean taking on duties or regularly participating in activities of the academic community. Nor does it mean attending departmental, faculty, and committee meetings. Rather, it simply means spending some time reading campus newsletters, memos, and other such materials that will help keep you informed about the professional life of your academic community. Or perhaps it might mean attending a few carefully chosen social or cultural events on campus.

In brief, arrange for a gradual transition, but without losing your concentration and focus, and without expending time and energy you should be devoting to your project. Some faculty set aside one day a week—often Friday—for conducting campus-related business, this set routine acting as a kind of quality control mechanism, allowing them to get needed chores done, but helping them resist the temptation of visiting campus too often. You will have to choose the approach that works best for you, but do employ some strategy for effecting a gradual reentry into campus life.

SHARE YOUR FINDINGS

Keep the flames of enthusiasm about your sabbatical project burning brightly by talking and writing about it. Take full advantage of post-sabbatical reporting opportunities: if your institution publishes a faculty newsletter, submit an article describing your sabbatical experience; if your office of faculty development sponsors a brown bag discussion series, offer to make a presentation on your sabbatical findings; if your department or division periodically schedules meetings for sharing scholarship, volunteer a presentation on your sabbatical; if you know of an appropriate journal, submit an article describing either some finding you've made on your leave or the personal and/or cultural enrichment you've experienced. In short, be proactive in your search for appropriate means by which to share with colleagues what you have learned. If your institution does not provide many vehicles for sabbatical sharing, suggest to the appropriate administrators some of the ideas mentioned above.

MAKE USE OF WHAT YOU'VE LEARNED

One of the best ways of prolonging the joy, excitement, and intellectual stimulation of the sabbatical is by making use of your newly-found knowledge in the classroom. Share your learning with your students. Don't miss an opportunity to enrich your class presentations with pertinent anecdotes, correspondence, documents, audio and videotapes, and any other information, resources, and materials your sabbatical research generates. Whenever possible incorporate sabbatical discoveries into your course syllabi through suggested readings, library reserve materials, as well as specific assignments and exercises. If you have kept a sabbatical journal, now is the time to review your entries. Sabbatical returnees report finding a wealth of potential teaching-learning materials there. Productive transfer of sabbatical learning to the classroom does not take place automatically, of course. Careful planning is necessary. Before the leave begins you should decide how and where you are going to record information potentially applicable to your courses.

DEVISE STRATEGIES FOR PROLONGING THE POSITIVE
EFFECTS OF THE SABBATICAL

Once you resume your teaching and collegial responsibilities, it will be impossible to continue doing all the wonderful things you enjoyed while on sabbatical. However, through careful planning—and a dash of ingenuity and resoluteness—you should be able to sustain some of the leave's excitement and intellectual stimulation. For example, setting up a program to continue your sabbatical reading schedule, even if in less concentrated form, will help maintain the flow of new ideas and concepts. Further, through letters, telephone calls, and visits you can carry on professional dialogues begun during the leave, thereby also helping nurture any new friendships you may have established. Some faculty point out they have helped maintain the leave's spirit of excitement by planning a series of short trips for a year or two following the sabbatical.

Unfortunately, even these relatively simple antidotes are not always easily administered once a demanding daily regimen of classes, committee meetings, and other such professional duties puts the squeeze on you. But while difficult, the situation is not impossible. Some sabbatical veterans point out that because the rearranging of priorities accomplished during the pre-planning stage left their lives less cluttered, they had more free time for the kinds of activities mentioned above.

MAKE CONTINGENCY AND FOLLOW-THROUGH PLANS

Due to a wide variety of factors, many sabbatical projects are not completed during the leave period. Some of the most frequently mentioned culprits include: miscalculating time needs; not being able to obtain requisite materials, equipment, and texts; discovering more foundation material than originally anticipated; encountering unforeseen research and logistical problems (and even unforeseen results); and suffering illness, accidents, and personal tragedy. Faculty in the sciences consider their projects especially vulnerable to unexpected delays. As one biologist put it, "In science, every experiment you do gives you more questions. You may be seduced by the dark side of research. In other words, while on leave you may stay in the research mode too long, ending up with mountains of data to analyze but only weeks or days in which to accomplish this" (Phythyon, 1993).

Considering all the things that can delay your completing a project, it is a good idea to draw up a contingency timetable. Do not let your project languish after the leave is over. Projects delayed have a way of getting pushed further and further aside, often never to enjoy closure. However, do not be too harsh on yourself if you do not complete your proposed project. Don't define the sabbatical by task alone. In the long run the product resulting from a completed project may not be nearly as important as the personal and professional development accruing from the research process itself.

REFLECT ON YOUR CAREER AND PERSONAL LIFE

Steve Langerud (1990), in "Re-entry Shock: A Career Dilemma," observes that students who have studied abroad frequently return with a fresh perspective on their life and the world around them: they have had their values challenged, they have been forced to examine their lifestyle, and they are trying to process what they've learned and how they've changed. Langerud could just as well have been describing the return of a faculty member from a sabbatical abroad, or even from an extended leave in some other culturally-distinct area of their own country.

The shock of experiencing a powerful challenge to one's perspective and long-held values can result in reassessing one's career, or at least the philosophical base of one's career. While such a reexamination may result in actually leaving one career for another, more often it results in effecting a change of direction within it. For example, after studying abroad a sociologist might decide to begin researching international cultural relationships; a biologist might wish to spend more time, both in terms of scholarship and teaching, dealing with global ecological problems; and an English professor might begin developing courses with an even stronger core of writings by Third World authors.

The post-leave period is also a good time for reexamining your lifestyle, your work habits, and your personal relationships. Indeed, close introspective reflection is as important *after* your leave as it was *before* it began. Now is the time to reflect back on the leave period in an attempt to determine how it affected you, and how you responded to your sabbatical lifestyle. Did you feel a renewed zest for life? Did you realize you were more exhausted and stressed-out than you had thought? Did you discover new interests? Did spending more quality time with your children help you to see that you really didn't know them as well as you should? Did you discover that you were allowing your profession to dominate your life? That you might even be a workaholic? Did you return with a clearer sense of your own talents…and limitations? Attempting to answer these kinds of questions honestly, although sometimes painful, can help put your life into clearer perspective and ultimately into better balance.

REVIEW YOUR INSTITUTION'S SABBATICAL POLICY

Many institutional sabbatical policies require that faculty returning from leave follow certain reporting and debriefing procedures. One of the most common requirements calls for submitting a formal sabbatical report to the departmental/divisional chair or academic dean within a specified time—usually about a month—after returning from sabbatical leave. However, some institutional policies call not only for written reports, but also for debriefing sessions with a departmental chair or, perhaps, dean of the college. Now is the time to review your sabbatical guidelines and policy statement to make sure you fulfill all the requirements. Failure to do so may jeopardize future sabbatical applications.

SOME FINAL OBSERVATIONS ON THE FIVE STAGES OF THE SABBATICAL EXPERIENCE

- While the actual leave period is undoubtedly the very heart and soul of the sabbatical, avoid glossing over the other vital stages of the enterprise. In fact, the leave itself will invariably suffer if any of the other stages is given short shrift.

- There is no substitute for careful planning. Start early and be willing to spend ample time thinking through your goals and objectives, as well as your plans for accomplishing them. Your return on this investment of time and thought will be substantial.

- Adopting the right attitude and approach are critical to the success of a sabbatical. A sabbatical should be seen as a grand adventure: a time to stretch the mind, rejuvenate the spirit, and perhaps even heal the body. The sabbatical is also a time for risk taking. Adopt a pioneering spirit. Boldly push into new research and teaching territory. But prepare yourself for setbacks and disappointments—they often come with the territory.

- The sabbatical, like so many other enterprises, returns proportionately what you put into it. Give, and give generously, to your sabbatical enterprise, but don't be unfair to yourself and to your institution by taking on an impossible task. Be ambitious, but define your project realistically and be reasonable in your expectations.

All of us hope for the perfect sabbatical. Perhaps if we plan carefully, adopt the right attitude, and have everything fall into place, we, too, can write as part of our sabbatical report what one fortunate recipient penned: "I don't believe I could have done more, or have done things differently, which would have improved my sabbatical. It was essentially everything I had hoped it would be."

SOME *DOs* AND *DON'Ts*

1. *Do* build a psychological adjustment period into the latter part of your leave.

2. *Do* devise strategies for prolonging the enjoyment and intellectual stimulation of your sabbatical leave.

3. *Do* share your findings with colleagues and students.

4. *Do* follow through on your project and make every effort to bring it to closure.

5. *Do* have a debriefing with your departmental/divisional chair, your director of faculty development, or your academic dean.

6. *Don't* let reentry shock get the best of you; there are ways of effectively combating it.

7. *Don't* wait for others to initiate dialogue about your sabbatical project; take the initiative.

8. *Don't* forget to submit a written report to the appropriate committee or academic officer.

A SABBATICAL CHECKLIST AND TIMETABLE

In the best of all possible worlds—a world without distractions, delays, emergencies, procrastination, burdensome committee duties, and the like—you would be able to pursue the following schedule methodically, giving ample time to each item in the sequence. However, because our lives are not always as orderly as we would like, and because circumstances beyond our control often thwart the best of plans and intentions, you may not be able to accomplish each of the checklist items within the suggested timeline. This is an ideal framework. Some modification, and even compression, is possible without jeopardizing your project.

ACTIVITIES	**TIMETABLE** Number of Months Before Application Deadline
1. Pre-Application Reflection and Planning *	
a. Clarify goals and objectives	18–24
b. Define your project	18–24
c. Determine feasibility	18–24
d. Discuss plans with departmental/divisional chair	18–24
e. Meet with departmental colleagues	18–24
f. Determine budgetary needs	18–24
g. Examine personal circumstances	18–24
h. Explore funding possibilities	18–24
i. Explore possibility of a faculty exchange	18–24
j. Consider applying for scholar-in-residence status	18–24
2. Application Process	
a. Request letters of support and begin gathering other supporting documents	3–6
b. Prepare proposal	3–6
1) Study sabbatical leave guidelines	
2) Consult with sabbatical veterans and attend informational sessions	
3) Study copies of successful sabbatical proposals	
4) Enlist a trustworthy proofreader	Institutional
c. Submit completed application to review committee	deadline
3. Pre-Sabbatical Preparation	Number of months before leave (assuming first semester sabbatical)
a. Begin following pre-sabbatical preparation schedule	8
b. Reassess your personal/professional life	8
c. Gather materials and do background reading	entire period
d. Find a sabbatical advisor/mentor	4–7

e.	Make travel and housing arrangements	4–7
f.	Set up a congenial work environment	2–4
g.	Make special arrangements	1–3
h.	Prepare in advance for a smooth return	1–3

4. The Leave Period
   a. Follow sabbatical leave timetable
   b. Remain flexible
   c. Break away from routine
   d. Keep a sabbatical diary or journal
   e. Savor the experience

		Number of months after the leave period
5.	Reentry and Follow-Through	
a.	Submit a written report to the appropriate academic officer	1–2
b.	Offer a seminar or presentation for interested colleagues	1–3
c.	Prolong positive effects of leave	ongoing
d.	Share your findings with colleagues and students	ongoing
e.	Make use of what you've learned	ongoing

* William Van Til (1971) suggests that if planning international travel and work you may need at least two years of lead time rather than the year to a year-and-a-half suggested here.

WORKS CITED

Franklin, T. (1993). Planning successful sabbaticals. *The Department Chair*, Spring, 8–9.

Jarecky, R., & Sandifer, M. (1986). Faculty members' evaluations of sabbaticals. *Journal of Medical Education,* 61(10), 803–807.

Langerud, S. (1990). Re-entry shock: A career dilemma. *Experiential Education,* 15(5), 6 and 17.

Phythyon, J. (1993). Unpublished interview. De Pere, WI: St. Norbert College, June 1993.

Reynolds, S.J. (1990). Sabbatical: The pause that refreshes. *The Journal of Academic Librarianship*, 16(2), 90–93.

Van Til, W. (1971). One way of looking at it: Anyone for international work? *Phi Delta Kappan,* 53, 154–155.

THE INSTITUTIONAL CONTEXT

7

The Role of Faculty Development

Many current indicators point to the critical need for continuous growth and renewal opportunities for faculty. Diverse societal demands on colleges, such as rapidly advancing technologies, greater accountability and productivity in academic quality, addressing highly diversified needs of students and especially of high-risk student populations, and preparing students for an ever-changing world-of-work, cause faculty to face continuous learning and self-development just to stay current.

Betty Kyger Miller

While not all institutions have full-fledged faculty development programs, most have at least a set of faculty development practices and some type of faculty development agent. At some institutions the agent is the director of faculty (or instructional) development, in others the departmental or divisional chair, and in still others the dean of the college or perhaps the associate academic dean. In some cases, the agent is the chair of a faculty development committee. This chapter is aimed primarily at these agents—faculty and administrators who have as their full- or part-time responsibility the task of promoting the personal and professional growth of faculty in all stages of their careers.

However, even those readers from institutions currently without faculty development programs or agents should find the following chapter of considerable value. For example, those currently planning faculty development programs may wish to incorporate some of the components described in this chapter. And those not yet in the actual planning stages, but hoping to gain approval for launching a program, may find this material useful in constructing a statement of rationale, or perhaps even a proposal. Faculty readers, whether enjoying the benefits of a program or not, will find references to helpful resources they can use to enrich their sabbatical experience.

Faculty development agents are in an excellent position to help their colleagues meet the challenges of the sabbatical. Although the role of faculty development will vary according to the special needs of each sabbatical program and the faculty it serves, the following discussion identifies some of faculty development's primary functions in leave programs. For purposes of economy, all faculty development agents will be subsumed under the descriptor *director* in the rest of this chapter. Further, the terms staff development, professional development, instructional development, and faculty development are used interchangeably. This chapter discusses the various roles played by the faculty development director.

SERVE AS FACILITATOR AND CONSULTANT

The faculty development director has ample opportunity, as facilitator and consultant, to assist colleagues throughout the sabbatical process. This assistance may take many forms.

Some applicants may need help interpreting institutional guidelines and policies governing sabbaticals. Thus, it is incumbent upon the director to study carefully all institutional materials pertaining to the sabbatical, or at least to know where to obtain this information. The director should also be familiar with the institution's sabbatical rotation and quota systems (both written and unwritten), as well as the policies, peculiarities, and politics of sabbatical review procedures, whether practiced by a committee or academic administrator. Since policies, procedures, and the like are often scattered throughout the institutional literature, the director can perform a valuable service by gathering these materials, organizing them in a reader-friendly format, adding a section or two on deadlines, helpful resources, and procedural tips—and then publishing them in the form of a sabbatical manual or handbook.

Other applicants may need assistance in identifying funding sources. A director with a good understanding of both internal and external funding sources and systems can prove invaluable to a colleague seeking support monies. Specific suggestions for the kinds of materials and information a director should have at hand are listed in a subsequent section on resource centers.

Applicants may also need assistance in formulating their sabbatical budgets. Putting together a detailed budget largely based upon extrapolative estimates can be tricky, especially for someone who has not done it before. While not all faculty development directors are expected to be financial whizzes, by virtue of their experience in helping others through the budget-making process most developers will probably have a better grasp of the technique than the typical applicant. Faculty embarking on overseas study for the first time are especially vulnerable to miscalculating costs. Well-informed directors, armed with good resources, can provide colleagues with information, tips, and references that may make the difference between a successful or failed study abroad project.

Still other applicants may ask the director for help in organizing the sabbatical proposal, or perhaps in reading a first draft and providing feedback. Once again, the experience gained from reading many such proposals can help make a director a knowledgeable and helpful critic. Further, because the director will probably be from outside the applicant's discipline, he or she can serve as a source of quality control, helping determine, for example, whether a proposal uses too much specialized jargon.

In addition to helping critique proposals, the director should set up an open file of successful sabbatical proposals. Reviewing these proposals with the sabbatical applicant can be an important first step in constructing a solid application.

The faculty development director may also assist in the sabbatical process through personal consultation. Few applicants are spared the stress and anxiety attendant upon drafting a major sabbatical proposal. These unsettling feelings are party crashers *par excellence*, deftly insinuating themselves into our lives before we even realize we've opened the door to them. But how can we remove them once they've taken up residence in our minds? Perhaps the most potent form of exorcism is dialogue, and part of the job of a director of faculty development should be to talk through the problems and concerns of their colleagues.

Most sabbatical recipients need someone with whom to discuss their projects, an objective, but sensitive, "coach" who will check the validity of methodologies and findings, monitor progress, and provide encouragement. This type of input is essential not only for the health of the project, but also for the psychological well being of the researcher. Directors should try hard to function in the role of a supportive colleague, helping bolster the faculty member's spirits through praise and encouragement. As one colleague noted on a sabbatical questionnaire aimed at defining the role of the director in the sabbatical process: "Keep in mind how delicate the buds of creativity can be and do your best to nurture, not prune" (St. Norbert College Sabbatical Survey, 1989).

The faculty development director can also be of immense help to faculty before, during, and after sabbatical leave by serving as a time management and "efficiency" consultant. In "Is Released Time an Effective Component of Faculty Development Programs," Robert Boice (1987) provides compelling evidence obtained from four demonstrational experiments that "campuses [funding] *conventional* programs of released time may be investing resources unwisely" (p. 315) if they do not also help faculty use their time more efficiently. Pointing out that "released time alone is not sufficient to ensure productivity in research and scholarship" (p. 323), Boice goes on to say that faculty can make good use of their released time only if they first cast aside their old, ineffective work habits. Most especially, faculty seem to be in need of better time management skills. Through time management workshops, faculty development agents trained in these skills can help sabbatical recipients become more efficient and confident time managers, thus protecting the faculty member's sabbatical investment, as well as the institution's.

Finally, the faculty development director can move beyond individual consultation into the realm of group activities. Through sabbatical workshops, for example, directors can provide a valuable service to entire groups of prospective applicants, an approach which might be particularly effective in large institutions with active sabbatical leave programs. The sabbatical workshop can be a real workhorse, helping faculty with all stages of the sabbatical, from planning to reentry. One approach might be to sponsor a series of workshops, devoting each one to a specific sabbatical stage or component. For example, the initial workshop could focus upon effective planning and goal-setting techniques, the next could involve hands-on exercises aimed at helping faculty organize and draft proposals, the next could focus on budget making, and so on. The possibilities are limited only by the director's imagination and resourcefulness.

Faculty developer Robert Boice (1993), for example, runs a special program for faculty on sabbaticals aimed at improving their writing. Pointing out that "sabbaticals strike many faculty at both research and comprehensive campuses as ideal times to get on track as writers," Boice forms one or two small groups (usually 4-6 members each) that meet with him biweekly for either the semester or academic year. Through these groups he helps sabbatical recipients "find fluency as writers" and links teaching with writing/scholarship by urging faculty participants "to attend to parallels between writing and teaching (e.g., the importance of moderate pacing; the value of letting other people do some of the work) and to write out some of their usual lecture presentations as scholarly, instructive pieces to be shared with students and colleagues." Boice reports that in the past few years "the program has helped all 17 sabbatical writers…finish a major writing project during their semester or two of participation" (p. 1).

Clearly, directors of faculty development can play important roles as sabbatical consultants and facilitators, but only if they conscientiously prepare themselves for the task. In order to be truly helpful to their colleagues they must do some homework. For example, a director should:

1. Carefully study the institutional guidelines and policies governing sabbaticals;

2. Read the model sabbatical proposals on open file;

3. Establish familiarity with internal and external sources of financial support;

4. Read some of the best "how to" books on grant writing;

5. Read the literature on sabbaticals; and

6. Become proficient in developing budgets.

This list is not meant to be definitive, but rather illustrative of the kind of preparation a director must undertake in order to enter into the role of facilitator-consultant in good faith.

PROMOTE THE SABBATICAL CONCEPT AND INSTITUTIONAL PROGRAM

One effective promotional strategy is to target the sabbatical as the focus of the faculty development program for a year or two. My own experience with this type of targeting may be instructive. Let us use as a kind of case study the strategy I used during the 1988–89 academic year at St. Norbert College.

I began by inviting colleagues recently returned from sabbatical to deliver presentations on their leave experiences. One of the best vehicles I found for this reporting was the Office of Faculty Development's "Food for Thought" program, a series of informal noon-hour discussion sessions dedicated to promoting an exchange of ideas about teaching and scholarship. I scheduled some of the presentations through that series, and others through various topical sessions. Secondly, I began a series in the faculty development newsletter called "Replenishing the Well: Reflections on the Sabbatical Experience." These retrospective essays, all written by recent sabbatical returnees, were not necessarily meant to be "how-to" articles, but based on the positive feedback I received from my readers, the insights and experiences the authors shared did prove helpful to those who later went on sabbatical. And, finally, I administered a questionnaire to all St. Norbert College faculty who had taken sabbaticals over the past decade, distributing the survey results to faculty colleagues.

In addition to the strategies outlined above, a faculty developer should work with appropriate unit administrators in getting sabbatical recipients both on- and off-campus publicity. As part of this promotional strategy, the director can feature articles on sabbatical awards in the faculty development newsletter. Another way of honoring sabbatical recipients is through a faculty development sponsored reception, at which sabbatical awardees are introduced and honored.

These are but a few of the things that can be done to promote the sabbatical through a faculty development program. Remember, too, that just because the sabbatical has been the center of attention for a year or two does not mean it should be forgotten at the end of that time period. The emphasis need not be as great, perhaps, but a director should still periodically schedule programs and presentations dealing with the sabbatical.

PREPARE A HANDBOOK OF TIPS AND GUIDELINES

While most colleges and universities publish detailed sabbatical policy statements, usually in the form of a section in the faculty handbook, far fewer make available additional information aimed at facilitating the sabbatical planning and application process. Fewer still offer suggestions to faculty on how to make best possible use of the sabbatical leave. The director of faculty development is in a good position to fill this void.

The task of putting together a pamphlet, brochure, or handbook for this purpose sounds arduous, but need not be. One way of proceeding is to administer a questionnaire to colleagues who have been on sabbatical, asking them to identify strategies, procedures, and methodologies which have worked for them. You can then analyze and compile the results, making them the core of your handbook.

There is no one format right for all institutions. Institutional culture, program size, administrative and governance style—all will help determine the form the handbook takes. The following list of possible components is meant to be illustrative, not definitive:

1. A copy of the institution's sabbatical policy and guidelines;

2. The philosophy and role of the sabbatical review committee;

3. The role of the office of faculty development;

4. A sabbatical checklist and timetable;

5. Tips on how to prepare for and take full advantage of the various stages of the sabbatical experience;

6. The benefits of a sabbatical;

7. Application/enrollment forms;

8. A few examples of sabbatical applications and reports; and

9. A selective bibliography of works on the sabbatical.

MONITOR POST-SABBATICAL PROGRESS

Frequently, the work begun on sabbatical is not completed during the leave proper. In such instances, the post-sabbatical period takes on particularly great importance in that unfinished projects can either be brought to fruition at that time—or can be left to die on the vine. Work remains to be done, the research is fresh in the mind of the scholar, and the momentum has been established, but now the vital ingredient of uninterrupted time has been snatched away. This difficult situation all too frequently ends with the sabbatical returnee pushing the project aside in favor of the more pressing concerns of a full teaching load and a wide array of collegial duties.

A director of faculty development can help bring about a more positive outcome. But this can be done only if a director closely monitors the reentry of a returning colleague and employs sensitive interventions. At the very least, a director should set up a debriefing session with sabbatical returnees, discussing their projects and sabbatical experiences, and offering to serve as a resource person and consultant. This initial session should be followed by periodic telephone calls or notes inquiring about the continuing work. The particular interventions employed will depend upon the problems and needs of each returnee. But one general rule applies across the board: without being intrusive or disruptive, directors should do their best to help returnees bring their sabbatical work to fruition.

A final note. The director should not forget about those whose proposals were turned down. These faculty should be encouraged to apply again. Rejection may lead to disillusionment and cynicism—even to a lack of faith in the system. Gentle counseling and support are crucial during these downtimes in a faculty member's professional life.

FACILITATE POST-SABBATICAL REPORTING

Most institutions require faculty returning from sabbatical leave to file a report. Many also require some type of public presentation. In fact, most sabbatical returnees want to make presentations, whether required to or not. Indeed, faculty returning from their leaves are eager to share what they've learned, to try out their new ideas, to reminisce about some of their scholarly and travel adventures. Interchange among peers constitutes a logical extension of the sabbatical experience. The director should facilitate this sharing.

The director's challenge is to develop a broad repertoire of reporting vehicles. The traditional forum for sabbatical sharing is the topical session or seminar specifically designed for the purpose of making sabbatical reports. These sessions are relatively easy to set up, and, if adequately publicized, usually draw well. Further, they can be made even more widely appealing through co-sponsorship with other offices. For example, a sabbatical project involving some aspect of cultural diversity lends itself to co-sponsorship with the institution's office of cultural diversity. Such cooperative programming helps universalize a topic, the resultant broadening of appeal often resulting in increased attendance. Further, co-sponsorship can help put a sabbatical topic, and the sabbatical program itself, into a broader institutional context. For instance, since enhancing cultural diversity is a key initiative on most campuses, the co-sponsored session mentioned above could serve to remind the entire academic community of how the sabbatical program can help enhance the institutional mission.

But besides the conventional sabbatical seminar, or some permutation thereof, what other vehicles can a director use to promote post-sabbatical sharing? Here are a few other possibilities.

- A brown bag *luncheon series* treating various pedagogical and scholarly topics lends itself nicely to a series of sabbatical reports.

- A regularly-scheduled *fall kickoff or semester-break faculty development conference* can be devoted to the sabbatical, featuring, as one possibility, a series of presentations on cutting-edge scholarship generated through sabbatical leaves.

- A *faculty development newsletter* is another effective vehicle for sabbatical sharing. Faculty development directors who edit these newsletters might consider inaugurating a special series consisting of articles written by faculty recently returned from sabbatical leaves. Such articles have fine potential for being both informative and entertaining, since sabbatical recipients can describe not only their sabbatical projects, but also what they learned about themselves, other cultures, and the process of scholarship or pedagogy. When laced with the colorful adventures faculty often experience on sabbatical leave, these articles take on a human interest dimension that makes them especially appealing, often even inspiring.

The director, however, should serve not only as a programming agent, but also as a motivator and facilitator. Some faculty are reluctant to initiate the setting up of a sharing session, thinking this might be viewed as self serving. In these cases, the director should take the initiative, warmly inviting (cajoling and coaxing, where necessary) colleagues to share what they have learned. Further, the director should help prospective presenters find an appropriate presentational format, one which will have the most universal appeal. If, for example, the sabbatical project is quite technical and specialized, the director ought to challenge the presenter to explain the concept in non-jargon terms understandable to a lay audience. In some cases, where the research is extraordinarily sophisticated, the director might want to recommend that the presenter focus not upon the research, but rather upon some other aspect of the leave—perhaps a commentary on the adventures encountered while working in a large corporate or government laboratory, or on the challenges and rewards of a scholar-in-residence position. Just talking about the project with an interested and sympathetic listener will assist sabbatical returnees in sorting out their feelings about their experiences, thus helping put the leave into proper perspective.

Finally, a faculty development director can perform a valuable function by serving as a kind of clearinghouse for returnees who wish to share what they have learned with students in their own and other's classes. One way of doing this is through compiling a directory of faculty willing to give presentations on topics drawn from their sabbatical research and experiences. The first step in this process might be to send out a memo inviting all sabbatical recipients of the past five years or so to submit a list of topics from which they would be willing to make classroom presentations. The director would place the names of these faculty, along with their topics, in a directory which would then be sent to all faculty. Such a directory would serve not only as a helpful resource to the entire academic community, but also would help promote and nurture the institution's sabbatical program. Perhaps most importantly, it would emphasize the pedagogical value of sabbaticals, demonstrating how faculty learning translates directly into enhanced student learning.

The sharing of what is learned from a sabbatical with the entire academic community constitutes a logical and productive extension of the sabbatical experience, and the office of faculty development can perform a valuable service by offering a broad array of opportunities to nurture this enriching dialogue. Such conversations not only make the sabbatical experience more satisfying, but also help foster collegiality and the spirit of community throughout the institution.

ACT AS LIAISON OFFICER

The role of the faculty development agent in a college or university depends in large measure upon the institution's governance system, administrative philosophy and style, as well as its culture, politics, and traditions. In some institutions, the faculty development director's role is purely facilitative. Other institutions place responsibility for leave programs, including policy making and administration, largely in the hands of the office of faculty development. Whatever the system or situation, the faculty development director should endeavor to set up a mechanism through which he or she can work closely with other academic officers in helping keep the sabbatical program strong, healthy, and responsive to faculty and institutional needs.

There are sound reasons for a faculty development agent assuming a central position in overseeing a sabbatical leave program. To begin with, the sabbatical leave is the "most common form of faculty renewal" (Boyer, 1987) and thus a sabbatical program is clearly within the bailiwick of the office of faculty development. Secondly, faculty developers, with their training and expertise in teaching-learning skills and issues, can be of particular value not only in helping faculty plan pedagogically-oriented sabbaticals, but also in helping wed research to classroom learning, thereby constructing a conduit for channeling sabbatical learning into the classroom. And, finally, faculty development personnel often get to know the faculty better than chief administrative officers, who are generally further removed from the academic trenches. However, the valuable information possessed by faculty developers is of little value if not regularly shared with other academic officers involved in administering the sabbatical program.

One way of ensuring a regular exchange of information is by creating a sabbatical coordinating committee which meets on a regular basis for the purpose of overseeing the institutional program. While the membership of this committee will vary from campus to campus, a representative body might include the academic dean, the chair of the sabbatical review committee, the director of faculty development, and two or three departmental/divisional chairs. This group would use its meetings to: (a) monitor faculty eligibility for sabbatical leaves (perhaps through a master list indicating the year each faculty member is eligible to apply for a leave); (b) study the record of sabbatical applications and leaves with an eye toward discerning significant patterns; (c) discuss the potential effects the taking of sabbatical leaves may have upon particular disciplines and academic programs; (d) help identify vehicles for post-sabbatical reporting; and (e) seek ways of strengthening the sabbatical program.

SET UP AND SUPERVISE A RESOURCE CENTER

Up to this point the emphasis has been upon the interpersonal functions of directors of faculty development, rather than upon their roles as collectors, caretakers, and disseminators of resource materials. In fact, there is a wide variety of texts, articles, and audio-visual aids that can prove helpful to faculty going through the various stages of the sabbatical experience. Directors of faculty development should obtain these materials, study them, and make them accessible to colleagues engaged in the sabbatical enterprise.

Most institutions with faculty or instructional development programs have some type of resource center, although it may go by another name—for example, the instructional development center, or teaching improvement center, or perhaps the learning enhancement center. Much of the material already housed in these centers will be pertinent to faculty engaged in sabbatical projects—especially those working on pedagogical or curricular development enterprises. In most cases, however, directors can substantially strengthen holdings of the kinds of materials, information, and equipment that will help faculty prepare for, and carry through, the extended leave. The following list identifies and briefly describes some of the primary resources and services a resource center can offer the sabbatical applicant.

Open file of successful sabbatical proposals

Few exercises are more valuable to a prospective applicant than examining firsthand a few successful sabbatical proposals. Studying the actual documents can provide answers to important questions: What type of project is likely to be approved? How long and detailed should my proposal be? How much time should I devote to providing a rationale for my project? How comprehensive should I make my projected timetable? How specific should I make my itemized budget? Which of my anticipated expenses are eligible for in-house funding support? What types of supporting documents should I include? What kind of tone and style should I strive for?

Setting up an open file of successful sabbatical proposals is not difficult. All a director need do is send a memo to sabbatical veterans asking for permission to place copies of their applications on open file in the resource center. Colleagues rarely refuse such requests. In fact, most faculty are pleased to be asked and are eager to share this material. If a response is not forthcoming, a telephone call or office visit is often all that is needed. The open file need not be voluminous. Five to ten applications will suffice, especially if they have been carefully chosen to represent a variety of proposals, from pedagogical and curricular enhancement projects, through artistic endeavors, to more conventional research activities. All proposals should be carefully screened, and only those representing a standard of quality worthy of emulation should be placed on public file.

In-house funding information

A resource center should house up-to-date information on all in-house funding sources, including official guidelines and application forms. It would also be a good idea to complement this file with an additional open file of successful applications to in-house funds most pertinent to sabbatical support (see Figure 1).

External funding information

In addition to in-house funding materials, a resource center should house a grant registry of external funding sources. Ideally, such a registry should hold information in alphabetically arranged folders on the major private foundations as well as primary corporate and government granting agencies (see Figure 1).

The registry should represent a broad spectrum of grant opportunities. Faculty from the natural sciences, for example, should be able to find information on such foundations and agencies as The Grass Foundation, The National Science Foundation, and The American Association for the Advancement of Science. Faculty from the social sciences should have access to folders on sources such as The American Institute for Economic Research, The American Council on Education, The Center for Advanced Study in the Behavioral Sciences, and The Social Science Research Council. Similarly, the registry should provide faculty from the humanities and fine arts with a variety of funding opportunities ranging from the Stanford Humanities Center and The National Endowment of the Humanities, to the National Endowment for the Arts.

In addition, the registry should contain information on the major philanthropic agencies, including such key sources as The Fulbright Scholar Program, The Danforth Foundation, and The John Simon Guggenheim Memorial Foundation; on specialized sources of funding, such as funds specifically aimed at supporting women scholars (e.g., The Mary Ingraham Bunting Institute and The Monticello College Foundation); and on funding sources for international studies and studies abroad projects.

FIGURE 1

SAMPLE LIST OF FUNDING SOURCES IN GRANT REGISTRY

American Council on Education

American Council of Learned Societies

American Institute for Economic Research

American Institute for Foreign Study

American Philosophical Society

American Scandinavian Foundation

Amoco Foundation

ARCO Foundation

Bunting Institute

Business & Professional Women's Foundation

Center for Advanced Study in the Behavioral Sciences

Council on International Educational Exchange

Council for International Exchange of Scholars

Council on Library Resources

Dana Foundation

Danforth Foundation

Dirksen Congressional Center

Dreyfus Foundation

Earhart Foundation

Eppley Foundation for Research

Feris Foundation of America

Folger Shakespeare Library

Ford Foundation

Fulbright Scholar Program

Fund for the Improvement of Postsecondary Education

German Academic Exchange Service

G. Paul Getty Trust

Grass Foundation

Guggenheim Foundation

Hastings Center

Hazen Foundation

Humanities Institute

Huntington Library Research Awards

Institute for Advanced Study

Institute for Research in the Humanities

International Research and Exchanges Board

Japan Foundation

Judicial Fellows Program

Kaiser Family Foundation

Kellogg Foundation

Life Sciences Research Foundation

MacArthur Foundation

Markey Charitable Trust

Marshall Fund of the U.S.

Mellon Postdoctoral Fellowships

National Academy of Education

National Council of Teachers of English Research Foundation

National Endowment for the Arts

National Endowment for the Humanities

National Geographic Society

National Science Foundation

Pew Charitable Trust

Randolph program for International Peace

Research Corporation

Rockefeller Foundation

Sage Foundation

Sinfonia Foundation

Sloan Foundation

Smithsonian Institute

Social Science Research Council

Spencer Foundation

Stanford Humanities Center

U.S. Department of Education

Wenner-Gren Foundation

Woodrow Wilson Fellowship Foundation

If carefully set up for the convenience of its users (it should contain not only informational brochures, but application kits as well) and regularly updated, the grant registry can be an important tool for faculty seeking external financial support for their sabbatical projects.

External funding reference texts

Faculty seeking financial support from external agencies may find it helpful to consult one or more of the many reference texts identifying sources for external funding, most notably *The Directory of Research Grants*, APA's *Guide to Research Support*, *The Foundations Directory*, and *Foundation Grants to Individuals*. Once sabbatical applicants have located the pertinent grant sources, they may then wish to consult helpful "how-to" handbooks such as Mary Hall's *Developing Skills in Proposal Writing*, Virginia P. White's *Grants: How to Find Out About Them and What to Do Next*, Mary Rubin's *How to Get Money for Research*, and David G. Bauer's *The Complete Grants Sourcebook for Higher Education* (please see Appendix D for a more complete listing of reference and "how-to" texts).

Applicants interested in sharpening their grant writing skills should study *Winning Grants: A Systematic Approach for Higher Education*, a cooperative project of ACE, David G. Bauer, and University of Nebraska Television. This impressive set of ten videotapes keyed to a *"How to" Grants Manual* provides a workshop-like experience in the comfort of either the resource center or the applicant's home.

The resource center should probably also subscribe to *News, Notes, & Deadlines*. Published six times a year by the Association of College and University Officers, this helpful newsletter constitutes an invaluable source of timely information on grant sources and application deadlines. Another excellent source of information is *The Grant Advisor*, a monthly newsletter (except July) containing timely articles on the national grant picture, detailed reviews of grant programs, and a helpful "Deadline Memo" listing hundreds of grant programs in deadline order.

Texts on financial matters pertaining to sabbatical leave

Most faculty need some help with the finances pertaining to a sabbatical leave, especially those involving income taxes. Thus, the director of faculty development should keep on the shelves of the resource center one or two up-to-date texts on taxes. One of the most useful is *The Tax Guide for College Teachers and other College Personnel* (published annually), which contains a helpful section detailing which sabbatical-related expenses may be deducted from your income taxes. Another excellent source of information is the Internal Revenue Service's Tax Guide for U.S. Citizens and Resident Aliens Abroad (Publication 54, Cat. NO. 14999 E). Texts like this are in heavy demand by faculty in general, so it is a good idea to order multiple copies and place them on a strict reserve or short-term checkout system.

Texts and handbooks on studying and traveling abroad

Faculty frequently undertake sabbatical projects involving travel and study abroad. International travel projects add a new dimension to sabbatical planning. The following texts serve as congenial and dependable guides to faculty doing their sabbatical work in foreign climes.

- Barbara Cahn Connotillo's (Ed.) *Teaching Abroad.* New York, NY: Institute of International Education, 1988.

- Crauford D. Goodwin and Michael Nacht's *Abroad and Beyond: Patterns in American Overseas Education.* Cambridge, England: Cambridge University Press, 1988.

- E. Marguerite Howard's (Ed.) *Academic Year Abroad: The Most Complete Guide to Planning Academic Year Study Abroad.* New York, NY: Institute of International Education, 1993.

- Sally Innis Klitz's *Faculty Handbook for Sabbaticals Abroad.* Storrs, CT: The University of Connecticut, 1984.

- Jayne and Tony Ralston's *The Sabbatical Book.* Buffalo, NY: The Roylott Press, 1987.

- UNESCO's *Study Abroad,* 1992–93. France: Unipub, 1991.

Time management newsletters and audiotapes

Careful time management is requisite to a productive sabbatical leave. The director of the resource center can help faculty hone their time management skills by first alerting sabbatical applicants to the importance of planning and managing time, and then by directing them to key resources in the center. Some helpful audiotapes include Janet Attard's *You Can Organize Yourself for Peak Productivity* and *Getting Organized: Overcoming the Roadblocks to Personal Organization.* Each set of tapes comes with a helpful manual. Harold Taylor's *The Time Management Report,* is a good monthly newsletter containing a wide variety of practical time management tips and strategies. There are a number of excellent full-length texts on time management, several of which are identified in Appendix C.

Reference texts and handbooks on writing, editing, and publishing

Most sabbatical projects involve considerable writing and editing, often with publication as a projected outcome. In light of this, the director ought to make the resource center a well-stocked scholar-writer's way station, its shelves holding a carefully chosen collection of reference texts, handbooks, and style manuals aimed at facilitating the writing, editing, and publishing process. Besides standard references such as an unabridged dictionary, a good thesaurus, a biographical dictionary, and a guide to abbreviations, the collection should contain widely-used style manuals (e.g., *The Chicago Manual of Style; The MLA*

Style Manual; Turabian's *A Manual for Writers of Term Papers, Theses, and Dissertations;* the APA *Style Manual;* and the *U.S. Government Printing Office Style Manual*); helpful guides to writing with word processors (including texts on preparing electronic manuscripts such as the *Chicago Guide to Preparing Electronic Manuscripts for Authors and Publishers*); and a broad spectrum of handbooks dealing with topics such as nonsexist writing, copyright laws and guidelines, research theory and practice, proposal writing, manuscript editing, and desktop publishing. If the budget is adequate, the center's collection should also contain the current edition of *Books in Print.*

Hardware resources

Some types of hardware may also prove useful to faculty on, or preparing for, sabbatical leave. For example, because many pedagogical and scholarly resources now appear in videotape form, sabbatical researchers will appreciate a resource center equipped with a television monitor and VHS recorder/player. With this type of equipment the center can serve as a convenient viewing room for tapes such as Bauer's *Winning Grants.*

For those faculty who use a microcomputer, but who do not yet own one, or for those whose microcomputers are off-campus, a state-of-the-art microcomputer and printer in the resource center will also prove quite useful. Further, the center could house a software library containing a wide array of software ranging from data management and spreadsheet systems to sophisticated word processing packages.

Faculty expertise

The director of faculty development should not neglect one of the most important human resources on campus—faculty colleagues. Faculty who have been on extended leave return with vast amounts of useful information about every aspect of the sabbatical. In particular, they return with a fine repertoire of travel information. The director of faculty development should tap this reservoir, inviting sabbatical returnees to submit a brief written statement about good places to stay, eat, and visit. These suggestions can then be compiled into a faculty travel guide which either can be housed in the faculty development resource center or published in pamphlet form and sent to all faculty.

CONCLUSION

As has been stated earlier, one of the great ironies involving the sabbatical leave is that this important professional growth opportunity is frequently treated with benign neglect. Both leave recipient and institution could receive more from sabbaticals if someone with the requisite knowledge, information, and concern, would provide guidance. The faculty development professional is in a position to help provide this valuable service.

If they are to succeed in enhancing the system, however, faculty development agents must take the initiative in setting up activities, programs, workshops, and services designed to promote and aid the sabbatical process. They must not only incorporate sabbatical assistance components into faculty development programs, but also attempt to integrate a faculty member's sabbatical planning into his or her total professional growth plan. And, just as importantly, they must take the time to become knowledgeable about the sabbatical system, its philosophy, and its procedures.

A final word of caution. Because the sabbatical is one of the oldest and most conventional components of an institution's faculty development program, directors may be tempted to give it short shrift, concentrating instead on fledgling programs seemingly in need of more nurturing. Assuming that longevity naturally results in peak efficiency or productivity, however, can be costly. Sabbatical programs need care and attention, too. Directors of faculty development must not take lightly their responsibility for nurturing sabbatical programs.

WORKS CITED

Anonymous response (1989). St. Norbert College Sabbatical Survey. De Pere, WI: St. Norbert College Office of Faculty Development.

Boice, R. (1987). Is released time an effective component of faculty development programs? *Research in Higher Education, 26,* 311–326.

Boice, R. (1993). Correspondence, January 6, 1993.

Boyer, E.L. (1987). *College: The undergraduate experience in America.* New York, NY: Harper & Row.

Miller, B.K. (1989). Individualizing faculty renewal. *The Journal of Staff, Program, and Organization Development, 7*(1), 33–37.

8

The Role of Departmental and Divisional Chairs

…a department chairperson plays a crucial role in joyously energizing and renewing the department.

Peter Frederick

It would be difficult to overemphasize the importance of the role of departmental and divisional chairs in the sabbatical process. To begin with, as disciplinary peers and teaching colleagues, departmental chairs* are particularly well prepared to understand the attitudes and needs of sabbatical applicants. Further, departmental chairs are in the best position to solve any replacement staffing problems created by an anticipated sabbatical leave. And, finally, because they monitor the progress and evaluate the achievements of all departmental staff, chairs are intimately familiar with their colleagues' career trajectories as well as their professional goals and objectives. In short, departmental chairs are uniquely positioned to be of invaluable help to the prospective sabbatical applicant.

What are the primary functions of the departmental chair in the sabbatical process? While not definitive, the tasks identified and discussed in this chapter represent the chair's chief responsibilities.

* For the sake of convenience, I will subsume both departmental and divisional chairs under the single rubric, departmental chair.

SABBATICAL COUNSELING

One of the most important, challenging, and rewarding tasks of the departmental chair is to serve as a sabbatical consultant/counselor, helping colleagues plan, prepare for, and carry out, sabbatical projects. Counseling, like teaching, is an acquired skill that is honed through training and practice. And just as teachers can enhance their craft through workshops and reflection, so too can chairs become better counselors by expending some time and effort on self-help and training programs. Here are a few things departmental chairs can do to prepare themselves for the role of sabbatical counselor.

Preparation

First, chairs should become students of adult and career development. Ideally, they should take some courses in this area, perhaps auditing those offered by their own institutional colleagues. Workshops can also be of genuine value, especially if they blend theory with practical application. Further, chairs should read some of the pertinent literature, especially seminal works such as G. Sheehy's *Passages: Predictable Crises of Adult Life.* New York, NY: Dutton, 1976; D.J. Levinson's *The Seasons of a Man's Life.* New York, NY: Knopf, 1978; R.L. Gould's *Transformations: Growth and Change in Adult Life.* New York, NY: Simon & Schuster, 1978; M. F. Belenky and Associates' *Women's Ways of Knowing: The Development of Self, Voice, and Mind.* New York, NY: Basic Books, 1986; M.F. Lowenthal, M. Thurner, D. Chiriboga, and Associates' *Four Stages of Life: A Comparative Study of Women and Men Facing Transitions.* San Francisco, CA: Jossey-Bass, 1975; D. Heath and H. Heath's *Fulfilling Lives: Paths to Maturity and Success.* San Francisco, CA: Jossey-Bass, 1991; F.M. Hudson's *The Adult Years: Mastering the Art of Self-Renewal.* San Francisco, CA: Jossey-Bass, 1991; J.W. Gardner's *Self-Renewal.* New York, NY: Norton, 1981; E.H. Erikson's *Identity and the Life Cycle.* New York, NY: International Universities Press, 1959; M. Fiske and D. Chiriboga's *Change and Continuity in Adult Life.* San Francisco, CA: Jossey-Bass, 1990; and W.H. Bergquist, E.M. Greenberg, and G.A. Klaum's *In Our Fifties: Voices of Men and Women Reinventing Their Lives.* San Francisco, CA: Jossey-Bass, 1993.

There are only so many hours in a day, of course, and considering all their other responsibilities it is unreasonable to expect departmental chairs to become experts on adult and career development. However, it is crucial for them to become aware of at least the fundamental tenets of developmental theory. Knowing, for example, that adults are continuously changing, and that they need certain kinds of renewal experiences at certain stages in their lives and careers can make the difference between effective and ineffectual counseling. Indeed, such knowledge can help chairs better understand why some faculty readily apply for sabbatical leaves and why others do not, even when they are actively encouraged to do so.

In order to become better counselors, chairs must also work at becoming better listeners and observers. These learned skills, often taken for granted, are key to the counseling process. Only through active listening and careful observation in one-on-one situations can a chair adequately monitor the professional lives of his/her departmental colleagues. Are there signs of exhaustion and stress? Has mid-career stagnation set in? Is a change of pace and scene needed? Has scholarship declined? Is retooling necessary? Distress signals are not always pronounced. Often the inside story manifests itself through inflections and tone of voice, fleeting facial expressions, subtle body language, and seemingly cryptic references: the chair must be alert and sensitive to what might be an important subtext. In particular, chairs must be on the lookout for faculty who are in obvious need of an extended leave, but who might not realize it...or who, for one reason or another, might be reluctant to apply. The burden of responsibility for encouraging these colleagues to apply rests squarely upon the shoulders of the chair.

Departmental chairs must also be systematic record keepers, composing and keeping an accurate and up-to-date sabbatical eligibility masterlist. Working from this masterlist, the chair can then, in a timely fashion, talk with colleagues about their professional goals and plans, and about how a sabbatical leave might fit into these plans.

The counseling process

In a particularly helpful article on sabbatical counseling entitled "Changing Collegial Conversation," Peter J. Frederick (1991) outlines a procedure he has found effective in guiding departmental colleagues through the sabbatical process. His systematic approach, summarized below, constitutes a useful and humane counseling paradigm.

Frederick begins with a caveat: because sabbaticals are "important events with enormous potential to be life and career-forming landmarks" chairs must put careful "thought and planning" into counseling conversations. Further, the conversations should be scheduled at key points in the process: (1) long in advance of the leave, (2) on the eve of departure, and (3) upon return.

Frederick describes the first conversation as the "most crucial one," explaining that the chair's goal must be to "clarify the options and opportunities of the leave in terms of the larger career goals and priorities of the faculty member." During this session the chair should "listen very carefully for an ambivalence between what faculty members *think* they should do...and what they really *want* to do...." In sum, the chair's primary role during this first meeting is to "ask holistic questions that open up and legitimate a variety of possibilities, to listen carefully for 'shoulds' and 'wants,'...to serve as a sounding board,...and to consider not just professional and institutional goals but also family or other personal obligations." Frederick also notes that a chair should "help the applicant identify every conceivable creative source of financial, family, and emotional support to plan a full year's leave in some other place."

And what about the conversation on the eve of departure? Frederick suggests that the chair "gently prepare the departing colleague for some of the unexpected dangers of a sabbatical leave," including: "excessive expectations," "loneliness," the inevitable "tensions" resulting from travel abroad with family in tow, and reentry shock.

Unfortunately, even the most careful preparation for reentry does not guarantee that the faculty member's return from sabbatical will be smooth and painless. Thus, as Frederick implies, the third counseling session is also very important. If the returnee achieves a smooth reentry, this session need be nothing more than a pleasant debriefing, during which the chair and faculty member discuss accomplishments, enriching experiences, and plans for sharing with colleagues and students what has been learned on sabbatical.

However, as Frederick points out, there is the good possibility—especially for "intercultural travelers"—that reentry will be "difficult." Indeed, Frederick states that "post-sabbatical depression is not unlike post-partum or post-tenure depression: the event long awaited and planned for is over, and now what?" Here again, the chair can be of considerable help by listening sympathetically, acknowledging the returnee's concerns, prescribing antidotes, and "suggesting various forums" through which the returnee can talk about his or her sabbatical experiences (Frederick, pp. 3–4).

Let us now look a little more closely at some of the key points in Frederick's strategy. First, Professor Frederick rightly stresses the importance of putting sabbatical conversations into a wider context. Sabbatical planning must not be done in a vacuum, but rather in the context of an individualized professional growth plan. Does the sabbatical build upon what the faculty member has already been doing? Will an extended leave help realize any of the applicant's chief teaching, curricular, and scholarly goals? The faculty member and chair should, in brief, not only talk about the short term logistical problems of sabbatical planning, but also the long term factors. While it is vital to deal with such matters as replacement needs, it is even more important to determine how the sabbatical leave project promises to help applicants achieve their long term professional goals.

Second, chairs must be very sensitive to a colleague's financial concerns, providing as much practical advice and help as possible. While chairs may be unable to solve all the financial problems applicants encounter, they can suggest possible solutions. For example, if a sabbatical candidate needs external funding support, the chair might suggest possible funding sources, or at least refer the applicant to personnel who can help in the search for support monies. Or, if an applicant needs the help of a research assistant, the chair might work toward satisfying the need through the use of departmental funds. Having a chair serve as advocate and counselor can go a long way toward ameliorating an applicant's doubts and worries about financial resources and constraints.

Third, and particularly important, the chair ought to help prospective applicants see the broad spectrum of sabbatical project possibilities. As Frederick points out, all too frequently faculty see only research projects as potential sabbatical projects, probably because of the "dominance of the research model in higher education" (p. 4). But what about projects aimed at classroom research and teaching enhancement? What about projects involving curricular development? And what about projects in an area outside the applicant's field of specialization? It may even be that the chair knows of some departmental or institutional programmatic needs congruent with the faculty member's own interests; such sabbatical projects often have high potential for approval, while also promising tremendous dividends for both the individual and the institution. Chairs, in short, must know what is good for both applicant and institution. It may be, for example, that promoting sabbaticals aimed at producing generalists, rather than sharply-focused specialists, is more congruent with a department's and institution's mission—and in the long run is also better for the prospective applicant.

Fourth, as mentioned earlier in this chapter, departmental chairs face the special challenge of convincing reluctant faculty to apply for an extended leave. Surveys and anecdotal evidence suggest that faculty come to chairs with a wide variety of reasons for not making application. Chairs must carefully consider the validity of the reasons, discuss them with applicants, and try to help them sort through their thoughts and feelings. If the reluctance to apply seems born of unreasonable (perhaps even irrational) self-doubt, anxiety, and apprehension, it is the chair's responsibility to help neutralize those concerns. Chairs must be especially sensitive to telltale signs of mental tiredness, stress, and incipient burnout. Faculty exhibiting these debilitating qualities need sabbaticals badly, but often fail to apply because their negative state of mind makes them particularly fearful of change and failure. Chairs must do their best in encouraging applicants to transcend these negative feelings and apply for leave.

While convincing reluctant colleagues to make application might sound easy, it usually is not. To begin with, some difficult things may need to be said. Telling colleagues, for instance, that they are not being honest with themselves about their reasons for perennially deferring application is awkward at best. Further, it may be next to impossible to dislodge some mid- or late-career colleagues from a comfortable status quo no matter how logical and compelling the argument for application. And, finally, to complicate matters even more, while doing their best to encourage colleagues to make application, chairs must at the same time prepare them for the possibility of the leave request being denied. One chair, partly in jest but mostly in earnest, remarked that a chair sometimes must assume the role not only of counselor, but also of "therapist."

Fifth, the chair plays a central role in smoothing the reentry of a sabbatical returnee. As Frederick mentions, one of the chair's most important functions during this crucial juncture is as debriefing agent. Shortly after the return of the faculty member on leave, the chair should schedule an initial debriefing session, allowing plenty of time for a leisurely visit. The setting should be comfortable and welcoming. Meeting for lunch in a cozy restaurant, for example, will do wonders to set the right atmosphere for the conversation. During this session the chair should not only find out how the project fared, but should also assess the mindset and general disposition of the returnee. Did the project go as planned, or did serious glitches prevent completion? Is the returnee now worrying about how he or she is going to complete the project? Is the faculty member apprehensive about returning to a demanding teaching regimen? Has the returnee worked too hard, getting burned out in the process? These are the kinds of things that can be determined only by intelligent—and sensitive—questioning, active listening, and close observation. The reentry conversation may reveal, of course, that everything went fine; but if not, this is the time for gentle reassurance and helpful suggestions.

This is also the time for encouraging returnees to share what they have learned with the wider academic community. The chair might begin this conversation by discussing ways of using sabbatical learning in the classroom. All too often what is learned on sabbatical is shared only in limited fashion—most often with professional disciplinary colleagues through publication, far less often with students through classroom presentations. The link between sabbatical and classroom learning should be of central importance, but, unfortunately, is often observed more in the breach than in the practice. Without being intrusive or autocratic, the chair should monitor and facilitate the application of sabbatical learning so that the entire academic community benefits. At the very least, the chair should be sure to schedule time for sabbatical reports during departmental meetings.

The chair can also help sabbatical returnees by being open to negotiating teaching load and schedule. While staffing constraints may prevent chairs from being as generous as they would like, they should do their very best to provide a returning faculty member with a light transitional course load. Ideally, a returnee should be released from one course to help ease reentry. If that is not possible, the chair might help arrange for a returnee to teach two sections of the same course in order to reduce time spent on course preparation; or help to set up a schedule that doesn't require any new course preparations; or at least to help set up a schedule with blocks of time appropriate for pursuing research which might have gone unfinished during the leave itself.

All these suggestions are aimed as a corrective to one of the most common misperceptions about the sabbatical experience: that faculty return to their jobs blissfully free from reentry problems. Yes, the sabbatical is a restorative. Yes, the sabbatical infuses an instructor with new enthusiasm and energy. But moving from a flexible, remarkably stimulating schedule back to a demanding routine can be a shock. The shock will wear off, of course, but support and sensitivity and understanding will be needed during that transitional period. The departmental chair can cushion the shock of reentry through a program of humane interventions aimed at helping the returnee effect as smooth a transition as possible.

Finally, as Frederick points out, the departmental chair must be sure to begin the counseling process "long in advance of the leave." But just how long is "long"? Although each chair will probably follow a slightly different timeline, there seems to be general agreement that faculty should be contacted about two years before eligibility. At this time exploratory conversations should begin so that by about a year before the application deadline the sabbatical candidate already has a good handle on the sabbatical project, including its scope, duration, and setting.

While two years in advance of eligibility may at first blush seem like a long time, in reality it is not. To begin with, prospective applicants in need of external funding will have to apply at least two years ahead of the projected leave period if they hope to receive support by the time it is needed. Second, busy faculty members will find that they will need at least this much lead time to create a schedule with enough time built in for adequately thinking through their plans and objectives. And, finally, the chair will need considerable time to arrange replacement coverage, a topic I will treat more fully later in this chapter.

HELPING APPLICANTS PREPARE THEIR APPLICATIONS

Assuming that the initial counseling sessions have resulted in the faculty member's decision to apply for sabbatical leave, the chair now takes on another facilitative role—helping applicants prepare their sabbatical applications. Faced with the potentially daunting task of developing a proposal—complete with detailed description of the project, timelines, budget, and appropriate supporting materials—applicants need all the help they can get, often turning to the chair for both advice and solace.

And chairs can help in several ways. To begin with, because of the experience they've logged in such matters, chairs are usually more familiar with institutional sabbatical policy than is the average faculty member. Knowing not only the details of a policy, but also its nuances and possible biases, puts the chair in a position to provide a prospective applicant with an invaluable "insider's" understanding of the process. Are research projects generally favored over other kinds of proposals? Is there a bias in favor of off-campus study proposals? Does the review committee expect applicants to identify *specific* project outcomes? Is favored treatment shown to projects boasting substantial institutional benefits, or to those addressing particular institutional needs? Chairs can help provide answers to these important questions as sabbatical applicants begin formulating their proposals. In brief, the chair can help demystify the application process, thereby removing some of the applicant's doubts and uncertainty.

The departmental chair's role in the application process involves not only counseling, but also recommending. There is probably no more important reference accompanying a sabbatical application than the letter from the departmental chair. The chair, after all, makes the definitive statement on replacement arrangements and is in the best position to make a substantive commentary on the candidate's career trajectory and how the sabbatical fits into it. Indeed, the chair's letter is the very linchpin of the application.

DEVELOPING A SABBATICAL ROTATION SCHEDULE

Creating a sabbatical rotation schedule is one of the most effective and dependable ways of ensuring an orderly and systematic sabbatical leave procedure. The process is simple, the results substantial. Just calculate the eligibility status of all full-time tenure track departmental faculty and then list their names in chronological order, starting with those faculty currently eligible for application. This system provides a convenient format for determining, at a glance, the number of potential applicants in any given year and allows both faculty and chairs to spot possible future congestion points when (especially in large departments) several faculty become eligible for application during the same year.

Because of the advance warning a sabbatical rotation schedule provides, a chair can do a much better job of solving logistical problems, particularly those resulting from two or more faculty from the same department planning to apply for a sabbatical the same year. With plenty of lead time the chair can plan alternative course offerings, do some preliminary work on finding replacements, and meet with the prospective applicants in an attempt to work out leave schedules which appeal to both applicants, and which do not compromise departmental programming. In some instances, the solution may be as simple as scheduling one leave in the spring and the second in the fall. It may be, too, that one faculty member may not mind delaying his or her sabbatical for a year. Rather than being viewed as a drawback, some chairs see two applications in the same year as a positive situation, since it is sometimes easier to hire good replacement faculty for a full-year rather than for a single semester.

BUILDING A WORKABLE REPLACEMENT POLICY AND SYSTEM

Perhaps the chair's most important task in the sabbatical process is finding replacements for colleagues going on leave. This task might not be so onerous if all the chair had to worry about was temporarily filling a staffing gap. But the situation is far more complicated. The chair must not only be concerned with making it possible for a colleague to go on leave, but also with maintaining the integrity of departmental offerings and programs.

The kinds of difficulties encountered will, of course, vary from situation to situation, but certain fundamental questions pertain to most departments and institutions. Can a replacement be found? Should the coverage be in-house by departmental colleagues, or by temporary staff brought in from the outside? How much will the replacement(s) cost? How will the faculty member's absence affect departmental and general education program offerings?

Institutional sabbatical policies severely limit some departmental chairs' replacement options. However, chairs not operating under particular policy strictures (e.g., some institutions mandate that all coverage must be in-house) at least have the freedom to use their ingenuity and creativity in coming up with a viable solution. Following are a few of the coverage options from which chairs may choose:

- If the courses that must be covered are typically not heavily enrolled, or are offered only once every two or three years, it might be possible simply to delay offering them until the sabbatical recipient returns;

- If some of the classes in question are part of multiple section courses they might be dropped and the enrollment ceilings of the remaining sections raised to accommodate student demands (given, of course, the consent of those departmental colleagues teaching the enlarged courses);

- Depending upon school policy and the willingness of the departmental staff, course coverage could be handled on an overload basis;

- If an institution has a graduate school, or has some connection with area graduate schools, chairs might be able to find qualified teaching assistants willing to teach a course or two;

- Or, if there are adequate replacement monies, chairs can seek part-time or adjunct replacements.

Although replacement coverage constitutes a difficult challenge for all chairs, some may experience a greater degree of difficulty simply because of the relative size of their institutions. Large universities with correspondingly large departments allow for more flexibility in arranging staff replacements for faculty on professional leave than do small colleges with small departments. In fact, the majority of departments in colleges of under 2,000 students have ten or fewer faculty, and it is not uncommon to find single-member departments. Obviously, there is less possibility for relocation within these small departments than within large university departments with fifty or more staff members.

But whether from a small or large institution, all departmental chairs share two primary concerns. First, they must try to set up a fair and workable replacement policy that clearly sets forth principles, procedures, and guide-lines. Second, all chairs must work toward obtaining monies to cover replace-ment costs. The goal is to have enough in the budget to guarantee flexibility in meeting replacement needs. Restrictive policies that prevent faculty from applying for leave unless the department can cover from within, for example, are not only limiting, but potentially unjust in the case of small departments.

If we are to solve the problem of underutilized sabbatical programs we must work toward removing restrictive policies, logistical obstacles, and other disin-centives. A sabbatical should not impose undue hardship on several colleagues so that one may enjoy the restorative effects of a sabbatical leave. Sabbatical recipients should not have to begin one of the most potentially enriching, satis-fying, and joyous junctures in their professional lives with the anguish born of knowing their colleagues are paying a steep price for their good fortune. An institution supporting a sabbatical program must go beyond rhetoric to provid-ing sufficient monetary support. The chair should serve as a strong advocate for adequate replacement funds.

FACILITATING DEPARTMENTAL COOPERATION

Because the viability of a sabbatical proposal often hinges upon whether coverage can be arranged from within the applicant's department, disciplinary colleagues frequently become key players in the planning and application process. Indeed, the fate of an application often depends upon the good will, cooperativeness, and flexibility of those colleagues. More often than not, depart-mental faculty are happy to help cover a colleague's courses and even to absorb his or her other collegial responsibilities. However, even among colleagues of good will, misunderstandings and misperceptions occur. Some departments handle coverage requests with more grace and generosity than do others.

Strong leadership and modeling on the part of the chair can help shape departmental response. Perhaps even more important than a chair's success in solving logistical difficulties is the ability to model cooperativeness and to foster a spirit of collegiality within the department. A chair must be sensitive, for example, to the feelings of resentment that an already overburdened faculty member might feel when asked to help cover the courses of a colleague—even if that colleague is well-liked and respected. A chair should anticipate such reac-tions and make sure departmental meeting time is set aside for open discussion of what an anticipated leave will mean to the department. Such discussions can promote and nurture a sense of collective ownership of the project, thereby neu-tralizing possible feelings of resentment and, in the best of situations, even fos-tering departmental unity.

PRESERVING THE INTEGRITY OF ACADEMIC PROGRAMS

Up to this point we have focused on the chair as facilitator of the sabbatical process, performing a number of functions aimed at helping the sabbatical applicant prepare a successful sabbatical application. The chair must also serve as the primary advocate and steward of the department's academic programs, making sure that staffing arrangements, or rearrangements, in no way jeopardize the integrity of the programs offered. Whenever a sabbatical request must be acted upon, not only the good of the faculty, but the good of the students, must be considered. This responsibility demands a wisdom in decision making and a sense of balance that would make a high-wire specialist proud.

CHRONOLOGY OF FACILITATIVE STEPS

The following chronological summary of facilitative steps chairs can take to help colleagues through the various stages of the sabbatical process may serve as a helpful reminder and checklist for the busy departmental chair. It is not meant to be definitive.

Invitation and notification

Each year, probably near the end of the spring term, send a memo to all departmental members inviting those intending to apply for a sabbatical to discuss their plans with you. If a faculty member eligible for sabbatical does not respond, follow up with a telephone call or an office visit. Stress your accessibility, pointing out that you're always available to discuss prospective projects and that the summer break would be an especially fine time to do this.

Conference

Next, schedule a leisurely session with each prospective applicant, during which you talk over the faculty member's short- and long-term goals, proposed sabbatical project, and timing of the projected leave.

Departmental meeting

Schedule a departmental meeting to discuss the projected leave. Give the prospective applicant an opportunity to describe her or his sabbatical plans and to invite reaction and constructive suggestions. We often waste the tremendous human resources at our disposal simply because we don't take the time to make good use of them. Finally, be sure to share with the departmental staff the coverage challenges presented by the proposed leave.

Letter of recommendation

Give adequate time to the vital task of writing a concrete and detailed letter in support of the applicant's proposal, being sure not only to comment upon the quality of the project and how it promises to fit into the applicant's short- and long-term plans, but also how it fits into the departmental and institutional mission. Clearly describe how the applicant's courses, advisement responsibilities, and collegial duties will be covered in her or his absence.

Sabbatical monitoring

Make clear to sabbatical recipients that you welcome their questions and visits during the leave period, and that you will try to help in any way possible.

Debriefing

As soon as possible after the sabbatical recipient's return, schedule a debriefing session. Ideally, such a meeting can be set up a week or two before the term begins.

CONCLUSION

Departmental and divisional chairs play a central role throughout the sabbatical process. The chair serves as sounding board to prospective applicants during the earliest stages of exploration and reflection; as counselor during the more earnest planning stage; as coach during the application process; as advocate and intercessor during the replacement process; as mentor during the leave period itself; and as confidant during the reentry stage. Chairs willing to prepare adequately for these roles, and also willing to expend the requisite time and energy on them, can perform an extraordinarily helpful service to the faculty member.

Further, chairs can serve as influential advocates of institutional sabbatical programs, simply by getting their colleagues to take advantage of leave opportunities. This, of course, is as it should be since the sabbatical leave program is a key faculty development component, and departmental and divisional chairs are some of academe's most effective and powerful faculty development agents.

WORKS CITED

Frederick, P. (1991). Changing collegial conversation. *The Department Advisor,* 6(4), 1–5.

9

The Role Of
Chief Academic
Officers

There is no one device that can do more to refresh a faculty member than a sabbatical leave. [Thus] the dean should do everything possible to encourage extended leaves for worthwhile purposes, including visiting lectureships, major consulting activities, foreign assignments, and other activities that will provide opportunities for the members of [his/her] faculty to gain new perspectives.

Ralph E. Fadum

Venerable programs, like time-honored friendships, are sometimes taken for granted. Just because they have been long-lasting and dependable, we expect them to maintain their youthful health and vigor. But programs, like friendships, need care and nurturing. We should not assume that sabbatical leave programs will thrive on automatic pilot. Further, just because an institution establishes a sabbatical program does not necessarily mean the program will naturally operate at peak efficiency. Indeed, sabbatical programs may become poor investments if carelessly administered. In short, benign neglect may not only produce anemic programs, but may constitute the single greatest threat to the future well being of the sabbatical in American higher education.

If the sabbatical leave system is to fulfill its vast potential, administrators must play active roles as stewards and nurturing agents. Happily, there are several practical action steps that chief academic officers can take not only to strengthen an institution's extended leave program, but also to help ensure that faculty experience enriching and productive sabbaticals. This chapter examines how chief academic officers such as deans, provosts, and presidents can effectively support, promote, administer, maintain, and evaluate extended leave programs.

SUPPORT THE LEAVE PROGRAM

Through their words and deeds, academic administrators determine the destiny of sabbatical programs. While it may be possible for a program to survive without the energetic support of an institution's chief academic officers, its chances for truly prospering are slim. Sabbatical programs can live up to their full promise only if an institution's key academic administrators provide the requisite monetary and moral support.

Monetary support

Without adequate funding, sabbatical leave programs degenerate into little more than institutional window dressing. Indeed, this is all too frequently the reality. From its infancy, the sabbatical system has been hobbled by lack of adequate funding. Randall (1922), in one of the first major reports on the sabbatical, bemoaned the plight of programs without adequate monetary backing: "It seems reasonable to say that institutions which grant the privilege of sabbatic leave and do not at the same time sufficiently provide for the needs of the professor...are doing little better than the institutions which make no provision whatever" (pp. 111–112). Approximately three decades later, Woodburne (1950), in his *Faculty Personnel Policies in Higher Education*, states: "One of the most startling aspects, which has come out of this study of leave-of-absence practices, has been how frequently an announced policy has not been supported with funds which are necessary for its operation" (p. 138).

Clearly, one of an academic officer's most serious responsibilities is to provide funding at a level sufficient to make the program more than a mere institutional gesture. This means creating a steady and dependable flow of monies into the program, rather than trying to squeeze a little cash out of a contingency fund each year. This means building a fund large enough to guarantee that no sabbatical recipient suffers financially as a result of a leave. This means vigilantly guarding against budget cuts, whether from the state legislature or the board of trustees. And this means eliminating "disincentives" to the sabbatical in the form of reduction in salary or benefits, especially retirement benefits. Most institutions genuinely committed to the concept of the sabbatical leave either allocate a set percentage (with built-in inflationary hedges) of the institutional budget, or create a sabbatical leave endowment fund, the interest of which goes toward leave support. No matter what monetary mechanism is used, it is imperative that it be formalized through institutional policy and that this policy be publicized prominently in a publication such as the faculty handbook.

Moral support

Although nothing is more important to a sabbatical program than a solid financial foundation, it also needs the strongly-articulated moral support of those administering it. What chief administrators choose to say about a program, and when and how they say it, profoundly influences the attitudes and perceptions of others in the academic community. If an administrator says little or nothing about a program, for example, the implication, whether intended or not, is that the program is not worth mentioning. And if a sabbatical program is discussed only in terms of fringe benefits rather than faculty and institutional renewal, faculty may assume a similar outlook, squandering the tremendous professional development opportunities of the extended leave. In brief, academic administrators must be sensitive to the power of their words and should make a conscientious effort to support verbally the concept of the sabbatical leave in general and of the institutional program in particular.

PROMOTE THE LEAVE PROGRAM

At first glance, it would seem that a sabbatical program needs about as much promoting as a luxury cruise in the Bahamas. However, despite the intrinsic attractiveness of a paid extended leave, surprisingly few faculty ever apply for a sabbatical. A recent survey of faculty in the University of Wisconsin System (Franklin, 1993) reveals that "most…will never take a sabbatical leave," and that "only 1% of the total faculty [in the System] took sabbaticals each year" (p. 8). Jarecky and Sandifer's (1986) study involving nineteen medical schools reveals a similarly lukewarm response to the sabbatical program, pointing out that the number of faculty taking sabbaticals "within a year of eligibility ranged from 2 to 16 percent" (p. 806).

Significantly, when Ingraham and King (1965) asked college presidents to identify the most common "leave problems" facing administrative officers, they listed "unwillingness of those who need them most to take leaves" (pp. 80–81) as one of the top four, the other three being (a) lack of funds, (b) difficulty of finding replacements for leave recipients, and (c) the failure of faculty members to return to their home institutions at the end of the sabbatical leave. Further, extensive anecdotal evidence suggests that those faculty who do not apply for sabbatical are often those in most desperate need of the restorative effects of an extended leave, empirical evidence supported by Ingraham and King (1965) when they note that "from the point of view of the college, the lethargic need leaves more than the avid" (p. 82).

But why don't more faculty take advantage of sabbatical programs? The reasons, of course, are as different and personal as the individuals involved. Once again we can turn to the Jarecky and Sandifer (1986) survey for some answers. When asked about why they had not taken advantage of their eligibility, faculty offered a broad spectrum of reasons:

> Some took the position that the section or division for which they were responsible would surely collapse if they were to leave for a year. Others pointed out that a sabbatical would not provide substantial opportunity for collaborative research that was not already available at home. Some, especially younger faculty members, thought that their advancement or status would be impaired by being away. A few others mentioned financial and family constraints. There were also those who were not willing to move elsewhere for a year (p. 806).

Add to the reasons given above a reluctance to apply because of uncertainty about a sabbatical project, a fear of having the application denied, insufficient funds, inertia, family problems, and "at times just the love of teaching" (Ingraham and King, 1965, p. 81) and it becomes apparent that promoting the concept of the sabbatical leave is not labor lost.

The reality of the situation, then, is that faculty frequently have to be persuaded, coaxed, and cajoled into applying for a sabbatical leave—for their own good and for that of the institution. While there is no surefire formula for convincing eligible faculty to apply for sabbatical leave, administrators can take a number of steps both to promote the concept of the sabbatical and to generate more active interest and participation in the institution's program.

Clearly communicate policies

One way of promoting a sabbatical program is to communicate clearly its philosophy, purpose, policies, and procedures. A necessary first step, of course, is to draft a statement of philosophy in which the intent and tenets (in effect a kind of mission statement) of the sabbatical program are put forth in a straightforward and unambiguous fashion. The statement ought to address in one way or another the following kinds of questions and issues: How does the sabbatical policy reflect and enhance the institutional mission? Does the institution view the sabbatical as a right or a privilege, an entitlement or an earned reward? Does the institution consider the sabbatical a fringe benefit or a professional growth opportunity? What outcomes does the institution see as desirable?

While the particular governance system and administrative style of an institution will determine how a philosophy statement is generated, a collegial approach, in which faculty play a key role in generating such a document, is probably the best way of gaining faculty ownership of the program. In institutions with collective bargaining units, chief academic officers should work closely with union representatives when formulating the philosophical foundation of the program.

Once the statement of philosophy has been drafted and distributed, it is time to work on policy and guidelines. It is important to demystify the process, to set forth, clearly and concretely, institutional expectations, procedures, and stipulations. In particular, make certain that terms are defined and the application process carefully outlined. In addition, draft reader-friendly guidelines that clearly explain how the sabbatical leave will affect such things as health plans, retirement benefits, and other institutional benefits. The objective should be to distribute a document that lucidly states all the provisions of the leave plan.

Finally, be sure to prominently place the philosophy statement, procedural guidelines, and policy statement in an official document such as the faculty handbook. Some institutions print the information in both the faculty handbook and a separate sabbatical handbook containing detailed information on application procedures and deadlines, lists of tips, and even representative samples of successful proposals. Applicants report finding these sabbatical handbooks of great value.

Publicize sabbatical awards

A press release or two announcing the recipients of sabbatical leaves will go a long way toward promoting a sabbatical program. In most institutions the awarding of sabbaticals is based upon a tough competitive process, and faculty who receive sabbaticals earn them through hard work, careful planning, and well-written proposals. Thus, recipients of these highly competitive awards deserve recognition. Unless an institution treats sabbaticals like an outright entitlement and does not apply high standards to applications (and this is hardly ever the case), sabbatical awards ought to receive the same type of recognition, and be publicized in the same manner, as prestigious institutional awards for outstanding teaching and scholarship.

Sabbatical awards can be publicized in several other ways: memos or voice mail announcements from the dean's or president's office; announcements in student newspapers and faculty newsletters; and articles in alumni magazines. Using such strategies to acknowledge sabbatical awards not only promotes the sabbatical program, but also enhances overall faculty morale through nurturing the institution's learning community. It is a win-win strategy costing relatively little, even in terms of time and energy.

Schedule informational sessions

A practical, efficient, and productive way of promoting the sabbatical program is to schedule an informational meeting for prospective sabbatical applicants, either late in the spring or early in the fall semester. The invitation to these sessions should come out of the office of the academic administrator in charge of the program, or, if a peer review system is used, from the desk of the faculty chair of the committee. Better yet, the sessions might be co-sponsored by the appropriate chief academic officer and the sabbatical review committee.

To be most effective, these sessions ought to be relaxed, informal, and inviting. Not much structure is needed. At the institution with which I am most
familiar (St. Norbert College), the Dean of Academic Affairs and members of
the Personnel Committee sit around a large table and field questions from those
in attendance. There are no formal presentations, although members of the
Committee make certain they share important information about review procedures, as well as about how the Committee has viewed, interpreted, and imple-
mented the College's sabbatical policies. Faculty ask a wide variety of questions
ranging from "How important are letters of recommendation when applying for
sabbatical?" to "Will my proposal have a better chance of being approved if I
conduct my research off-campus?" Many questions deal with the "relative
weight" given to a particular criterion.

Such meetings serve a number of vital functions. For applicants nearing
completion of their proposals, the sessions provide information useful in making final revisions. For faculty just beginning the planning process and anticipating making application in the following year, the information gleaned can be
put to good use in developing their sabbatical proposals. Perhaps most importantly, this type of meeting helps demystify and validate the review process itself,
emphasizing its openness and the accessibility of the review committee and
administrative officers responsible for overseeing the program. This, in turn,
helps diminish the anxiety, doubts, and apprehension some faculty may have
about the application and review process.

Publish sabbatical reports

One way of promoting the sabbatical program while concomitantly providing a valuable service to faculty is to develop an open file of sabbatical reports.
Many institutions are already following this practice, with excellent results.

Eugene Rice (1983), when describing the sabbatical program inaugurated
at the University of the Pacific in the early 1980s, stresses the importance of the
final report in the sabbatical process. Explaining that sabbatical reports are "put
on file and made available to all faculty," Rice goes on to say that each report
"includes reasons for failing to achieve the goals that one projected in the planning process as well as an account of achievement" (p. 80). This approach not
only nudges the reporter into a more analytical and reflective state of mind, but
also, Rice goes on to say, makes each report more helpful to other faculty "doing
their own planning." Further, explains Rice, the departmental chair or academic
dean then responds to the report in writing, this assessment becoming "a part of
the regular periodic evaluation of each faculty member." Finally, Rice makes the
point that the Academic Vice President includes information on leave activities
in his/her annual report, these descriptions becoming "sources of conversation
and a means for making connections across departments and schools." One of
the final outcomes, according to Rice, is enhanced "colleagueship across depart-

ments and schools" (p. 80). This paradigm, with its clean and simple lines, provides a model worthy of our consideration.

ADMINISTER THE LEAVE PROGRAM

Institutional governance systems and mission statements, state legislation, bargaining agreements, campus traditions and culture—all influence, and in some cases actually determine, the administration of a sabbatical program. Approaches differ markedly. At some institutions, department or divisional chairs make the decisions on sabbatical applications; at others, the academic dean (or perhaps president) serves as both screening committee and decision maker; and at still other colleges and universities, the peer review system prevails.

The peer review system is not as widely used as one might expect. Ingraham and King (1965), in their classic study of faculty compensation, point out that in general, decisions on sabbatical applications (depending on the size of the institution) are made by chief academic officers rather than by peer review committees: "the person whose 'yes' or 'no' sticks is either the president or the dean" (p. 80). Of late, however, a change seems to be occurring. In one national study on the sabbatical, Hayward Daugherty, Jr. (1979) reported that "the majority of the respondents, 66.1%, indicated that either faculty committees or department chairmen were given the initial requests for sabbatical leaves" (p. 93). Further, in comparing his results with a major study conducted seven years earlier by Eberle and Thompson (1972), Daugherty found that the only major change in how sabbaticals were reviewed involved the use of sabbatical leave committees. In 1972, only 14.7% indicated that such committees were used, but in 1979 the percentage more than doubled, with 35.1% reporting the use of peer review committees.

Work with the sabbatical review committee

As Daugherty's study indicates, the trend in American colleges and universities seems to be toward full faculty participation in the administration of sabbatical programs—from developing leave policy (Ingraham, 1965) to reviewing and judging sabbatical applications. Does this mean, then, that chief academic administrators have little or nothing to do with the administration of sabbatical programs? Not really. Even when an institution uses a peer review system, the academic administrator shoulders important responsibilities.

Perhaps most importantly, chief academic officers have an obligation to work with faculty in developing and maintaining systems that are efficient and fair. Although no one formula can be universally applied to all institutions, the following guidelines drawn from several dozen faculty handbook statements are worth considering.

The sabbatical review committee should:

1. Be elected, representative of its constituency, and comprised of tenured peers. Some institutions, for example, stipulate that committee members must consist only of faculty either who are not eligible for leave or who are eligible but not making application; others specify that only tenured faculty who have had sabbatical leave experience are eligible to serve on the sabbatical review committee; and still others stipulate that any information dealing with replacement staffing, including projected costs, be kept from committee members and not be used in the decision-making process in any form.

2. Draft and publish a statement of its philosophy, tenets, procedural guidelines, and criteria for evaluation of sabbatical proposals.

3. Formulate guidelines that are clear and user-friendly.

4. State clearly its funding guidelines, letting applicants know the extent of in-house funding and the items and activities eligible for funding.

5. Sponsor an informational session to which prospective applicants may come for information and counsel.

6. Work toward de-politicizing the decision-making process, making sure only the merits of the proposal count.

7. Make sure artistic and creative projects are given the same respect and weight as more conventional scholarly and pedagogical projects, ultimately working toward a reliable and viable system of scholarly equivalency.

8. Make the system as humane as possible, giving applicants an opportunity to clarify their proposals, and providing applicants with suggestions for making their proposals stronger.

9. Be flexible, open-minded, and creative, approving proposals that may depart from conventional approaches, but that show promise of achieving the desired ends.

10. Help academic administrators promote the sabbatical concept and institutional program.

11. Make sure that selection criteria and priorities are congruent with the institutional mission.

The academic administrator's role in the peer review system, however, often goes beyond simply instituting and monitoring the system. In many institutions the academic dean or equivalent officer actually serves on the sabbatical review committee, although usually in an *ex officio* capacity. As a committee member, a chief academic officer can perform a vital function in the deliberative process, effectively serving as a liaison between the committee and the president or provost, as well as providing the committee with helpful information about applicants—information to which faculty colleagues may not be privy.

And what about institutions where the decision-making process resides with an administrative officer? In general, the key guiding principles described in regard to the sabbatical review committee also apply. Whether a faculty committee is used or not, decision-making should be de-politicized, the funding guidelines and application procedures should be clearly described and defined, and the system should be as just and humane as possible.

MAINTAIN AND MONITOR THE LEAVE PROGRAM

Once a program has been well promoted and effectively administered, it must be maintained and nurtured through careful monitoring. While a sabbatical review committee can perform the task of evaluating sabbatical proposals, it usually doesn't monitor, manage, and evaluate the program itself. Thus, another managing agency is necessary, a vigilant and dedicated overseer specifically charged with acting as the program's guardian.

Form a sabbatical program advisory committee

Sabbatical programs are inherently complex systems, in part because of the magnitude of the financial support involved, and in part because of the potentially powerful affect the programs may have upon staffing and programming. Further, they are programs involving the entire college or university community. Because of their scope and complexity, chief administrative officers often need help in effectively monitoring and managing them. Perhaps the best vehicle is some sort of administratively-appointed committee comprised of both administrators and faculty.

No one committee model is exactly right for every institution. However, for small to moderately large colleges and universities, a committee comprised of the chief academic officer as chair, the divisional chairs (or several representative departmental chairs), the director of faculty development, and the chair of the sabbatical review committee (or its equivalent) should work well. In some institutions it might be possible for an already constituted committee such as a faculty development committee to perform this advisory function, provided the committee is sufficiently representative.

The chair (let us assume it is the dean of the college) would call meetings regularly, perhaps two to three times a semester, to monitor all aspects of the sabbatical program. More specifically, the committee would probably take up the following kinds of matters:

- First, the committee should carefully monitor faculty eligibility and patterns of sabbatical leave awards (e.g., Are there some mid-or late-career faculty who have never taken a sabbatical, or who haven't taken one for many years?). In order to do this type of monitoring, the dean will have to compile a comprehensive list of faculty by starting date, so that the committee can determine how many faculty are eligible for sabbatical leave in a given year.

- Second, the committee should discuss how many sabbaticals the institution can support, both from a monetary standpoint and from the standpoint of the health of the institution's academic programs. At what point do disciplinary or general education programs begin suffering as a result of reduced staffing? Is the welfare of students being adequately considered? Should limits on the number of leaves granted be imposed? If so, what should the limit be? And what criteria should be used to determine who goes, and who does not go, on sabbatical? These questions demand careful consideration.

- Third, the committee should address the crucial matter of sabbatical replacements. The committee must be particularly sensitive to the plight of faculty in small (e.g., one to three member) departments. It is possible that faculty in these small departments will continually be denied leaves because either there aren't enough colleagues to cover for them, or there isn't enough money for a replacement.

- Fourth, the committee should periodically assess the review process to determine if it is just, sensitive to the needs of faculty, and functioning efficiently.

In brief, the overarching responsibility of this advisory group is to maintain the health of the institutional sabbatical system while seeking creative means of enhancing it. In addition, it should make certain the sabbatical program is congruent with the mission of the institution.

Combat legislative pressures

As stated earlier, an academic administrator's role in promoting, administering, and maintaining a sabbatical program will vary according to the type of institution involved. The chief academic officers of a private liberal arts college, for example, must face the challenge of obtaining financial support adequate to the needs of a sabbatical program from private donors. On the other hand, academic administrators of large land grant universities must be prepared to go head-to-toe with legislators determined to reduce, or even eradicate, sabbatical programs. Further, if the state legislature regulates sabbatical funding (and many states have at one time or another enacted sabbatical leave laws) administrators have as their responsibility the task of finding alternative funding. When state legislatures enact statutory provisions on sabbatical and other kinds of professional leave, and when state legislative budget committees get into the act, the primary line of institutional defense is rooted in the offices of an institution's chief administrative officers. If this line of defense crumbles, the territory lost is very difficult to recover.

Thus, administrators in most public institutions must not only adopt a proactive stance in protecting the integrity and vitality of sabbatical programs; they also must be diligent students of state policies and politics, closely monitoring legislation and legislative acts dealing directly or indirectly with faculty leaves.

Work with the collective bargaining unit

If a college or university has a teacher's union, the sabbatical might well become a matter of negotiation in collective bargaining agreements. It is incumbent upon administrators in such institutions to become familiar with the bargaining process and how the sabbatical fits into it.

EVALUATE THE PROGRAM

Earlier in this chapter I mentioned that benign neglect constitutes one of the greatest dangers to the sabbatical system. One way that neglect can manifest itself is through insufficient programmatic evaluation. Sabbatical programs should be periodically evaluated—either by the appropriate administrative officer, by the sabbatical review committee, by an advisory committee, or by some combination of these agencies. Following are some questions such an evaluation should address:

- Are full-year sabbaticals more productive than semester leaves?

- Are off-campus leaves more enriching and productive than on-campus leaves?

- What approaches or components seem to contribute most to a successful sabbatical?

- Is the in-house funding system sufficient to support sabbatical projects?

- Do sabbaticals have a demonstrably beneficial effect on teaching and academic programs?

- Is there a responsive and humane system in place for replacement coverage?

- If many eligible faculty are not applying for sabbaticals, why not? Are the reasons financial? personal? familial? Are the review procedures intimidating and formidable?

- Are certain cohorts being neglected? For example, would young faculty be helped by a pre-tenure sabbatical program? Would a "mini-sabbatical" program help scholars more than a traditional sabbatical program?

Answers to these and similar evaluative questions are not always easy to come by, but there are a number of sources to which administrators and faculty responsible for institutional sabbatical programs may turn, including: sabbatical reports; classroom use of sabbatical learning; tangible outcomes such as books, articles, and creative works; pedagogical and curricular enhancements;

and feedback from the sabbatical review committee. Further, evaluators may wish to broaden the assessment process by comparing the scope and productivity of their programs with those of similar institutions. Whatever the method used, the overseers of the sabbatical program should first develop criteria for evaluating the program, subsequently using the criteria as a vehicle for maintaining quality control.

Approximately eighty years ago, the AAUP set up a Committee on Systems for Sabbatical Years. This group, referred to as "Committee K," conducted sabbatical surveys in a stretch from 1917 to 1923 and from these surveys generated a list of questions and suggestions (Scott, 1925). Two of these key questions were: (1) How do faculty on leave "actually spend their time and how much good does it do them?" and (2) "Do our absentee professors really improve? Do they come back sounder, saner, more zealous for learning, more contented with their service and their salaries, or do they come back fagged, impatient, averse to life at home and the problems of a harassed academe?" (p. 91). Good questions then, and good questions today. Indeed, they deserve to be at the heart of the evaluation process.

CONCLUSION

Clearly, chief administrative officers play a vital role in the sabbatical leave system. They are responsible for its financial well being, for its tone and reputation, for its credibility, and for its creativity and flexibility. Further, they are responsible for putting the sabbatical into the proper institutional context. Whether a sabbatical is seen as a discrete faculty fringe benefit or as an intrinsic part of an institution's mission is largely up to administrative leaders. They, too, determine whether or not the sabbatical program is built into the institution's faculty development program, becoming "part of an overall plan to meet professional, personal, and organizational goals" (Wheeler, p. 2), or whether it remains on the fringe of the institution's efforts in this area. It is also up to the chief academic officers to see that benefits from the sabbatical accrue to *both* the individual and the institution, as well as to convince members of the academic community that faculty vitality and growth is a shared responsibility of the individual *and* the institution. Finally, it is the job of administrative leaders to help those outside the academic community better understand the sabbatical.

Serving as a good steward for the sabbatical system is both time and energy consuming. Is it worth the effort? The answer is a resounding "yes." To begin with, a sabbatical program constitutes one of the largest investments in faculty development an institution makes, and large investments demand special treatment. But beyond this, a well-functioning sabbatical program offers tremendous benefits to an institution. It can significantly improve faculty morale, promote scholarship, enhance teaching, strengthen curricular offerings and programs, promote internationalism, foster collegiality, and enhance institutional image and reputation. A good sabbatical program can also be used as an inducement for candidates to sign a contract and for senior faculty members to maintain their allegiance, thus helping ensure a strong future for an institution. In short, a sabbatical program is a vital part of an institution's investment in the future and should be placed high on the priority list of chief academic officers.

WORKS CITED

Fadum, R. (1971). The role of the dean in faculty development. *Engineering Education*, 62, 104–106.

Franklin, T. (1993). Planning successful sabbaticals. *The Department Chair*, Spring, 8–9.

Ingraham, M., & King, F. (1965). *The outer fringe: Faculty benefits other than annuities and insurance.* Madison, WI: University of Wisconsin Press.

Jarecky, R., & Sandifer, M. (1986). Faculty members' evaluations of sabbaticals. *Journal of Medical Education*, 61(10), 803–807.

Randall, O. (1922). Report on the commission on sabbatic leave. *Association of American Colleges Bulletin*, 8, 104–118.

Rice, R.E. (1983). Leaves and other institutional resources for maintaining faculty vitality. In D.T. Bedsole (Ed.), *Critical aspects of faculty development programs: Proceedings of the invitational seminar on faculty development* (pp. 77–81). Sherman, TX.

Scott, F. (1925). Report of Committee K: Systems for sabbatical years. *AAUP Bulletin*, 11, 90–91.

Wheeler, D. (undated publication). *A prospectus on faculty leaves: Opportunities for renewal and growth.* University of Nebraska, Lincoln: IANR Office of Professional and Organizational Development.

Woodburne, L.S. (1950). *Faculty personnel policies in higher education.* New York, NY: Harper & Brothers.

CONCLUSION

10

The Benefits Derived
From Sabbatical Leaves

It is necessary to discuss not only the vitality of societies but the vitality of institutions and individuals. They are the same subjects. A society decays when its institutions and individuals lose their vitality.
                                                                    John Gardner

Discussing the benefits derived from extended leave programs is a delightful task, but not without its challenges. Part of the problem is that there are so many benefits which accrue to the faculty member, the student, and the institution as a whole, it is nearly impossible to do justice to the subject without turning a chapter into a book. In addition, many benefits are project specific. The faculty member who travels widely on sabbatical, meeting new people and soaking up new cultures, enjoys some benefits not experienced by the scholar who spends most of the leave cloistered in a basement study working on a lengthy manuscript. On the other hand, the sabbatical traveler may not experience the particular kind of satisfaction the cloistered scholar may derive from intense research uninterrupted by any kind of outside interference, even if potentially enriching and stimulating. Finally, it is difficult to convey adequately the passion with which faculty recount the beneficent influences of their sabbatical leaves. A good sabbatical, like a good book, has the power to change one's life. Trying to recapture the compelling tone of a colleague who has experienced a sabbatical epiphany demands an expressive vehicle more akin to poetry than expository prose.

Despite these difficulties, however, it is possible to identify several primary benefits faculty derive from sabbatical leaves, no matter what their projects. Further, the challenge of adequately reflecting the enthusiasm of those experiencing good sabbaticals can be met in part by using some of their own words.* The benefits discussed in this chapter reflect the responses of scores of faculty to the interview question: "What are the greatest benefits you derived from your sabbatical?"

FACULTY BENEFITS

Serves as an agent of rejuvenation and renewal

Although the sabbatical may not virtually be a time for "resting" on the seventh year, breaking away from the routine of academic life and the regimen of a full schedule of classes can provide the faculty member on sabbatical with a rare opportunity for genuine renewal. Indeed, when faculty are asked about benefits derived from the sabbatical, most comment upon its importance as an agent of renewal and rejuvenation, stressing its potency as an antidote to stagnation, stress, and burnout. Faculty returning from sabbatical are infused with new vitality and energy, qualities essential to effective classroom performance and the carrying out of collegial duties.

The degree of rejuvenation generated by a sabbatical seems to go well beyond a simple recharging of one's intellectual battery, to a more profound type of renewal affecting the very core of one's being. Faculty returning from sabbatical frequently speak of "spiritual rejuvenation" and "spiritual elevation," not in a strictly religious sense, but rather in the broader sense of profound psychological and emotional uplift resulting in a renewed sense of self-esteem and self-confidence. Many faculty point out that the change of pace and environment afforded by a sabbatical translate into a state of renewed creativity, often resulting in new ideas, fresh approaches, and bold innovation. In brief, a good sabbatical experience has enormous restorative potential, renewing faculty not only physically, but mentally and spiritually as well.

Provides time for reflection

Many faculty consider having more time to reflect on their lives and careers one of the primary benefits of the sabbatical leave. Faculty, like other busy professionals, seldom seem to have the time—or take the time—to step back and reassess their professional (and personal) lives, to measure their accomplishments, to redefine their goals, and to take stock of their relationships with family, colleagues, and friends. And yet this kind of stock taking can play a large part in determining not only the success of one's career, but the happiness of one's life. The sabbatical leave, with its relatively uncluttered and potentially more

* The quotations in this chapter appearing without attribution were gleaned from anonymous responses to various questionnaires the author administered from 1984 to 1994.

contemplative lifestyle, provides an invaluable opportunity for putting careers and personal lives back into focus and balance.

Furnishes a fresh perspective

One of the happy outcomes of being freed from the tyranny of the clock and appointment book is gaining a clearer perspective through reflection. Faculty newly returned from sabbatical leaves often speak of having gained a clearer focus on their personal priorities and of having formulated plans for building these priorities into their lives. In interviews, respondents describe how the time they spent in reflection had resulted in a "new focus and perspective on ideas and movements" in their fields. Still others comment on how a fresh perspective often translates into a new appreciation for colleagues and academic community.

But contemplation and reflection while on sabbatical are not the only activities capable of generating a fresh perspective. Travel is also a potent catalyst for creating a change, perhaps even reversal, of perspective. For example, one faculty member who had studied abroad pointed out that his sabbatical provided him with an opportunity to witness how heavily Europeans depend upon the print media for their news. While overseas, he, too, began spending more time reading newspapers, noting how much more in-depth the coverage was than the typical television treatment. Another sabbatical veteran who had spent her sabbatical studying an ancient Asian culture, enthusiastically described her renewed sense of history, now seeing her role as teacher and artist from a fresh—and more meaningful—historical vantage point. And still another sabbatical returnee reported she had returned to the United States with a greater understanding of, and appreciation for, our system of higher education, an epiphany resulting from her first-hand experience with systems of higher education in several European countries.

Perhaps one additional type of new perspective ought to be mentioned. Several faculty described the leave as a kind of "touchstone experience," an opportunity for "testing one's personal limits." One sabbatical returnee put it this way: "A sabbatical helps you come to realize just what you're able and not able to accomplish as a scholar and teacher. In other words, you gain a clearer perspective on your skills and abilities, your strengths and weaknesses. You truly discover what you are, and are not, capable of...and how well motivated you are."

Builds new professional relationships

Sabbatical projects are not undertaken and pursued in a vacuum—at least they should not be. Indeed, many faculty returning from sabbatical speak of how their professional lives have been substantially enriched through professional relationships and friendships developed during their leaves. Sorcinelli's (1987) study of leave participants reveals that faculty considered the opportunity to "create networks with individuals in other universities, research laboratories, government, or industry" one of the primary benefits of extended leaves (p. 13). And these are not simply short term arrangements. Sabbatical veterans have discovered that the professional relationships developed during the leave period sometimes last a lifetime, frequently resulting in collaborative ventures.

Affords an opportunity for maintaining current

One of the most distressing discoveries teacher-scholars can make is that they have fallen behind in their fields of specialization. Unfortunately, this is something that can happen rather quickly, and with depressing frequency, especially in rapidly-changing fields such as those in the natural sciences (e.g., chemistry, molecular biology, genetics, human ecology, biotechnology). The sabbatical is an excellent vehicle for moving back into the professional loop through studying cutting-edge scholarship and developing state-of-the-art technical skills. Sabbaticals often provide, as one faculty member put it, that rare opportunity to be "brought up-to-date in the field by those who are in present practice and who are at the top level of the profession."

The extended leave is particularly important to faculty in areas where it is difficult to maintain currency (for instance, aeronautical engineering) simply through reading journals, texts, and attending professional meetings. In some areas it is necessary to spend time in the field, to actually work in laboratories and industrial settings where state-of-the-art experimentation and innovation are going on (Brodsky, 1979). Thus, for some faculty the sabbatical leave may be one of the only means of dodging the bullet of technical obsolescence. This type of experiential learning has the added benefit of helping bring the world of practice and theory closer together in the classroom, thereby helping ensure that students are the ultimate beneficiaries of the sabbatical leave.

Enhances teaching

A sabbatical leave provides faculty with a superb vehicle for improving teaching. To begin with, scholarly updating not only brings a new credibility and relevance to classroom presentations, but also a renewed sense of self-confidence, often accompanied by a fresh resolve to practice more innovative pedagogical techniques. Indeed, many sabbatical returnees—perhaps because of their new level of self-confidence, enthusiasm, and energy—seem more willing to become greater risk-takers. And while risk taking does not in itself guarantee improved teaching, it often helps transform bland and routinized classrooms into dynamic and lively learning laboratories.

However, expanding and updating one's knowledge and skills are not the only factors responsible for enhanced classroom performance. Because many faculty audit courses while on sabbatical they have an excellent opportunity to observe and study peer pedagogy. One faculty member described his sabbatical as being like a "teaching clinic," during which he had a chance to study how other instructors "captured student attention and interest, generated discourse, phrased questions, and developed and used syllabi."

Not only technical skills are enhanced through peer observation. By virtually becoming students again, faculty who audit courses often experience a healthy reversal of perspective. Sophie Freud Loewenstein speaks for many faculty when she poignantly describes her role reversal while on sabbatical:

> My new role of trainee reminded me of what it means to be a student (a person of low power) and of the kind of risks that this role entails....As a teacher of adult students who come to study after some years of successful work, I find it enormously useful to experience for myself the sense of powerlessness, helplessness, fear of exposure, and fear of disciplinary authority that students confront. My students had tried to convey this to me, but I had forgotten such feelings and they had seemed unreal. I am happy that my empathy and sensitivity to their vulnerabilities has thus increased (p. 8).

Teachers experiencing what Loewenstein describes can never be the same again. After such an experience, it would take a very calloused and insensitive instructor not to identify more closely with students' struggles, not to empathize with their doubts and apprehensions, not to sympathize with their feelings of powerlessness. This kind of sensitivity and understanding ultimately results in a more humane and nurturing pedagogy. In short, it is difficult to develop a true understanding and respect for the learning process until we learn to see things through the eyes of our students.

INSTITUTIONAL BENEFITS

Trying to differentiate between faculty and institutional benefits is a tricky business because in one way or another every benefit a faculty member derives from a sabbatical almost always translates into institutional renewal and growth. When a faculty member returns from sabbatical with a repertoire of newly-acquired knowledge and renewed vigor, for example, aren't an institution's students the ultimate beneficiaries? When a faculty member receives accolades for pioneering research, aren't an institution's reputation and prestige enhanced proportionately? Despite the overlapping of faculty and institutional benefits, however, it is important to list institutional benefits separately if for no other reason than to emphasize the significant role a sabbatical program can play in enhancing the health and vitality of an institution.

Increased faculty efficiency, versatility, and productivity

One of the most striking qualities faculty report bringing back to their academic communities is a renewed sense of self-confidence—both as teachers and scholars. Faculty frequently speak of a dramatic "return to confidence" in their intellectual and scholarly capabilities, and of their "renewed sense of reconnection with the scholarly network and vocation." Further, many faculty report "more efficiency and productivity," both as teachers and scholars, as a result of their leaves. More specifically, by broadening and sharpening their professional skills and increasing their knowledge, faculty are often able to teach new courses, help plan new academic majors and general education programs, and serve as resource persons in areas ranging from grant writing to international study opportunities. This versatility significantly enhances a faculty member's value to the institution.

And sabbaticals bring not only immediate returns, but long-term benefits extending throughout the institution. Even in times of retrenchment, the sabbatical can serve the institution well by functioning as a primary vehicle for retraining faculty to assume other roles in the system, as well as by helping them develop new disciplinary and research interests.

Strengthened institutional programs

Sabbatical projects are not limited to an individual's specialized research interests. In fact, faculty frequently undertake sabbatical projects aimed at enhancing either departmental course offerings or institution-wide initiatives such as general education, leadership, and honors programs. Although the author knows of no national study that attempts to calculate the number of new courses created as a result of extended leaves, anecdotal evidence indicates the statistics would be impressive. Impressive, too, would be a count of the number of institutional programs sparked by sabbatical returnees bringing back new ideas and helpful information gleaned from conversations with colleagues at other colleges and universities. Looked at from this perspective, an institution's sabbatical program assumes the function of a nurturing wellspring, helping supply the entire academic community with a steady source of revitalizing and rejuvenating ideas and innovations.

Enhanced learning environment

Instructors returning from sabbatical with newly-acquired knowledge, restored vigor, and renewed enthusiasm for the classroom experience, are almost sure to become more dynamic and effective teachers. After a while this infusion of energized faculty has a collective effect, producing a kind of synergy or gestalt, with the whole becoming greater than the sum of its parts. Enthusiasm is contagious, and an infrastructure of reenergized faculty can help create a vital learning climate that positively affects others in the academic community.

Improved morale

High faculty morale is perhaps the most precious of institutional attributes. With good morale nearly anything is possible, even under the most difficult of circumstances; without it little is possible even if the circumstances are auspicious.

Unfortunately, there is no magic formula for enhancing morale. Unique institutional cultures demand unique nurturing.

However, both experiential and survey evidence reveal that one core ingredient of almost every high faculty morale success story is a professional growth program. For example, in an article entitled "High Faculty Morale: What Exemplary Colleges Do Right," Eugene Rice and Ann Austin (1988) list faculty development programs among the most important factors that "can make a significant difference" in fostering faculty satisfaction and morale. Even more specifically, Harry Kershen (1968) identifies improved morale as one of the most significant benefits of the sabbatical leave, pointing out that creating a "core of experienced professionals with up-to-date knowledge of their subjects and an awareness of modern teaching methods and innovations brings improved instruction and leads to an esprit de corps among the staff, which in turn enhances [the] ability to attract and retain new teachers of high caliber" (p. 20).

In short, while the sabbatical leave alone is not enough to lift faculty spirit from the abyss to the mountain top, when offered in conjunction with other professional growth opportunities it can prove to be a tremendously potent catalyst for raising morale.

Enhanced loyalty to the institution

Among all the intangible benefits derived from the sabbatical, the matter of institutional loyalty is perhaps the most difficult to measure and analyze. In fact, extrapolation and anecdotal evidence weigh in more heavily here than statistical studies, of which there are none currently. When interviewed, sabbatical recipients frequently report returning from sabbatical with a greater appreciation for, and stronger loyalty to, their institutions. There is little mystery in this response. When an institution is willing to invest in a faculty member's professional growth and satisfaction, that individual is likely to reciprocate by investing in the institution.

Enhanced faculty recruitment and retention

In their classic study, *American Professors*, Howard R. Bowen and Jack H. Schuster (1986) emphasize the point that "the availability of leaves is one of the features of academic life that attracts and holds capable people..." (p. 247). As recruiters quickly find in their interviews with teaching candidates, few things impress prospective colleagues more than strong institutional support of professional growth programs. Indeed, when it is time for candidates to ask their questions, many inquire first about whether they will be given released time and monetary support for their scholarly projects. Some ask about the sabbatical program in particular, viewing it as a kind of touchstone of the institution's attitude toward the professional and personal well being of its faculty. Thus, institutions interested in finding and holding the most desirable candidates (that is,

those displaying a desire to learn and grow and become productive teacher/
scholars), would do well to offer as many attractive opportunities as possible for
professional and personal development. The sabbatical represents one of the
most effective tools for attracting new, and retaining seasoned, faculty.

Enhanced intellectual climate

The more faculty on the cutting edge of scholarship in their disciplines, the
more faculty engaging in classroom research and other kinds of productive scholarship, the livelier an institution's intellectual climate. As has already been shown,
the sabbatical leave provides a vehicle for promoting this type of intellectual
activity. Sabbatical programs also produce some important spinoffs that contribute to a college or university's intellectual climate. For example, the public
reports given by sabbatical returnees typically feature cutting-edge scholarship.
Further, faculty returning from sabbatical often invite to their home institutions
noted educators and scholars they met while on leave, thus enriching the institutional climate.

Enhanced academic reputation of the institution

While some sabbatical benefits are intangible, most sabbatical outcomes
can be seen and measured. Sabbaticals result not only in new attitudes and perspectives, in renewed vigor, and in better physical and emotional health—they
also result in articles, books, paintings, poems, short stories, novels, plays, sculptures, and scientific discoveries. These tangible products enhance not only the
reputation of the scholar/teacher, but also the reputation of the institution as a
whole.

CONCLUSION

Because many of the primary benefits derived from the sabbatical experience are not easily quantifiable, they are difficult to measure. What type of
barometer can we use, for example, to gauge a heightened sense of self-confidence and self-esteem? By what yardstick do we measure an enhanced sensitivity
toward, and appreciation for, other cultures? What formula can we use to figure
the end results of clearer perspectives and priorities? How do we quantify
improved morale? How do we statistically measure the spirit of hope and excitement engendered by a program promising to help transform dreams into reality? How do we weigh enhanced incentive? How do we gauge a sabbatical program's potency as an antidote to stress and burnout, stagnation and mediocrity?
And how can we begin to measure the enhanced image of an institution which
demonstrates its humaneness and concern for the learning of its students by
strongly supporting a program promoting professional and personal growth?
Only when we arrive at a formula for measuring these kinds of outcomes will we
be able to take the true and full measure of sabbatical programs.

WORKS CITED

Bowen, H., & Schuster, J. (1986). *American professors: A national resource imperiled.* New York, NY: Oxford University Press.

Brodsky, R.F. (1979). A new type of faculty improvement leave. *Engineering Education,* 70(3), 271–76.

Gardner, J. (1983). *Self renewal: The individual and the innovative society.* New York, NY: W.W. Norton.

Kershen, H. (1968). A board member looks at sabbatical leaves. *New York State Education,* 55, 19–20, 47.

Loewenstein, S.F. (1983). *Last sabbatical: A midlife journey.* Grand Forks, ND: University of North Dakota Office of Instructional Development.

Rice, R.E., & Austin, A.E. (1988). High faculty morale: What exemplary colleges do right. *Change,* March/April, 1988.

Sorcinelli, M.D. (1987). Sabbaticals and leaves of absence: Critical events in the careers of faculty. *Journal of Higher Education Studies,* 2(1), 9–14.

11

An Overview

*The sabbatical leave is the most common form of faculty renew-
al, but...sabbaticals are far from universal and leaves are rarely
available for junior faculty. We urge that a sabbatical leave policy be
available at every institution, with the understanding that such
leaves will be competitively awarded and will be used in ways that
will promote faculty growth and assume benefits to the institution
and its students.*

Ernest L. Boyer

The 1990s is not a particularly happy decade for higher education. Indeed, academia often seems more like a battle zone than the proverbial ivory tower. From the surrounding heights constant sniping comes from caustic critics representing both the print and electronic media. From both left and right come attacks launched by legislators and parents demanding accountability, fiscal responsibility, and greater productivity. And as if these external forces weren't destructive enough, sporadic fighting within academic ranks over such issues as "political correctness" creates enmity among those who should be standing shoulder-to-shoulder against a formidable opposition.

All members of the academic community have felt the deleterious effects of public disenchantment and of fiscal austerity, but none more than the faculty. The roll call of problems and issues facing educators is abundant: salaries that are not keeping up with the cost of living; growing numbers of underprepared and unmotivated students; pessimistic enrollment projections; increasing pressure to find outside funding to support research projects; a growing cohort of nomadic temporary faculty; limited opportunity for promotions and in-house grants; uncertainty about the future of academic programs; retrenchment;

institutional closings; and the list goes on. Add to this the overarching challenge of trying to create with limited resources a nurturing environment for an increasingly diverse student population and one gets some idea of the potentially demoralizing climate in which faculty have to work. At the very least, the situation demands adequate incentives and rewards to help sustain morale. The sabbatical leave, while certainly not a panacea, is a potent antidote to the burnout and disillusionment that currently plague college and university faculty.

SOME RECOMMENDATIONS FOR MAINTAINING HEALTHY SABBATICAL PROGRAMS

As I have mentioned previously, sabbatical programs need care and nurturing if they are to realize their full potential for providing faculty with professional growth opportunities. But how, exactly, do we go about strengthening our sabbatical programs? How can we become more effective caretakers? The following recommendations are just a few of the things faculty and administrators must do to protect and enhance the sabbatical system.

Working toward a shared vision

If we are to strengthen significantly our sabbatical system, we must try to reach philosophical agreement on the purpose and place of the sabbatical. All too frequently the sabbatical is viewed either as a motivational carrot administrators dangle before the noses of faculty, or as a faculty entitlement about which administrators should have little or nothing to say. Perhaps a more balanced, and productive, approach is to view the sabbatical as a professional growth opportunity benefitting not only faculty but also students and the institution as a whole: in short, a program for the good of the entire academic community. As Maganzini (1987) suggests, faculty "must recognize the mutuality of institutional interests and self-interest..." (p. 13); administrators, in turn, must recognize the mutuality of faculty growth and institutional vitality.

Sharing responsibilities and assuming accountability

Faculty and administrators, however, must not only share the same vision in regard to the sabbatical. They must also share responsibility for maintaining the system. At first glance, the burden of responsibility seems to rest chiefly on the shoulders of chief administrators. But faculty also bear considerable responsibility. Sabbatical recipients, for example, must help maintain programmatic integrity. This means engaging not only in conscientious sabbatical leave planning, writing well-articulated proposals, and doing one's best to fulfill project goals, but also fulfilling all policy requirements (e.g., abiding by the rules governing compensation received while on sabbatical, and delivering concrete and detailed sabbatical reports on schedule). Further, it means seeking opportunities to share the knowledge gained on leave with colleagues, students, and the wider public.

And what of those faculty who have not as yet received a sabbatical? They, too, have a responsibility. Indeed, it is in the best interests of all faculty to play active roles in nurturing their institution's sabbatical program. For example, faculty should volunteer to serve on sabbatical review committees. In addition, they should make every effort to attend sabbatical report presentations. And, finally, they should study sabbatical policy statements and guidelines. Only when well informed and knowledgeable about their sabbatical program will faculty be in a position to monitor and help strengthen it through constructive suggestions and action.

Asking tough questions

We must continue asking tough, fundamental questions about the sabbatical, beginning with a close examination of the concept itself. The sabbatical variously has been called an "entitlement," a "right," a "fringe benefit," a "necessity," a "luxury," a "privilege," a "vacation," and even a "boondoggle." Which is it? Ideally, which ought it to be? Beyond this basic question, the following also demand our consideration:

- Should the sabbatical review system be in the hands of administrative officers or peer committees? What are the advantages and disadvantages of each system?
- Why don't more faculty who are eligible for sabbaticals apply?
- What are the long term benefits of sabbatical leaves?
- What can be done to bolster sabbatical funding?
- How can institutions effectively counter legislative regulation of sabbatical programs?

Only by asking hard questions about the sabbatical can we arrive at solutions to some of the problems facing the sabbatical system in our colleges and universities.

Integrating sabbatical programs

If the sabbatical leave program is to realize its full potential, administrators and faculty must work together to place it into a broader faculty development context. The following case study helps illustrate how and why this should be done.

While at the University of the Pacific, Eugene Rice (1983) helped direct a program in which the traditional leave program had been "redefined." According to Rice, the university moved from a "competitive" sabbatical program to a "faculty development leave" system in which both tenured and untenured faculty were eligible to apply for extended leave every five years. The leave was for one semester with full pay. Just as noteworthy as the generosity of the program, however, was its integrative nature. Rice described the redefined leave program as the "point around which all professional development activities at the university center." Further, the program was factored in to all "systematic long range academic planning in the institution." In short, the program served not only as the linchpin of all professional growth activities, but it also became an organic part of institutional programming. As Rice pointed out, this type of program "can become a pivotal resource in meeting the individual faculty member's personal and professional needs while, at the same time, strengthening the institution" (pp. 77–81).

Being flexible, creative, and innovative

A leitmotif running through the literature on the sabbatical is the call for greater flexibility, creativity, and innovation on the part of those administering sabbatical programs. A sampling of comments is both instructive and compelling. In her study of sabbaticals and other leaves of absence, Mary Dean Sorcinelli (1987) strongly recommends both expanding opportunities (i.e., more released time of different types) and providing greater flexibility (i.e., more "creative means" for pursuing traditional leave opportunities). Schuster and Wheeler (1990), in *Enhancing Faculty Careers: Strategies for Development and Renewal*, commend those institutions creative and flexible enough to "provide sabbatical leaves for non-tenured, junior faculty," thus affording them the "opportunity to organize [their] research agenda when it is most needed" (p. 34). Thomas Maher (1981), in *Designing New Roles Within Academe*, suggests that colleges and universities must not only review their policies regarding the sabbatical, but that they should "provide 'living' examples of creative alternatives to the traditional uses of sabbaticals" (p. 92). Harry Kershen (1968), looking at the sabbatical from the perspective of a school board member, praises sabbatical leave policies in general, but stresses they fail in "not going far enough." Kershen explains that "present policies prevent teachers from using their sabbatical year in free-ranging exploration of ideas outside their fields, thus limiting and frustrating individuals—often the most gifted and imaginative—and discouraging them from applying for leaves." If our teachers are to be "widely-informed, well-rounded persons," Kershen concludes, "they should, therefore, be permitted—no, urged—to study widely beyond the narrow confines of their fields" (p. 20). And Ingraham and King (1965) echo Kershen's view by stating they are "depressed by the terrible purposefulness of leaves" (p. 86). It is tempting to apply the old bromide about not fixing something that isn't broken to the conventional seven year sabbatical system now in place at so many U.S. institutions of higher learning. However, even unbroken objects and systems sometimes need fine tuning and sprucing up. In short, there is room for creativity. Not creativity for creativity's sake, certainly, but creativity aimed at generating a rich repertoire of professional growth opportunities that best respond to the needs of faculty now and in the future.

Innovative leave programs do not necessarily have to replace conventional sabbatical programs. Rather, they can complement existing programs, thus providing faculty with a greater variety of professional growth opportunities designed to address a mosaic of needs and talents. The possibilities are limited only by the creativeness and imagination of those administering sabbatical programs.

Such creative approaches have the potential to solve some of the problems facing academia today. Andrew Cherlin, Professor of Sociology at the Johns Hopkins University, illustrates how this can be done in a November 22, 1989, article in *The Chronicle of Higher Education*. Cherlin writes: "If colleges and universities are serious about easing the conflict between work and family life for women on their faculties, they could take the simple and inexpensive step of allowing untenured faculty members to take advance sabbatical leaves for pregnancy and infant care." Cherlin goes on to explain that "the crunch time for having children is also the crunch time for getting tenure," thus making this innovation a particularly helpful and humane one for young, harried faculty. Indeed, Cherlin suggests that such advance sabbaticals be granted to both male and female assistant professors "so they [can] be at home during pregnancy or with a new baby." A key to this program would be that during the advance sabbatical the "tenure clock would stop," the time off not counting in the "usual six-year period of research allowed prior to the tenure decision." Finally, pointing out that the "cost to institutions would be modest," Cherlin concludes that such a program would not only allow those eligible to "compete for tenure on an equal basis," but also ensure that the "children of faculty members are not short changed because of the demands of their parents' careers" (p. B2).

More flexibility is also needed in the sabbatical review system. Not only administrators, but also sabbatical review committees ought to rethink the conventional approach to proposal evaluation. Perhaps as a result of the sabbatical leave's traditional association with research (Rudolph, 1962; Geiger, 1986; Frederick, 1991), review agents have had a tendency to view the sabbatical as a vehicle for research. Anecdotal evidence suggests that research projects are considered "textbook cases," while projects aimed at pedagogical or curricular enhancement, or aimed at cultural enrichment in general, are considered problematic.

All of this is understandable. Reviewers find it easier to judge conventional research proposals promising tangible outcomes. But there are good reasons for taking a sabbatical other than the production of an article, monograph, or book. What if a faculty member already has an excellent publication record and is more in need of some cultural enrichment or a broadening of perspective and outlook? Perhaps the candidate is close to burning out and desperately needs a change of venue—not an arduous research schedule. In this instance, just getting away from the rigors of collegial life and experiencing another culture for a semester or two may be far more beneficial than undertaking a new research project, no matter how promising the outcome. In brief, there are a wide variety of sabbatical needs and an equally broad range of legitimate sabbatical topics. If the rationale is sound, why shouldn't such proposals be approved, despite their unconventionality?

A FINAL OBSERVATION

Most of us tilling the fields of academia have a good idea of how valuable the sabbatical leave is to the professional and personal well being of the teacher-scholar. My own sabbatical leaves represent two of the brightest moments in my professional career and have left me with a healthy respect for a sabbatical's potential for providing renewal, enrichment, and enlightenment.

However, it is difficult to appreciate fully the potency of this growth opportunity until one reads, and hears, the words of colleagues who have experienced it. My study of the sabbatical has reinforced my conviction that one of the best decisions an institution can make is to develop and support a strong sabbatical program. Such a decision would be well justified even if the only members of an academic community who benefitted from sabbaticals were faculty. But not only faculty benefit. Perhaps the greatest beneficiaries of a sabbatical program are our students. Better informed and reenergized teachers returning to their classrooms with self-confidence, fresh knowledge, and a livelier bounce to their step are better prepared to create a fertile learning environment in which deep and long-lasting learning takes place. Students expect, and deserve, a quality education. The sabbatical helps us maintain that quality.

WORKS CITED

Boyer, E. (1987). *College: The undergraduate experience in America.* New York, NY: Harper & Row.

Cherlin, A. (1989, November 22). Needed: Early sabbaticals for pregnancy and infant care. *The Chronicle of Higher Education,* p. B2.

Frederick, P. (1991). Changing collegial conversation. *The Department Advisor,* 6(4), 1–5.

Geiger, R. (1986). *To advance knowledge: The growth of American research universities, 1900–1940.* New York, NY: Oxford University Press.

Ingraham, M., & King, F. (1965). *The outer fringe: Faculty benefits other than annuities and insurance.* Madison, WI: University of Wisconsin Press.

Kershen, H. (1968). A board member looks at sabbatical leaves. *New York State Education,* 55, 19–20, 47.

Maganzini, A. (1987). Retraining faculty at the community college. In *Policy issues at the community college: Essays by fellows in the mid-career fellowships program at Princeton University.*

Maher, T. (1981). Designing new roles within academe. In Baldwin, R., et al. (Eds.), *Expanding faculty options: Career development projects at colleges and universities* (pp. 87–98). Washington, DC: AAHE.

Rice, R.E. (1983). Leaves and other institutional resources for maintaining faculty vitality. In D.T. Bedsoe (Ed.), *Critical aspects of faculty development programs: Proceedings of the invitational seminar on faculty development* (pp. 77–81). Sherman, TX.

Rudolph, F. (1962). *The American college and university: A history.* New York, NY: Random House.

Schuster, J.H., Wheeler, D., & Associates (1990). *Enhancing faculty careers: Strategies for development and renewal.* San Francisco, CA: Jossey-Bass.

Sorcinelli, M.D. (1987). Sabbaticals and leaves of absence: Critical events in the careers of faculty. *Journal of Higher Education Studies*, 2(1), 9–14.

APPENDICES

APPENDIX A

THE SABBATICAL: A SELECTIVE BIBLIOGRAPHY

Anderson, C., & Atelsek, F. (1982). *Sabbatical and research leaves in colleges and universities* (Higher Education Panel Report No.53). Washington, DC: American Council on Education.

Anthony, R., & Roe, G. (1984). *Educators' passport to international jobs: How to find and enjoy employment abroad.* Princeton, NJ: Peterson's Guides.

Arden, E. (1969). A sabbatical plan for deans. *AAUP Bulletin,* 55(2), 267–269.

Asbrand, D. (1985). Sabbaticals are not just for scholars: Time off rejuvenates engineers and managers. *Electrical Design News,* 30, 291–292.

Astin, A., Comstock, C., Epperson, D.C., Greeley, A.M., Katz, J., & Kauffman, J.F. (1974). *Faculty development in a time of retrenchment.* The Group for Human Development in Higher Education and *Change Magazine.* Washington, DC: Heldref Publications.

Avakian, A.N. (1987). Planning for innovative leave opportunities. *Planning for Higher Education,* 15, 23–28.

Baer, J., & Stenersen, S. (1985). If wishes were fishes, this proposal to liberalize teacher sabbatical policies would be a whale of a good idea for your school board. *The American School Board Journal,* 172, 28–29.

Baldwin, R. (1979). Adult and career development: What are the implications for faculty? *Current Issues in Higher Education,* 2, 13–20.

Barrows, A. (1919). *Report upon a questionnaire concerning the organization and facilities for research issued by the division of educational relations of the national research council.* (Confidential). Washington, DC: The National Research Council.

Bast, R. (1992). A sabbatical? Do it! *BioScience,* 42(7), 546–547.

Belcher, K. (1913). The sabbatical year for the public school teacher. *Educational Review,* 45, 471–484.

Bennett, H., & Scroggs, S. (1932). Sabbatical leave: The status of sabbatical leave in publicly controlled institutions of higher learning. *Journal of Higher Education,* 3, 196–199.

Blaisdell, T. (1923). The small college and the sabbatical year. *School and Society,* 18, 589–590.

Bluhm, H. (1976). The sabbatical leave plan: Is it meeting faculty and institutional needs? *Improving College and University Teaching,* 24(4), 207–209.

Boice, R. (1987). Is released time an effective component of faculty development programs? *Research in Higher Education*, 26(3), 311–326.

Booth, S., & Higbee, E. (1974). A comparative study of sabbatical leave practices in selected commonwealth and U.S. universities (Unpublished Report). Hamilton, Ontario: McMaster University.

Bowen, H., & Schuster, J. (1986). *American professors: A national resource imperiled.* New York, NY: Oxford University Press.

Boyer, E. (1987). *College: The undergraduate experience in America.* New York, NY: Harper & Row.

Brodsky, R.F. (1979). A new type of faculty improvement leave. *Engineering Education*, 70(3), 271–276.

Brooks, D., Fuller, R.G., James, H.J., Lewis, L.C., Debry, J., Johnson, J.W., & Silberman, R.G. (1980). Sabbatical leaves in pedagogy. *Journal of Chemical Education*, 57(12), 845–846.

Bucher, G. (1983). Scheduling of more frequent sabbaticals. In *Critical aspects of faculty development programs: Proceedings of the invitational seminar on faculty development.* Bedsole, D. (Ed.), (Sherman, TX, April 25–26,), 71–76.

Burke, E. (1990). A year in Germany: A sabbatical dream. *English Journal*, 79, 67–69.

Campbell, O. (1931). Systems of sabbatical leaves. *AAUP Bulletin*, 17, 219–234.

Cardozier, V.R. (1987). *American higher education.* Brookfield, VT: Avebury.

Centra, J. (1978). Faculty development in higher education. *Teachers College Record*, 80(1), 188–201.

Centra, J. (1985). Maintaining faculty vitality through faculty development. In S. Clark & D. Lewis (Eds.), *Faculty vitality and institutional productivity* (pp. 141–156). New York, NY: Teachers College Press.

Cherlin, A. (1989, November 22). Needed: Early sabbaticals for pregnancy and infant care. *The Chronicle of Higher Education*, p.B2.

Chronister, J. (1987). A perspective on issues facing the professoriate. *Educational Considerations*, 14(1), 19–20.

Coleman, J. (1974). *Blue-collar journal: A college president's sabbatical.* New York, NY: J.B. Lippincott.

Cooke, D., & Ayers, A. (1943). Sabbatical leave. In H. Rivin & H. Schueler (Eds.), *Encyclopedia of modern education* (pp. 698–699). New York, NY: Philosophical Library of New York City.

Cooper, L. (1932). Sabbatical leave for college teachers. Unpublished doctoral dissertation, University of Cincinnati, 1931. Abstract as University of Florida Publication (Gainsville, FL), Education Series, 1(1), 88 pp.

Cope, H. (1958). Fringe benefits and prestige items. *College and University Business,* 25, 35–37.

Daugherty, H., Jr. (1979). *Sabbatical leaves in higher education.* Unpublished doctoral dissertation, Indiana University, Bloomington, IN.

Dees, B. (1957). Opportunities for faculty study in engineering. *Journal of Engineering Education,* 47, 558–564.

Delattre, E. (1981, April). The survival of teachers and administrators. Paper Presented at the Meeting of the Community College Humanities Association, Washington, DC.

Deutsch, M. (1952). *The college from within.* Berkeley, CA: University of California Press.

Dumser, P.M. (1991). Mini-sabbaticals widen a teacher's world. *Educational Leadership,* 49, 77–78.

Eberle, A., & Thompson, R. (1972). *Sabbatical leaves in higher education.* Bloomington, IN: Indiana University Student Association of Higher Education.

Eble, K. (1978). *Professors as teachers.* San Francisco, CA: Jossey-Bass.

Eble, K., & McKeachie, W. (1985). *Improving undergraduate education through faculty development.* San Francisco, CA: Jossey-Bass.

Eells, W.C. (1962). The origin and early history of sabbatical leave. *AAUP Bulletin,* 48, 253–255.

Eells, W.C., & Hollis, E. (1962). *Sabbatical leave in higher education: Origin, early history, and current practices* (Bulletin No. 17). Washington, DC: U.S. Office of Education.

Eiesland, G. (1991). Sabbatical success: Program enriches lives, careers. *Trial,* 27, 56–59.

Eisenstein, H. (1986). New criterion for determining the worth of a university. *College Student Journal,* 20, 331–334.

Fadum, R. (1971). The role of the dean in faculty development. *Engineering Education,* 62, 104–106.

Foreman, J. (1976). The 'mini'-sabbatical concept: To upgrade college faculties at low cost. *Kappa Delta Pi Record,* 13(2), 34–35 and 65.

Frank, C. (1966). Of sabbaticals in general, particularly mine. *Liberal Education,* 52, 144–148.

Frank, C. (1967). *Six Franks abroad: One man's sabbatical.* Cleveland, OH: World Publishing.

Franklin, T. (1993). Planning successful sabbaticals. *The Department Chair.* Spring, 8–9.

Frederick, P. (1991). Changing collegial conversation. *The Department Advisor,* 6(4), 1–5.

Furniss, W.T. (1981). *Reshaping faculty careers.* Washington, DC: American Council on Education.

Gaff, J. (1978). *Toward faculty renewal: Advances in faculty, instructional, and organizational development.* San Francisco, CA: Jossey-Bass.

Geiger, R. (1986). *To advance knowledge: The growth of American research universities, 1900–1940.* New York, NY: Oxford University Press.

Geis, G., Wilburn, M., & Mellor, G. (1981). Preparing for teaching in colleges and universities: In-service support in Canada and the United States. *Studies in Higher Education,* 6(1), 47–57.

Goldberg, T. (1988). An academic in practice—or how about a sabbatical doing social work? *Journal of Social Work Education,* 24(3), 211–220.

Good, C.(Ed.). (1959). *Dictionary of education (3rd ed.).* New York, NY: McGraw-Hill.

Good, H. (1992, June). The frustrations and satisfactions of a sabbatical. *The Chronicle of Higher Education,* 24, pp. B2–3.

Grieder, C. (1961). Sabbatical leaves for administrators? *Nation's Schools,* 68, 6 and 8.

Heiges, R. (1954). On sabbatical leave. *Peabody Journal of Education.* 32, 6–8.

Hendel, D., & Solberg, J. (1983, April). Sabbatical and leave experiences of female and male faculty at a large research university. Paper presented at the Annual Meeting of the American Educational Research Association, Montreal, Canada.

Henry B. (1974). A sabbatical tale. *AAUP Bulletin,* 60, 296–298.

Holleman, J.(1981). Developing an alternative sabbatical leave policy. Unpublished. Ed.D. Practicum, Nova University, Fort Lauderdale, FL.

Ingraham, M., Brown, J.D., & Megaw, N. (1967). A statement on leaves of absence. *AAUP Bulletin,* Autumn, 270–273.

Ingraham, M. & King, F. (1965). *The outer fringe: Faculty benefits other than annuities and insurance.* Madison, WI: University of Wisconsin Press.

Jarecky, R., & Sandifer, M. (1986). Faculty members' evaluations of sabbaticals. *Journal of Medical Education,* 61(10), 803–807.

Jensen, I. (no date). *Sabbatical leave: A selected bibliography.* College Hill, UT: Merrill Library and Learning Resource Program, Utah State University.

Johnstone, W. (1980). Faculty retrenchment in the 1980's: A question of how many? and how managed? *Journal of the College and University Personnel Association,* 31(1), 22–30.

Jubak, J. (1990). Work sabbaticals: Taking time off to recharge. *Self,* 12, 118–120.

Kershen, H. (1968). A board member looks at sabbatical leaves. *New York State Education,* 55, 19–20, 47.

Kessell, W., & Muse, P. (1951). A study of sabbatical leave in teacher training institutions. *Teachers College Journal,* 22, 70–71.

Kimball, B. (1978). The origin of the sabbath and its legacy to the modern sabbatical. *Journal of Higher Education,* 49(4), 303–315.

Kirkpatrick, E. (1916). The sabbatical year in state educational institutions. *School and Society,* 3, 783–784.

Kleiman, C. (1992 December). More firms add up pluses of sabbaticals. *Chicago Tribune,* Section 8, 1.

Klitz, S. (1984). *Faculty handbook for sabbaticals abroad.* Storrs, CT: The University of Connecticut.

Koelsch, W. (1987). *Clark University.* Worcester, MA: Clark University Press.

Konrad, A. (1983). Faculty development practices in Canadian universities. *The Canadian Journal of Higher Education,* 13(2), 13–25.

Kuramoto, A. (1990). A sabbatical abroad: Planning the trip, enjoying your stay. *Adult Learning,* 2, 29.

Langerud, S. (1990). Re-entry shock: A career dilemma. *Experiential Education,* 15(5), 6 and 17.

Lawson, R. (1979). Sabbatical leave: Don't fear it. *NJEA Review,* 53(3), No.3, 25–26.

Laycock, F. (1955). ...And one to grow on. *AAUP Bulletin,* 41, 733–41.

Lemon, A. (1927). The leave of absence in universities and colleges. *Journal of Educational Research,* 16, 210–212.

Lloyd, R., & Walker, G., Jr. (1948). Sabbatical leave in negro colleges and universities. *School and Society,* 68, 190–191.

Loewenstein, S.F. (1983). *Last sabbatical: A midlife journey.* Grand Forks, ND: University of North Dakota Office of Instructional Development.

McKenna, D. (1977). Ten lessons of a recycled president. *Liberal Education,* 63, 423–434.

McVey, F., & Hughes, R. (1952). *Problems of college and university administration.* Ames, IA: Iowa State College Press.

Maganzini, A. (1987). Retraining faculty at the community college. In *Policy issues at the community college: Essays by fellows in the mid-career fellowship program at Princeton University.*

Magrath, C.P. (1983). Letting go—even briefly. *Change,* 15, 5–6.

Maher, T. (1981). Designing new roles within academe. In Baldwin, R., et. al. (Eds.), *Expanding faculty options: Career development projects at colleges and universities* (pp. 87–98). Washington, DC: AAHE.

Marker, D. (1983). Faculty leaves. In J.W. Fuller (Ed.), *Issues in Faculty Personnel Policies* (pp. 37–46), 11, *New Directions for Higher Education.* San Francisco, CA: Jossey-Bass.

Marsee, S. (1961). Sabbatical—full or half salary? *Junior College Journal,* 31, 333–336.

Matoney, J., Jr., & Weston, M. (1985). Planning a sabbatical? These tips can save taxes. *AAHE Bulletin,* 38, 11–13.

Maul, R. (1954). Encouragement to further study. *NEA Research Bulletin,* 32, 176–79.

Mayberry, M.A. (1987). Objective sabbatical: A time for self-renewal. *Nursing Administration Quarterly,* 11, 9–12.

Meyer, A. (1929). Leaves of absence in American universities. *School and Society,* 2, 356–360.

Miller, B.K. (1989). Individualizing faculty renewal. *The Journal of Staff, Program, and Organization Development,* 7(1), 33–37.

Mitchell, J.L. (1981). Faculty development and first principles. *The CEA Critic,* 43(2), 8–13.

Mulrow, P. (1989). Sabbatical leave: An important mechanism for revitalizing faculty. *The Journal of Laboratory and Clinical Medicine,* 113, 537–540.

Murphy, R. (1959). Sabbaticals and fringe benefits. *Quarterly Journal of Speech,* 45, 99–103.

Neidle, E. (1978). Sabbatical policies and their implementation at United States dental schools. *Journal of Dental Education,* 42(11), 604–608.

Olivero, M. (1989). The corporate sabbatical: A win-win approach. *Working Woman,* 14, 22–24.

Olney, K. & McGrath, E. (1990). Time off for good behavior. *Savvy Woman,* 11, 62–65.

Patton, B. (1981, November). Continued development of tenured faculty. Paper presented at the Annual Meeting of the Speech Communication Association, Anaheim, CA.

Ponzo, Z. (1989). The endless vita: You can't get enough of what you don't need. *Journal of Counseling and Development, 67,* 414–415.

Professional leave report, 1971–1972 (1972). Washington State Council on Higher Education: Olympia, WA.

Ralston, J., & Ralston, T. (1987). *The sabbatical book.* Buffalo, NY: The Roylott Press.

Randall, O. (1922). Report of the commission on sabbatic leave. *Association of American Colleges Bulletin, 8,* 104–118.

Randall, O. (1923). Report of the commission on sabbatic leave. *Association of American Colleges Bulletin, 9,* 188–202.

Randall, O. (1924). Report of the commission on sabbatic leave. *Association of American Colleges Bulletin, 10* (May), 137–140. Also in *AAUP Bulletin, 10* (April, 1924), 210–212.

Reuler, J. (1989). Sabbatical. *JAMA, 261*(3), 408–10.

Reynolds, S.J. (1990). Sabbatical: The pause that refreshes. *The Journal of Academic Librarianship, 16*(2), 90–93.

Rice, R.E. (1983). Leaves and other institutional resources for maintaining faculty vitality. In D. Bedsole (Ed.), *Critical aspects of faculty development programs: Proceedings of the invitational seminar on faculty development* (pp. 77–81). Sherman, TX.

Riely, M.G. (1971). Sabbatical leave: The teacher's R and R. *The Independent School Bulletin, 30*(3), 68–70.

Robinson, J.S. (1983, August 31). Impressions from my first sabbatical. *The Chronicle of Higher Education,* p. 28.

Rossi, A. (1973). Sabbatical leave for teachers: Should it be compulsory? *Education Digest, 90,* 36–37.

Rubin, B.M. (1987). *Time out: How to take a year (or more or less) off without jeopardizing your job, your family, or your bank account.* New York, NY: W.W. Norton.

Rudolph, F.(1962). *The American college and university: A history.* New York, NY: Random House.

Ruebsam, E. (1947). Sabbatical leave in land-grant institutions. *AAUP Bulletin, 33,* 717–720.

Sabbatical leave for teachers. (1976). PAR Analysis No. 211. Baton Rouge, LA: Public Affairs Research Council of Louisiana.

A sabbatical on full salary. (1958). *School and Society, 86,* 421–422.

Schrammel, H.E. (1937). Length of the employment year and sabbatical leaves of absence in teachers colleges. *School and Society, 45,* 454–456.

Schuster, J., Wheeler, D., & Associates. (1990). *Enhancing faculty careers: Strategies for development and renewal.* San Francisco, CA: Jossey-Bass.

Schwartz, L.L. (1983). Nurturing an endangered species: A constructive approach to faculty development. *Improving College and University Teaching,* 31(2), 65–68.

Scott, F. (1925). Report of Committee K: Systems for Sabbatical Years. *AAUP Bulletin,* 11, 90–91.

Scott, J. (1992). Planning and implementing a sabbatical leave abroad. *Journal of Education for Business,* 67, 238–242.

Shanker, A. (1985). Sabbaticals: A good teacher lure. *American Teacher,* 69, 5.

Simpson, E. (1990). *Faculty renewal in higher education.* Malabar, FL: Robert E. Krieger Publishing.

Sorcinelli, M.D. (1987). Sabbaticals and leaves of absence: Critical events in the careers of faculty. *Journal of Higher Education Studies,* 2(1), 9–14.

Statement of principles on leaves of absence. (1972). *AAUP Bulletin,* 58, 244–245.

Stickler, W.H. (1965). How 59 major institutions conduct faculty sabbatical leave programs. *College and University Business,* 39(4), 52–54.

Stickler, W.H. (1958). Sabbatical leave in the state universities and land-grant institutions 1957–58. *Higher Education,* 14, 118–119.

Stright, I.L. (1964). Sabbatical leave: A critique. *Journal of Higher Education,* 35, 388–390.

Sullivan, R. (1972). A sabbatical to teach. *Contemporary Education,* 44(1), 44–45.

Toll, J. (1980). Rewards to stimulate faculty excellence. *National Forum: Phi Kappa Phi Journal,* 60(2), 3–4.

Toomey, E., & Connor, J. (1988). Employee sabbaticals: Who benefits and why. *Personnel,* 65, 81–84.

Turner, M.A. (1988). Tax consequences of faculty leaves for professional development. *College Teaching,* 36(4), 149–152.

Van Meter, E. (1984). Eight ways to recruit the teachers you want for the jobs you've got. *American School Board Journal,* 171(2), 27–28.

Van Til, W. (1971). One way of looking at it: Anyone for international work? *Phi Delta Kappan,* 53, 154–155.

Vasiliauskas, J. (1978). *The development of recommendations for College of DuPage faculty sabbatical leave policy.* Unpublished Study. College of DuPage, Glen Ellyn, IL.

Walrath, N.D. (1985). Sabbaticals: A time to reflect, a time of discovery. *English Journal, 74*(2), 40–41.

West, D.C. (1982). The value of a sabbatical. *AGB Reports, 24*, 33–35.

Wheeler, D. (undated publication). *A prospectus on faculty leaves: Opportunities for renewal and growth.* University of Nebraska, Lincoln, NE: IANR Office of Professional and Organizational Development.

White, K. (1981). Deferred maintenance or institutional renewal?: Professional development leaves at Valencia Community College (Unpublished paper). Valencia Community College, Orlando, FL.

Woodburne, L. (1950). *Faculty personnel policies in higher education.* New York, NY: Harper & Brothers.

Woods, T. (1961). The college instructor, the sabbatical leave, and the school district. *Journal of Secondary Education, 36*, 461–463.

Zahorski, K.J. (1990). *The St. Norbert College sabbatical handbook.* DePere, WI: St. Norbert College Press.

APPENDIX B

(The Faculty Personnel Committee reviews and makes recommendations on all sabbatical proposals, thereby playing a central role in the application process. While the Faculty Handbook *rather broadly outlines the functions of the Committee, the following statement, drafted by members of the 1989–90 Personnel Committee, more concretely delineates its philosophy, expectations, and procedures. In brief, it is an explanation of how the Faculty Personnel Committee reaches its decisions regarding sabbaticals.)*

A STATEMENT ON THE PHILOSOPHY AND ROLE OF THE ST. NORBERT COLLEGE FACULTY PERSONNEL COMMITTEE

THE INFORMATION SESSION

Each September, the Faculty Personnel Committee schedules an informational meeting for prospective applicants with questions about policies and procedures. Most applicants have probably completed a substantial portion of their applications prior to this meeting, but it may provide information useful in final revisions. This meeting is potentially of greater service to those faculty contemplating applications in the following year.

PROCEDURES

The Personnel Committee begins its deliberations immediately after the September 30 application deadline. Its first item of business is to consider sabbatical proposals. Each Committee member receives a copy of each proposal and any supporting material to read prior to the meeting at which it is considered. Usually from one to two hours are spent discussing a proposal before it is voted upon. Voting is by secret ballot, and a sabbatical is approved or denied by a simple majority. If a sabbatical is approved, the Committee then considers and votes on its budget. The Committee will reconsider any decision at the request of any of its members up until the end of its deliberations in December.

WHAT THE COMMITTEE LOOKS FOR IN SABBATICAL PROPOSALS

All else being equal, Personnel Committee members would prefer to see a faculty member spend a sabbatical leave away from campus and its day-to-day distractions, they would prefer to see a sabbatical project somehow related to the faculty member's discipline, and they would prefer to see a faculty member on sabbatical in a position to interact with colleagues in the same field of endeavor.

Nevertheless, the scope of successful sabbatical applications is broad. Within the last ten years, some faculty members have spent sabbaticals on campus, some have commuted from home to nearby institutions, some have moved shop out-of-state, and some have traveled abroad. Sabbaticals have been used to bring ongoing projects to fruition and to set out in new directions of scholarship. Faculty on sabbaticals have engaged in research directed toward publication and in study directed toward pedagogical and curricular enhancement. It is up to the applicant to convince the Personnel Committee that a particular course of action is most suited to that applicant's needs and objectives and that it will benefit the College. The Committee for its part is willing to be convinced.

The applicant should clearly state the objectives of the proposed sabbatical and should provide concrete evidence that these objectives can and will be met. Tangible and intangible outcomes should be described. Although the primary purpose of a sabbatical may be research, retooling, or renewal, it may have other, indirect, benefits as well. Some Committee members seem more willing than others to read between the lines ("This person really *needs* a sabbatical," or "This research will undoubtedly benefit this person's classes"), but it is probably safer to make explicit even those points that "go without saying."

The applicant should provide a carefully detailed timetable, which should not necessarily be restricted to the period of the sabbatical itself. For example, significant planning or other groundwork may occur during the summer or semester prior to the actual sabbatical, and listing that activity may help convince the Committee of the applicant's dedication to the project. On the other hand, there may be perfectly understandable reasons why an applicant's obligations require that all sabbatical-related activity be confined to the sabbatical semester. It would be prudent to explain these reasons to the Committee. It would also be prudent to make clear how the proposed sabbatical activity is something more than could be accomplished during the summer or during the course of a regular semester.

The sabbatical applicant should solicit supportive correspondence from outside the campus community. For example, a letter would be expected from any person named in the proposal as a collaborator, as would a letter from an official at any proposed host institution. If the intent of the sabbatical applicant is to produce a textbook, a letter from a publisher who expresses interest or from a colleague attesting to the need for such a book might be helpful. Some applicants have used surveys to provide similar evidence.

All applicants should work closely with their Division Chairs and provide them with adequate notice of their intentions well before the September 30 deadline. Among other things, the Division Chair is expected to provide an analysis of the impact of a sabbatical on the applicant's discipline. With additional time for consideration, the Division Chair may be able to produce a more effective argument on the applicant's behalf.

Finally, the Committee expects to see a complete proposal, as described in the *Faculty Handbook*. We feel compelled to point this out only because we have received proposals missing such requirements as a *curriculum vitae* and budget.

THE BUDGET

There are few hard and fast rules or traditions in this area. The *Faculty Handbook* indicates that the faculty member is expected to contribute and that any outside salary must be reported. The Committee has not approved funding in excess of roughly $2,500. It does not usually pay for food or for more than one round trip to the city of the host institution. Automobile mileage is reimbursed at the College rate (currently 24¢/mile).

The Committee may impose on a particular budget category an upper limit beyond which expenses will not be reimbursed. However, it has also on occasion recommended that a particular budget line item be increased. The Committee expects the sabbatical applicant to economize when possible and has sometimes questioned hotel rates or other figures. It is sometimes worthwhile, however, to spend money in the name of efficiency. Flying between two sites, for example, may save valuable research time. As in other parts of the sabbatical proposal, it is up to the applicant to justify unique needs, and it is worthwhile for the applicant to demonstrate "having done some homework."

The Faculty Personnel committee
February 8, 1990

(From Kenneth J. Zahorski, *The St. Norbert College Sabbatical Handbook*. DePere, WI: St. Norbert College Press, 1990.)

APPENDIX C

Time Management Resources

Collins, C. (1987). *Time management for teachers: Practical techniques and skills that give you more to teach.* West Nyack, NY: Parker Publishing.

Culp, S. (1991). *Streamlining your life.* Cincinnati, OH: Writer's Digest Books.

Davidson, J. (1991). *Breathing space: Living and working at a comfortable pace in a sped-up society.* New York, NY: Master Media.

Fanning, T., & Fanning, R. (1990). *Get it all done and still be human: A personal time management workshop.* Menlo Park, CA: Kali House, Open Chain Publishing.

Hobbs, C. (1988). *Time power: The revolutionary time management system that can change your professional & personal life.* New York, NY: HarperCollins.

Hochheiser, R. (1992). *Time management.* Hauppauge, NY: Barron Publishing.

Kozoll, C. (1982). *Time management for educators.* Kappa Publishing.

Lakein, A. (1973). *How to get control of your time and your life.* New York, NY: Peter Wyden, Inc.

Mayer, J. (1990). *If you haven't got the time to do it right, when will you find the time to do it over?* New York, NY: Simon and Schuster.

Moskowitz, R. (1983). *Total time management.* Second Edition. U.S.: American Management Association (Cassette).

Rutherford, R. (1978). *Administrative time power.* Mentor, OH: Learning Concepts, Inc.

Stanton, S. (1990). *The 25-hour woman.* New York, NY: Bantam Books.

Taylor, H. (1993). *The administrator's guide to personal productivity.* Princeton Junction, NJ: Eye on Education.

Taylor, H. *Getting organized.* Eight cassettes to help you become organized.

#1 Set Goals and Priorities	#5 Don't Be a Packrat
#2 Plan and Schedule	#6 Organize Your Environment
#3 Write Things Down	#7 Work Smarter, Not Harder
#4 Don't Procrastinate	#8 Avoid Tyranny of Urgent

Taylor, H. *Making time work for you.* Willowdale, Ontario: The Time Management Consultants, Inc.(Cassette).

Taylor, H. *101 ways to save time.* Willowdale, Ontario: The Time Management Consultants, Inc. (Cassette).

Taylor, H. *The time management report.* Published monthly by Harold Taylor Time Consultants, Inc.
    2175 Sheppard Ave. East, Ste. 110
    Willowdale, Ontario M2J 1W8
    Canada

APPENDIX D

GRANT SEEKING AND GRANT WRITING RESOURCES

The following lists are not meant to be definitive. Rather they are meant to identify some of the resources helpful to the sabbatical applicant seeking grant monies. My goal is to point the way to some major sources without overwhelming the reader with too much information.

The reader should remember the following points: (1) Many directories are updated on an annual basis; the edition listed here may have been superseded by a more recent volume. (2) Some of the choices listed below may appeal only to a specialized audience. (3) Many states have a directory of foundations which lists not only the major foundations which will have made it into the national directories, but also the smaller foundations, including family foundations. These are especially good sources for projects that reach out into the community or for smaller scale projects. (4) The items in *Some Key Granting Agencies* represent only a few of the hundreds of foundations that make grants for individuals and projects in higher education. Indeed, these are just some of the stars in a constellation of philanthropies. (5) Rather than beginning your search in the myriad of subdirectories, you may wish to turn immediately to the following kinds of core directories: *The Foundation Directory, The Corporate Giving Directory, The Foundation 1000, The Foundation Reporter,* and *The Foundation Grants Index.* Three serials—*Corporate Giving Watch, Foundation Giving Watch,* and *Federal Grants and Contracts Weekly*—provide timely updates of deadlines.

SOME KEY GRANTING AGENCIES

American Council of Learned Societies
228 East 45th Street
New York, NY 10017-3398

American Institute for Foreign Study
102 College Division
Greenwich Avenue
Greenwich, CT 06830

American Philosophical Society
104 South Fifth Street
Philadelphia, PA 19106

Amoco Foundation
206 East Randolph Drive
Chicago, IL 60601

The ARCO Foundation
515 South Flower Street
Los Angeles, CA 90071

Council on International Educational Exchange
205 East 42nd Street
New York, NY 10017

Council for International Exchange of Scholars
3007 Tilden Street, NW
Suite 5M
Washington, D.C. 20008-3009

The Camille and Henry Dreyfus Foundation
Suite 1305
555 Madison Avenue
New York, NY 10022-3301

The Eppley Foundation for Research
575 Lexington Ave.
New York, NY 10022

Fulbright Scholar Program
Suite 5M
3007 Tilden Street, NW
Washington, DC 20008-3009

The Fund for the Improvement of Post-Secondary Education (FIPSE)
U.S. Department of Education
Washington, DC 20202-5175

German Academic Exchange Service
950 Third Avenue, 19th Floor
New York, NY 10022

Harry Frank Guggenheim Foundation
527 Madison Avenue
New York, NY 10022-4304

John Simon Guggenheim Memorial Foundation
90 Park Avenue
New York, NY 10016

The Humanities Institute
4701 Willard Ave, #1715
Chevy Chase, MD 20815

International Research and Exchanges Board
1616 H Street, NW
Washington, DC 20006

The Japan Foundation
New York Office, 39th Floor
152 West 57th Street
New York, NY 10019

The Henry J. Kaiser Foundation
2400 Sand Hill Rd.
Menlo Park, CA 94025

W.K. Kellogg Foundation
One Michigan Avenue, East
Battle Creek, MI 49017-4058

Life Sciences Research Foundation
C/O Lewis Thomas Laboratories
Princeton, NJ 08544

Lilly Endowment Fund
2801 N Meridian St.
PO Box 88068
Indianapolis, IN 46208

Lucille P. Markey Charitable Trust
Southeast Financial Center, Suite 4300
Miami, FL 33131-2379

The German Marshall Fund of the U.S.
11 Dupont Circle, NW
Washington, DC 20036

Andrew Mellon Postdoctoral Fellowships
University of Pittsburgh
910 Cathedral of Learning
Pittsburgh, PA 15260

National Council of Teachers of English Fellowships
1111 Kenyon Road
Urbana, IL 61801

National Endowment for the Arts
The Nancy Hanks Center
1100 Pennsylvania Ave., NW
Washington, DC 20506

National Endowment for the Humanities
1100 Pennsylvania Avenue, NW
Washington, DC 20506

National Science Foundation
The Fellowship Office
2101 Constitution Ave.
Washington, DC 20418

The Newberry Library
Committee on Awards
60 W Walton Street
Chicago, IL 60610-3380

Office of Naval Research
Arlington, VA 22217-5660

Pew Charitable Trust
One Commerce Square
2005 Market Street, Suite 1700
Philadelphia, PA 19103

Randolph Program for International Peace
U.S. Institute of Peace
1550 M Street, NW, Suite 700
Washington, DC 2005-1708

Research Corporation
6840 East Broadway Blvd.
Tucson, AZ 85710-2815

Resources for the Future
1616 P Street, NW
Washington, DC 20036

Rockefeller Foundation
1133 Avenue of the Americas
New York, NY 10036

Smithsonian Institute
Office of Fellowships and Grants
Washington, DC 20560

Social Science Research Council
605 Third Avenue
New York, NY 10158

The Spencer Foundation
900 North Michigan Avenue, Suite 2800
Chicago, IL 60611

Stanford Humanities Center
Mariposa House
Stanford University
Stanford, CA 94305-8630

U.S.A.F. Summer Faculty Research Programs
Universal Energy Systems, Inc.
SFRP/GSRP Office
4401 Dayton-Xenia Rd.
Dayton, OH 45432

U.S. Department of Defense Grants
ODDDR&E (R&TAT/RLM)
Pentagon Room 3E114
Washington, DC 20301

U.S. Department of Education
Office of Educational Research and Improvement
Washington, DC 20208-5646

U.S. Department of Health & Human Services
Agency for Health Care Policy and Research
2101 E Jefferson St., Suite 501
Rockville, MD 20852

University Exploratory Research Program
The Proctor & Gamble Company
Miami Valley Laboratories
P.O. Box 398707
Cincinnati, OH 45239-8707

Alexander von Humboldt-Stiftung
Jean-Paul-Strabe 12
D-53173 BONN
Germany

Wenner-Gren Foundation
1865 Broadway
P.O. Box 398707
New York, NY 10021

Woodrow Wilson Fellowship Foundation
Newcombe Dissertation Fellowships
CN 5281
Princeton, NJ 08542

SEEKING GRANTS AND FELLOWSHIPS:
A SELECTIVE BIBLIOGRAPHY OF SOME IMPORTANT REFERENCE WORKS

FEDERAL SOURCES

Catalogue of Federal Domestic Assistance. Can be accessed via computer on: Dialog, SPIN, FAPRS, IRIS, and SDC.

Federal Grants and Contracts Weekly: Project Opportunities in Research, Training, and Services. Alexandria, VA: Capitol Publications, Inc.

The Federal Register: What It Is, and How to Use It. Washington, DC: U.S. Government Printing Office. (periodically updated).

Guide to Federal Assistance. Rock Hill, SC: Wellborn Associates, Inc., 1992.

Guide to Federal Assistance Newsletter. Rock Hill, SC: Wellborn Associates, Inc., 1993.

FOUNDATION & CORPORATE SOURCES

Corporate Giving Directory. 14th Ed. Rockville, MD: Taft, 1993.

Corporate Giving Yellow Pages, 1992: Guide to Corporate Giving Contacts. Rockville, MD: The Taft Group, 1991.

Foundation Directory. Compiled by the Foundation Center. 14th Ed. New York, NY: Foundation Center, 1992.

Foundation Giving Watch. Detroit, MI: The Taft Group, 1993.

The Foundation 1000: In-Depth Profiles of the 1000 Largest U.S. Foundations: 1992–1993. New York, NY: The Foundation Center, 1992.

Foundations Grants Alert. Alexandria, VA: Capitol Publications, Inc., 1993.

Foundation Grants Index. Compiled by the Foundation Center. New York, NY: Foundation Center, 1993.

Foundation Grants to Individuals. New York, NY: The Foundation Center, 1984.

Foundation News. New York, NY: The Foundation Center, 1993.

Foundation Reporter. Rockville, MD: The Taft Group, 1992.

International Foundation Directory, Third Ed. Detroit, MI: Gale Research Company, 1991.

NSF Bulletin. Washington, DC: National Science Foundation, 1993.

Philanthropic Digest. Washington, DC: Brakeley, John, Price, and Jones, 1993.

Science Trends. Washington, DC: Trends Publishing Company, Inc., 1993.

GENERAL SOURCES

Annual Register of Grant Support: A Directory of Funding Resources. Wilamette, IL: National Register Publishing Co., 1992.

Blum, Laurie. *Free Money for People in the Arts.* New York, NY: Collier Books, 1991.

Cassidy, Daniel J. *The Graduate Scholarship Book: The Complete Guide to Scholarships, Fellowships, Grants, and Loans for Graduate and Professional Studies.* Englewood Cliffs, NJ: Prentice Hall, 1990.

Cassidy, Daniel J. *The International Scholarship Book: The Complete Guide to Financial Aid for Study Abroad.* Englewood Cliffs, NJ: Prentice Hall, 1990.

Chronicle Financial Aid Guide. Moravia, NY: Chronicle Guidance Publications, Inc., 1991.

Chronicle of Higher Education. Washington, DC: The Chronicle of Higher Education, Inc., 1993.

Directory of Grants in the Humanities. Phoenix, AZ: Oryx Press, 1988.

Directory of Research Grants 1993. Phoenix, AZ: The Oryx Press, 1993.

Financial Resources for International Study: A Definitive Guide to Organizations Offering Awards for Overseas Study. Princeton, NJ: Peterson's Guides, Inc., 1989.

Grants. Phoenix, AZ: The Oryx Press, 1992.

Grants and Aid to Individuals in the Arts. Fifth Ed. Washington, DC: Washington International Arts Letter, 1991.

The Grants Register 1991–1993. ed. Lisa Williams. New York, NY: St. Martins Press, 1990.

Higher Education Opportunities for Minorities and Women—Annotated Selections. 1985–86 Ed. Compiled by William C. Young. Washington, DC: U.S. Department of Education, 1986.

Humanities. Washington, DC: National Endowment for the Humanities, 1993.

International Funding Guide: Resources and Funds for International Activities at Colleges and Universities. American Association of State Colleges and Universities, 1985.

IRIS Data Base of Sponsored Opportunities. University of Illinois at Urbana-Champaign, IL: Research Services Office.

Jankowski, Katherine E., ed. *Inside Japanese Support, 1992.* Rockville, MD: Taft, 1992.

Kirby, Debra M., ed. *1992–93 Scholarships, Fellowships, and Loans: A Guide to Education-Related Financial Aid Programs for Students and Professionals.* Detroit, MI: Gale Research, Inc., 1992.

Minority Funding Report. Arlington, VA: Government Information Services, 1993.

The National Directory of Grants and Aid to Individuals in the Arts, International. Washington, DC: Washington International Arts Letter, 1987.

News, Notes and Deadlines. Washington, DC: Association for Affiliated Colleges and University Officers, 1993.

Peterson's Grants for Post-Doctoral Study. Princeton, NJ: Peterson's Guides, 1992.

Schlacter, Gail Ann. *Directory of Financial Aid for Women 1991–92.* San Carlos, CA: Reference Service Press, 1987.

Schlacter, Gail Ann. *How to Find Out About Financial Aid: A Guide to Over 700 Directories Listing Scholarships, Fellowships, Loans, Grants, Awards, Internships.* Los Angeles, CA: Reference Service Press, 1991.

Schlacter, Gail Ann and Sandra E. Goldstein. *Directory of Financial Aid for Minorities 1991–93.* San Carlos, CA: Reference Service Press, 1991.

Schlacter, Gail Ann and David R. Weber. *Financial Aid for Research, Study, Travel, and Other Activities Abroad: 1992–1994.* San Carlos, CA: Reference Service Press, 1992.

GRANT PROPOSAL WRITING: SOME KEY REFERENCES

WORKS

Bauer, David G. *The "How To" Grants Manual: Successful Grantseeking Techniques for Obtaining Public and Private Grants.* 2nd Edition. Phoenix, AZ: ACE/Oryx Press. 1988.

Belcher, Jane C. and Julia M. Jacobson. *From Idea to Funded Project: Grant Proposals that Work.* Phoenix, AZ: The Oryx Press, 1992.

Bowman, Joel P. and Bernadine P. Branchaw. *How to Write Proposals that Produce.* Phoenix, AZ: The Oryx Press, 1992.

Coleman, William, David Keller, and Arthur Pfeffer, eds. *A Casebook of Grant Proposals in the Humanities.* New York, NY: Neal-Schuman Publishers, 1982.

Ezell-Kalish, Susan, ed. *The Proposal Writer's Swipe File III: 15 Professionally Written Grant Proposals.* Washington, DC: The Taft Corporation, 1981.

Gilpatrick, Eleanor. *Grants for Nonprofit Organizations: A Guide to Funding and Grant Writing.* New York, NY: Praeger, 1989.

Hall, Mary K. *Getting Funded: A Complete Guide to Proposal Writing.* Portland, OR: Continuing Education Publications, 1988.

Lefferts, Robert. *Getting a Grant in the 1990's—How to Write Successful Grant Proposals.* NY: Prentice Hall Press, 1991.

Locke, Lawrence F., Waneen Wyrick Spirduso, and Stephen J. Silverman. *Proposals that Work: A Guide for Planning Dissertations and Grant Proposals.* 2nd Edition. Newbury Park, CA: Sage Publications, 1987.

Margolin, Judith B. *Foundation Center's User-Friendly Guide: A Grantseeker's Guide to Resources.* New York, NY: The Foundation Center, 1992.

Margolin, Judith B. *Foundation Fundamentals.* New York, NY: The Foundation Center, 1991.

VIDEOS

Winning Grants: A Systematic Approach for Higher Education. A cooperative project of ACE, David G. Bauer, and University of Nebraska Television. Consists of ten videotapes keyed to the *"How To" Grants Manual,* as well as a leader's guide.

Application Forms

UNIVERSITY OF RHODE ISLAND

REQUEST FOR LEAVE

NAME _____ RANK/TITLE _____

COLLEGE _____ DEPARTMENT _____

TYPE OF LEAVE: (Check one, please)

LWOP _____ EDUCATIONAL _____ OTHER _____ SABBATICAL_____

PERIOD OF LEAVE:

FALL_____ SPRING_____ ACADEMIC YEAR ____ OTHER _____
                                                    (Specific dates)

SABBATICAL APPLICANTS, please complete the following:

Date of initial appointment_____Rank at initial appointment _____

Effective date of tenure (must be effective prior to start of leave) _____

Types of previous leaves _____ Date_____

_____ Date_____

Number of years of *full-time service* at URI since returning from last sabbatical leave (partial years of service are not cumulative and cannot be counted)_____

ATTACH A STATEMENT WHICH INCLUDES THE FOLLOWING INFORMATION:

I. Background for sabbatical leave proposal; specific intended outcomes of leave activity (short term and long term goals);

II. A specific outline of the sabbatical leave proposal, including dates, location of study, specific arrangements for laboratory space, studio space or library facilities, and activities to be conducted;

III. Supporting materials: Letters confirming support or agreement to cooperate, an evaluation of the project, if applicable, a bibliography relevant to the activity being prepared; and

IV. An updated résumé limited to material related to the requested leave.

APPLICATIONS FOR LEAVES (<u>six</u> <u>copies</u>) SHOULD BE FORWARDED <u>TO THE</u>
<u>DEAN</u> BY <u>SEPTEMBER 15</u> OF THE ACADEMIC YEAR PRECEDING THE LEAVE.

_____   _____
APPLICANT'S SIGNATURE   DATE

The following section is to be completed by the Department Chairperson:

EVALUATION OF THE PROPOSAL (include its worth and contribution to
the department as well as the individual's professional growth)

Chairperson's Recommendation: _____

_____   _____
Chairperson's Signature   Date

Dean's Recommendation: _____

_____   _____
Dean's Signature   Date

UNIVERSITY OF SOUTH FLORIDA

APPLICATION FOR SABBATICAL LEAVE

Date_____

TO: Chair, Sabbatical Committee
ADM 226
University of South Florida
Tampa, Florida

In accordance with the purpose, eligibility, and terms of the sabbatical program as established in the BOR/UFF Agreement, I hereby apply for a sabbatical for:
(Please check)

☐ One semester at Full Pay

_____ Fall

_____ Winter

☐ Two semesters at One-Half Pay

_____ Fall and Winter

☐ Either of the Above

For Academic Year _____

NAME _____

RANK _____

DATE OF RANK _____

COLLEGE _____

DEPARTMENT _____

DATE OF INITIAL

USF EMPLOYMENT _____

Account for all absences from full-time teaching since date of initial USF employment (e.g., leave without pay, Fulbright, departmental release time, sponsored research, etc.)

DATES	PURPOSE	PAY*
_____	_____	_____
_____	_____	_____
_____	_____	_____

*Indicate "with" or "without" pay

Present below a detailed outline of your planned sabbatical program:

Enumerate benefits of your program to:

(a) YOURSELF:

(b) THE UNIVERSITY:

(c) THE PROFESSION:

Report here or by accompanying letter any additional information which you deem worthy of consideration by the selection committee:

Do you know of any other leave that would conflict with your Sabbatical Leave?

_____ yes _____ no   (if yes, please describe)

I attest that the above information is correct.

_____

Applicant's Signature

(© University of South Florida 1993. Reprinted with permission of University of South Florida.)

TEXAS A&M UNIVERSITY
APPLICATION FOR FACULTY DEVELOPMENT LEAVE

APPLICANT INFORMATION FORM

1. Name: _____

2. Academic Rank or Title: _____

3. Department: _____

4. College: _____

5. Employment in Texas A&M University System

   Number of years consecutive employment: _____

   Total number of years in System: _____

   Tenure status:_____

   Date of Tenure if applicable: _____

6. Have you previously received a Faculty Development Leave? _____

   If so, please give dates_____

7. Dates of projected leave:

   From _____,   19 _____

   To   _____,   19 _____

8. Compensation requested:

   Full Salary _____

   Half Salary _____

9. Outside funding applied for_____Yes_____No

   Source: Amount:

10. Will other funding sources be used to supplement any aspect of the requested leave?

    Yes_____   No_____

    If yes, identify source of funds and how they could be used:

    If no, do you plan to attempt to secure additional support funding? Identify the source of possible funding and how it could be used.

11. Location(s) where leave will be taken:

12. a. Describe as fully as possible (in technical terms) what you plan to do during the leave period.

    b. If the above description would be unclear to a lay person, sum-marize in one brief paragraph what you propose to do during the leave period.

13. What are your reasons for wishing to undertake the leave?

14. How do you project the purpose of the leave will benefit you profes-sionally (if not covered in question 13)?

15. How do you project the purpose of the leave will benefit your col-lege?

16. How do you project the purpose of the leave will benefit Texas A&M University?

TERMS OF LEAVE

17. The Undersigned acknowledges an understanding of the University's expectations that all recipients of an academic study leave will return to service as a member of the Texas A&M University faculty for a period of at least one year following completion of the leave. The undersigned agrees not to accept employment from any other person, corporation, or government, unless the Board of Regents finds that it is in the public interest and that it otherwise meets requirements of law. It is understood that the leave of absence for faculty development will be subject to cancellation for violation of the conditions under which the leave was granted.

_____
Signature of Applicant

Date: _____

CLARKE COLLEGE

Sabbatical Request Form

Sabbaticals at Clarke College are granted to Professors and Associate Professors who have been teaching successfully at the College for at least seven (7) years. The purpose of the sabbatical is to encourage further professional growth. It may lead to curricular change, new specialization occasioned by departmental need, publication, or artistic creations.

If you are interested in applying for a sabbatical, please fill out this form and return it to the Academic Affairs Office by October 31.

APPLICATION

Name of Applicant: _____ Date: _____

Department: _____ Office Phone:_____

Date of Last Sabbatical or Leave (Semester and Year): _____

Application Instructions: Describe your sabbatical plans by stating the items listed below.

1. Goals of the sabbatical project (state the purposes you intend to achieve).

2. Procedures (state as precisely as you can the procedures or process you will follow to achieve the goals stated above, e.g., describe the resources you will utilize, the time you will devote to each stage of your sabbatical project, etc.).

3. Describe the importance of the sabbatical project to the department, college, and/or your own professional growth.

4. Evaluation (indicate the means you will use to evaluate the accomplishment of your goals).

THE UNIVERSITY OF WISCONSIN-STEVENS POINT

PROGRAM FOR THE DEVELOPMENT OF UNIVERSITY PERSONNEL

DO NOT FILL IN
Proposal Number_____
Account Number _____

DATE OF APPLICATION   _____

TYPE OF GRANT: SABBATICAL

TITLE OF PROPOSED
PROJECT OR STUDY   _____

_____

SUBMITTED BY   _____

DEPARTMENT OR OFFICE _____

PHONE NUMBER   _____

COLLEGE, SCHOOL
OR ADMINISTRATIVE
AREA   _____

PROJECTED FUNDING DATE (check one; please explain any contingencies)

_____ Fall semester (full time)

_____ Spring semester (full time)

_____ Academic year (65% compensation)

THE APPLICANT FOR A SABBATICAL IS A (please check all those which are appropriate):

_____ Member of an Ethnic Minority

_____ Woman

SABBATICAL LEAVE FORM

Submitted by _____ Date _____

Department/Unit _____ Date _____

Leave Requested: Semester(s)_____ Year _____

Title of proposal_____

Type of Proposal

    1. primarily enhancement of teaching/curriculum development _____

    2. primarily research_____

    3. other (explain)_____

Departmental and College assurances (complete one of the following)

A. I support this application for a sabbatical leave. The Department has committed the resources to support the personnel expenses related to this sabbatical leave request.

      Signature _____
                   Unit Chair/Head/Associate Dean

      Signature _____
                   Dean of College

                   OR

B. I cannot support this application for sabbatical leave (please attach a letter of explanation).

      Signature _____
                   Unit Chair/Head/Associate Dean

      Signature _____
                   Dean of College

PROPOSAL NARRATIVE

*General
instructions:*

Please follow the format outlined below. Be specific, concise, and coherent. *Your proposal must be written so that it can be readily understood by someone outside your field.* Make certain it is clear how your objectives relate to the project you describe in your background, as well as how your activities will accomplish these objectives.

1. *Summary*

Describe your project in no more than a sentence or two. This summary will be used to report your approved sabbatical to the Board of Regents.

2. *Abstract*

Describe your project, its value, and the expected outcomes in a paragraph or two.

3. *Background*

Describe the project you propose to undertake. Show how it fits within the broader context of your discipline. Say why it seems to you to be worth doing.

4. *Objectives*

Specify what you plan to accomplish on your sabbatical.

5. *Activities*

List the activities you will be engaged in to accomplish your objectives, making certain to show how these activities are related to your objectives. Indicate the approximate amount of time to be spent on each.

6. *Results*

Identify those who are likely to benefit from the results of your project. Explain what the benefits are likely to be. *Note*: Recipients of sabbaticals are subject to the UW System Policy on Copyright of Instructional Materials (see University Handbook, pp. IV 7–11). Submission of a sabbatical application will be understood to imply that you have read and agree to this policy.

7. *Evaluation*

Describe how the product(s) of your sabbatical might be evaluated. Some examples:
- Original research or a book manuscript will probably be sent to reviewers prior to being published.
- A laboratory manual might be sent to instructors of similar courses at other institutions for evaluation (and possible adoption).
- A colleague might be requested to attend (and evaluate) lectures or performances derived from sabbatical activities.

VITA SUMMARY

NAME: _____

DEPARTMENT:_____

RANK OR TITLE: _____ DATE HIRED: _____

HIGHEST ACADEMIC DEGREE AND DATE AWARDED: _____

1. Provide a brief résumé of professional experience which will give evidence to the reader of your ability to undertake the intended project.

2. List previously awarded grants of any type in the past five years.

3. List related publications, exhibits, performances in the past five years.

4. Likelihood of patentable or publishable results: (See pages G. 20–21 of the University Handbook for UW-System Policy on Copyright of Instructional Materials).

(Please, do not send a complete résumé.)

SABBATICAL APPLICATION CHECK-OFF SHEET

The sabbatical application should include the following sections in order. This form is provided to insure completeness of the grant application. Do not include with the application at time of submission.

_____ Sabbatical Cover Sheet completed

_____ Sabbatical Leave Form completed and signed by appropriate individuals in either "A," "B," or "C."

_____ Letter(s) of Support (strongly recommended)

_____ Proposal Narrative completed according to guidelines.

_____ Summary   _____ Activities
_____ Abstract   _____ Results
_____ Background   _____ Evaluation
_____ Objectives

_____ Vita summary completed (do not send/submit a complete vita/résumé).

_____ Sabbatical Proposal Critique form with top three lines completed.

(Sabbatical form courtesy of the University Personnel Development Committee, University of Wisconsin—Stevens Point.)

SACRED HEART UNIVERSITY

SABBATICAL APPLICATION

NAME:_____DATE: _____

Faculty Area: _____

Sabbatical Leave Requested: (Please check appropriate box)

_____ Full year at half pay (1992-1993 academic year)

_____ Half year at full pay

_____ Fall 1992 Semester

_____ Spring 1993 Semester

GUIDELINES

Please include the following information with your application:

1. Goals and objectives of sabbatical leave

2. How will the sabbatical leave enhance your effectiveness as a faculty member at the university?

3. How will the university benefit from your sabbatical leave?

4. What do you hope to contribute to your faculty area after having been on sabbatical leave?

5. Obtain a recommendation from your faculty chair. He/she must indicate the impact leave could have in your area.

Completed Applications

THE UNIVERSITY OF RHODE ISLAND

REQUEST FOR LEAVE

NAME _Robert Rohm_____ RANK/TITLE _Professor_____

COLLEGE _Arts and Sciences_____ DEPARTMENT _Art_____

LWOP _____ Educational _____ Sabbatical _XXX__

Full Year _____ Fall Semester _____ Spring Semester _XXX__

Other _____

Date of Initial Appointment _July 1, 1965_____

Rank at Initial Appointment _Assistant Professor___

Effective Date of Tenure _____July 1, 1969_____
(Tenure must be effective prior to the start of the leave.)

Dates and Types of Previous Leaves: _9/71-8/72 — Sabbatical Leave_____

_Spring 1974 — LWOP (Educational)___

_Spring 1980 — Sabbatical Leave____

Number of Years of Full Time Service at URI Since Returning from Last Sabbatical Leave: (partial years of service are not cumulative and cannot be counted) _6__

ATTACH A STATEMENT WHICH INCLUDES THE FOLLOWING INFORMATION:

I. Background for sabbatical leave proposal; specific intended outcomes of leave activity (short term and long term goals);

II. A specific outline of the sabbatical leave proposal, including dates; location of study, specific arrangements for laboratory space, studio space or library facilities; and activities to be conducted;

III. Supporting materials: Letters confirming support or agreement to cooperate; an evaluation of the project, if applicable; a bibliography relevant to the activity being prepared; and

IV. An updated résumé limited to material related to the requested leave.

APPLICANT'S SIGNATURE _(Signature)_____

DATE _September 10, 1985_

APPLICATIONS FOR LEAVES (six copies) SHOULD BE FORWARDED TO THE DEAN BY SEPTEMBER 15 OF THE ACADEMIC YEAR PRECEDING THE LEAVE.

The following section is to be completed by the Department Chairperson:

EVALUATION OF THE PROPOSAL (Include its worth and contribution to the department as well as the individual's professional growth.)

This is a very worthwhile proposal. In his past work Robert Rohm has taken his observations of everyday objects and re-interpreted them into intellectually provocative and finely crafted sculptures which have received the highest critical acclaim. Observing and recording such objects and architectural forms in foreign cultures will expand the variety of sources on which he can draw. An extended period of travel is essential for the project which can furnish the kind of material necessary for his professional, creative development. The consistently high quality of his work, national recognition and strong exhibition record demonstrate the likelihood of future exhibitions and creative activities.

WILL A REPLACEMENT BE NECESSARY? YES__XX__NO_____

HOW WILL THE PROFESSIONAL ASSIGNMENT OF THE APPLICANT BE CARRIED OUT DURING THE PERIOD OF LEAVE?

A replacement will be necessary to teach the following courses during spring semester, 1987:

> Art 207 Drawing (1 section)
> Art 103 Three-Dimensional Studio I (1 section)
> Art 243/344 Three-Dimensional Studios II and III
>   (1 section taught simultaneously)

CHAIRPERSON'S RECOMMENDATION I strongly recommend this proposal.

CHAIRPERSON'S SIGNATURE _____(Signature)_____

DATE _September 5, 1985__

DEAN/DIRECTOR'S RECOMMENDATION _____

DEAN/DIRECTOR'S SIGNATURE _____

DATE _____

SABBATICAL PROPOSAL

September 1984

PROFESSOR ROBERT ROHM, DEPARTMENT OF ART

SABBATICAL PROPOSAL: *SPRING SEMESTER, 1987*

Introduction

I plan to spend seven months (Spring Semester, 1987: January through July) traveling primarily in the Far East and Italy with particular interest focused in viewing vernacular architecture, common street constructions, and cultural/religious sites. I will record these interests with extensive journal notebooks, drawings, and 35mm color slides, returning with a greatly enhanced visual vocabulary to fuel the making of my sculpture.

I. *Background for the Proposal*

Travel in the United States and other countries has provided a major source of inspiration for my sculpture throughout my career. The importance of this activity has increased over the last several years as my sculpture has focused more on common objects such as furniture, tools, carts, etc., for its basis. The immersion in foreign cultures provides a rich visual source for new, and/or unique combinations of three dimensional forms, enhancing my visual vocabulary. While my sculpture does not attempt to literally imitate the forms of other cultures, the visual vocabulary I gather from these travel experiences gets synthesized through my personal aesthetic, culminating in new, individual, and unique sculptural expressions.

During my sabbatical in the spring term of 1980, I took a ten week trip visiting Japan, Hong Kong, Thailand, India, Greece, Italy, and England. I made numerous notes and drawings of architectural details, objects, and peculiar juxtapositions of three dimensional forms. That experience also provided insights as to where I would want to spend more time if given the opportunity. In the fall term of 1980, following that sabbatical, I exhibited nine new sculptures in a solo exhibition on campus in the Main Gallery of the Fine Arts Center. These sculptures, which were directly inspired by my sabbatical travel experiences, were subsequently exhibited in galleries in New York and Boston.

A. *Short Term Goals*

To view and record with drawings, notebooks, and 35mm color slides the sites proposed under II. C., locations.

B. *Long Term Goals*

To return to the University of Rhode Island and my studio to digest the visual information gathered during the proposed travels, and to make sculptures based on these experiences. I will mount a solo exhibition of new sculpture in the Main Gallery of the Fine Arts Center within the year following the sabbatical. I would expect that this new work will then be shown at the galleries in New York (O.K. Harris) and Boston (Nielsen) which represent my work.

II. *Proposed Sabbatical Leave Activity*

A. *Description of the Project*

I propose to travel primarily in the Far East and Italy for seven months during the spring semester of 1987, January through July. While the itinerary is primarily selected for major cultural/religious sites, I am equally interested and inspired by viewing the vernacular architecture and common street objects and constructions one finds while walking the streets and market places of exotic foreign lands. My recorded observations of three dimensional forms combined or used in ways new to me form the basis for an enhanced visual vocabulary which will serve the making of my sculpture in the years ahead.

B. *Schedule of the Project*

I plan to travel extensively for the months of January, February, and March visiting India, Thailand, Burma, and Indonesia. I will then live in Japan for approximately two months, April and May, before returning west to Italy for the months of June and July. These two extended stays will provide the opportunity to live in another country where one can experience the subtle nuances often missed during continuous travel. Establishing a temporary home base will also provide time to digest and further develop drawings and notes accumulated during other portions of the trip. Upon returning home, I will begin making new sculptures based on my travel experiences.

C. *Locations*

Some of the major locations that I intend to visit are: Southern India, Bombay, Aurangabad and the Ellora and Ajanta cave temples carved from solid rock from the top down, Varanasi, the capital of the Hindu faith, and numerous temples and shrines. Madras and Kumbakonam with many temples and 10th Century frescos, Majurai and the Meenakshi temple with its hall of a thousand columns. Thailand: a revisit of Bangkok with its impressive wats and the Royal Palace complex, much of which was closed for restoration during my 1980 trip. Chiang Mai in northern Thailand as the departure point for the hill tribe villages of Meo, Yao, and Ekaw. Bangkok is also the most accessible departure point for entry to Burma. Burma: Rangoon, the capital. Mandalay, seat of

Burmese arts, Buddhism, and the Shive Nadaw monastery with elaborate wood carvings.

My projected two month stay in Japan will be centered in Kyoto to have adequate time to view in depth the many temples and gardens with their supremely refined sense of design. A one-week visit to Japan during my trip in 1980 made it a "must" place to view in depth.

In Italy, I am specifically interested in seeing the stone villages of Alberobello, Trani, Bisceglia and Molfetta on the Apulian coast (the heel of Italy). These villages contain outstanding examples of trulli buildings. The trulli are circular stone buildings constructed without mortar or squaring off of the stones. Many have conical roofs while others have an outside stone staircase leading to flat roofs.

It is important to note that weather conditions in Southern India and Southeast Asia make our winter months of January, February, and March the ideal time to travel to these locales, avoiding intolerable heat and monsoons. Therefore, a trip to this part of the world would not be advisable during University summer vacations.

All of the places I propose to visit are open to the public, eliminating the need for special arrangements which would have curtailed the spontaneity I plan to achieve. Further, the visual recording process I propose while traveling can be accomplished without a studio, leaving me considerable flexibility in selecting accommodations.

I am confident that this proposed sabbatical leave will be as potent a force as the last one was in terms of propelling my growth as an artist. The book, *Robert Rohm, Selected Work 1975–1985*, which is included in this presentation shows some samples of sculptures made following my last sabbatical in 1980. The travel notebooks I keep are discussed in the enclosed article titled, "A Dictionary of Assumptions: Drawings by Contemporary Sculptors," by Ronald J. Onorato.

In addition to growth as an artist, I believe my extensive travels have also helped me to grow in personal ways and I'm a better teacher for having had these experiences.

III. *Supporting Materials*
(Attached)

IV. *Updated Résumé*
(Attached)

III. *Bibliography:*

New York Times, "Art People," (photograph), Vivien Raynor, August 1, 1980.

Providence Journal, "Art Review: Sculpture by Robert Rohm," (photograph), Edward J. Sozanski, February 16, 1981.

Art Express, "Art Review: Robert Rohm, O.K. Harris (New York)," (photograph) May/June, 1982.

Drawing, "A Dictionary of Assumptions: Drawings by Contemporary Sculptors," Ronald J. Onorato, November/December, 1983.

New York Times, "Art Review: Robert Rohm and Ted Weller," John Russell, February 24, 1984.

Art in America, "Art Review: Robert Rohm at O.K. Harris," Kenneth Baker, May, 1984.

Arts Magazine, "Robert Rohm," (photograph), Ronald J. Onorato, January, 1985.

The Boston Globe, "Perspectives: Rohm's Sculptures a Show to Savor," (photograph), Christine Temin, January 31, 1985.

"Robert Rohm: Selected Works 1975-1985," (catalogue), Nielsen Gallery, Boston, Massachusetts, Text: Kenneth Baker, 1985.

The Narragansett Times, "Feature: Sculptures Both in and Out of Our Everyday World," (photographs), Bill Rodriguez, April 4, 1985.

Providence Journal, "Art Review: At U.R.I., a Potpourri," (photograph), Bill Van Siclen, June 21, 1985.

IV. *Résumé:*

Robert Rohm
Professor of Art
Department of Art, Fine Arts Center, URI

PROFESSIONAL HISTORY

1956–1959	Instructor, Columbus College of Art and Design, Columbus, Ohio.
1960–1965	Instructor, Pratt Institute, Brooklyn, New York.
1965–1970	Assistant Professor, University of Rhode Island, Kingston, Rhode Island.
1970–1974	Associate Professor, University of Rhode Island, Kingston, Rhode Island.
1974–present	Professor, University of Rhode Island, Kingston, Rhode Island.

RÉSUMÉ: Since Sabbatical Leave in 1980 (Note: A complete résumé is included in the back of my *Selected Works: 1975–1985* book which is included in the material being represented).

SOLO EXHIBITIONS

1980	O.K. Harris, Works of Art, New York, NY.
1981	Main Gallery, Fine Arts Center, University of Rhode Island, Kingston, RI.
1982	O.K. Harris, Works of Art, New York, NY.
1984	O.K. Harris, Works of Art, New York, NY.
1985	Nielsen Gallery, Boston, MA.
1985	La Jolla Museum of Contemporary Art, La Jolla, CA.

GROUP EXHIBITIONS

1980	*Other Media*, Florida International University, Miami, FL.
1980	*Perceiving Modern Sculpture: Selections for the Sighted and Non Sighted*, Grey Art Gallery, New York University, New York, NY.
1981	*New Dimensions in Drawing: 1950–1980*, Aldrich Museum of Contemporary Art, Ridgefield, CT.
1982	*New York/ New York*, Myers Fine Arts Gallery, State University College, Plattsburgh, NY.
1983	*O.K. at Zone*, Zone Gallery, Springfield, MA.
1983–84	*The Sculpture as Draftsman: Selections from the Permanent Collection*, Whitney Museum of American Art, New York, NY; Visual Arts Gallery, Florida International University, Miami, FL.
1985	*Gallery Artists*, Nielsen Gallery, Boston, MA
1985	*Faculty Exhibition*, Main Gallery, Fine Arts Center, University of Rhode Island, Kingston, RI.

COLLABORATIVE PERFORMANCE PIECES

1985	*Untitled 1985 (if you don't now, you'll never)*. Alice Kaltman, Choreographer; Robert Rohm, Sculptor. Performed by Alice Kaltman, Lissy Trachtenberg, and Douglass Dunn:
	University of Rhode Island, Kingston, RI, April 11 and 12, 1985.
	540 Broadway, New York, NY April 21, 1985.
	La Jolla Museum of Contemporary Art, La Jolla, CA, (November 15, 1985).

GRANTS

1982	Rhode Island State Council on the Arts, Individual Artist Grant, Sculpture.

THE UNIVERSITY OF WISCONSIN-STEVENS POINT

PROGRAM FOR THE DEVELOPMENT OF UNIVERSITY PERSONNEL

DO NOT FILL IN
Proposal Number _____
Account Number _____

DATE OF APPLICATION   September 25, 1991 _____

TYPE OF GRANT: SABBATICAL

TITLE OF PROPOSED
PROJECT OR STUDY   Arnold Gesell: The Man Behind the Norms _____

_____

SUBMITTED BY   Janet L. Malone _____

DEPARTMENT OR OFFICE Human Development and Nutritional Sciences ___

PHONE NUMBER   346-2108 _____

COLLEGE, SCHOOL
OR ADMINISTRATIVE
AREA   College of Professional Studies _____

PROJECTED FUNDING DATE (check one; please explain any contingencies)

_____ Fall semester (full time)

_____ Spring semester (full time)

__X___ Academic year (65% compensation)

THE APPLICANT FOR A SABBATICAL IS A (please check all those which are appropriate):

_____ Member of an Ethnic Minority

__X___ Woman

SABBATICAL LEAVE FORM

Submitted by <u>Janet L. Malone</u>   Date <u>September 25, 1991</u>

Department/Unit <u>Human Development and Nutritional Sciences</u>

Leave Requested: Semester(s) _____ Year <u>1992–93</u>

Title of proposal <u>Arnold Gesell: The Man Behind the Norms</u>

Type of Proposal

     1. primarily enhancement of teaching/curriculum development _____

     2. primarily research <u> X </u>

     3. other (explain) _____

Departmental and College assurances (complete one of the following)

A.   I support this application for a sabbatical leave. No replacement money will be requested from the Sabbatical Support Fund.

           Signature <u>(signature)</u>_____
                              Unit Chair/Head/Associate Dean

           Signature <u>(signature)</u>_____
                              Dean of College

OR

B.   I support this application only if support for replacement salaries is available. An application for such support will be made to the Sabbatical Support Fund in the amount of $_____.

           Signature _____
                              Unit Chair/Head/Associate Dean

           Signature _____
                              Dean of College

OR

C.   I cannot support this application for sabbatical leave (please attach a letter of explanation).

           Signature _____
                              Unit Chair/Head/Associate Dean

           Signature _____
                              Dean of College

ARNOLD GESELL: THE MAN BEHIND THE NORMS

Summary

The goal of this project is the preparation of a manuscript detailing the life of Arnold Gesell which will document the events in his life which led to his distinguished contributions to the study of human development.

Abstract

Gesell and his colleagues have authored over 30 books which describe and document his significant contributions to the study of child development. There is, however, virtually no published information which allows students and professionals to study Gesell's work within the historical perspective of his life. The goals of this project are: (1) To prepare a manuscript detailing the life of Arnold Gesell which will document the events which led to his distinguished contributions to the study of human development, and (2) To disseminate this information in a form which may be used by students and professionals. Three sources of data will be collected for the project. Data sources include: a comprehensive review of professional literature, a series of oral interviews with individuals familiar with Gesell, and investigations into previously unpublished materials. Data collected will be analyzed and categorized into a framework established by the proposer. Formative evaluation will be provided by external reviewers with expertise in the area of child development/early childhood education. Summative evaluation will come as the final product is accepted (or not accepted) by publishers and from reactions by professionals who use the materials in teaching or in further research.

TABLE OF CONTENTS

ARNOLD GESELL: THE MAN BEHIND THE NORMS

Background

Few individuals have made more significant contributions to the study of child growth and development than has Arnold Gesell. Of particular importance to professionals in this field of study is Gesell's position that development is the result of a child's genetic inheritance which is governed by a set of fundamental patterns common to all members of the species. This belief led Gesell and his colleagues to establish sets of developmental norms which have been used for some 60 years to measure the normalcy with which a child is developing (Berger, 1991; Berk, 1991; Salkind, 1990).

The work done by Arnold Gesell is well described and documented in the 30 or more books which were authored by him and his colleagues. Consequently, there is little need for further investigation of his work. Missing from the literature, however, is any substantial documentation of the events in his life which led him to achieve what he did. In fact, research for the brief introduction which follows was gleaned from newspaper articles and various unpublished papers—materials which are not accessible to the student of child development outside of this geographic area. There is virtually nothing available in the professional literature which would allow the study of Arnold Gesell, the man, from a historical perspective.

That someone with ties to Wisconsin and to the University of Wisconsin/ Stevens Point should write the story of Gesell's life seems fitting. This is where he spent his time during the period of life that he, himself, would say was most critical in determining what he would become. He was born and spent his boyhood days in the small Mississippi River town of Alma, Wisconsin. His college education began in what was then known as the Stevens Point Normal School. While enrolled at Stevens Point, he distinguished himself as a scholar; as editor of the newly established school newspaper, The Normal Pointer; and as the winner of an inter-state oratorical contest.

Upon graduation from the Stevens Point Normal School in 1899, Gesell was appointed to teach German and history in the Stevens Point High School. He then enrolled at the University of Wisconsin/Madison where he graduated with the class of 1903. After graduation from Madison, he became principal of the Chippewa Falls High School. In 1906, he received a Ph.D. in psychology from Clark University and in 1915 a Doctor of Medicine Degree form Yale. After receiving the M.D., Gesell remained at Yale where he founded the Clinic of Child Development and served as its head until his retirement in 1948. Two years later, he founded the Gesell Institute of Child Development in New Haven, Connecticut. Until his death in 1961, Gesell remained with the Gesell Institute where he devoted his time to the study of children and to the writing of a daily newspaper column on topics related to child rearing (Buehler, 1961; Gesell, 1986; Gesell, 1991).

In 1971, the Gesell family accorded to the University of Wisconsin/ Stevens Point the privilege of using the Gesell name in renaming the Campus Laboratory School. Members of the family and close friends were on campus as the school was rededicated with a new name and a new mission. The school became known as the Gesell Institute for the Study of Early Childhood. The new mission focused on early childhood education and learning disabilities—those areas which Dr. Gesell and his colleagues emphasized in their work (*Stevens Point Journal*, 1971 and 1971a).

I am interested in this project for two reasons. I served as Director of the Gesell Institute on this campus for eight years and have taught courses in Child Growth and Development and Theories of Development for ten years. During this time, I have been surprised by the meager amount of information available to pass on to students about the man whose portrait hangs on the wall of the laboratory. I think that Arnold Gesell is a part of our students' academic heritage about which they should feel great pride. The material should not, however, be limited to students on this campus, but should be made available to all students of human growth and development who wish to study the roots of their discipline.

I have always had an interest and a fondness for anything historical. I enjoy collecting data via archival investigations, reviews of old textbooks and journals, and oral interviews and in searching for connections between past, present, and future events. In recent years, I have found that the excitement I feel when such connections are uncovered may be passed on to the students so that they, too, feel this sense of excitement. Participation in this study will provide me with valuable experience which will increase my skills as a historical researcher in addition to providing me with new insights which can be passed on to students and other professionals.

Objectives

The overall goals for this project are: (1) To prepare a manuscript detailing the life of Arnold Gesell which will document the events which led to his distinguished contributions to the study of human development and (2) To disseminate this information to students and professionals. Specific objectives for the project include:

I. Data Collection

   1) To review available biographical and autobiographical information included in textbooks and professional journals published during the years when Gesell was doing his work.

   2) To conduct a series of oral interviews with individuals acquainted with Arnold Gesell.

   3) To review previously unpublished materials (letters, photographs, school records, etc.) and newspaper articles which document important events in Gesell's life.

II. Manuscript Preparation

1) To identify a framework within which the data collected may be organized and analyzed.

2) To categorize data according to the identified framework.

3) To prepare a manuscript titled "Arnold Gesell: The Man Behind the Norms." (At this point, I am not certain whether the manuscript would be for a monograph, a chapter in a book, or a book.)

III. Dissemination

1) To submit the completed manuscript to the Publications Department of either the Society for Research in Child Development, the National Association for the Education of Young Children, or the Association for Childhood Education International.

2) To submit proposals for oral presentations to a minimum of two of the professional organizations listed above. (All of these organizations have history sections and accept proposals for reporting historical research.)

3) To incorporate appropriate aspects of the study into the classes which I teach.

Activities

In order to meet the objectives of this project, the following activities will be completed: (Numbers preceding each activity refer to the above listed objectives. Predicted timelines follow each activity.)

Activity

I.1   Conduct a complete library search for materials which include references to the life of Arnold Gesell. Of particular interest will be the journals of the Society for Research in Child Development and the American Home Economics Association. (Academic year preceding sabbatical leave: 1991–92)

I.2   Contact the following individuals to request oral interviews:

Blanche Schnieder (early acquaintance of Gesell)	Alma, Wisconsin
Katherine Gesell Walden (daughter)	Larchmont, New York
Anne Walden Weiss (granddaughter)	Waukesha, Wisconsin
Judge Gerhard Gesell (son)	Washington, DC

Carry out as many interviews as possible (Summer, 1991 and Summer, 1992. Initial interview with Judge Gesell has been completed. Additional interviews with him may follow.)

I.3   Review the following unpublished materials and newspaper accounts:

Materials available in the archives at UW-SP and UW-Madison (Summer, 1991).

Original Gesell papers in the Library of Congress (See summary of interview with Judge Gerhard Gesell for description of materials available: Appendix B) (September and October, 1992).

Photographs taken by Gesell's father (Collection housed in Madison) (Summer, 1992).

Early editions of the Alma newspaper, The Buffalo County Journal (Summer, 1992).

II.1–3 Review the materials collected and identify common themes which will serve as a framework for organizing the materials (November and December, 1992). Organize materials according to themes (January and February, 1993). Write manuscript (March through August, 1993).

III.1   Contact the Publications Department of the professional organizations to determine their respective interests in the manuscript. If none indicates an interest, contact the commercial publishing companies (Summer, 1991). Submit manuscript (September, 1993).

III.2   Prepare proposals for conference presentations according to guidelines of the organization. If accepted, present appropriate materials at national meetings. Solicit feedback from conference participants (According to deadlines established by organizations).

III.3   Incorporate appropriate materials about the life of Arnold Gesell into two of my classes: Child Growth and Development and Theory to Practice in Human Development. Respond to requests from other Human Development professors to provide guest presentations in their classes (Research Methods and Recent Advances in Child Development) (Fall semester, 1993).

Results

The results of this project will be a completed manuscript which will be available to both students and professionals in the field of human growth and development. The exact form that the manuscript will take is unknown at this point as I do not know for sure how much material will be available to me. However, I feel relatively confident that the project will be publishable. The project will result in the following benefits:

To students of child growth and development: I firmly believe that one cannot understand and appreciate the present if one does not understand and appreciate the past. The contributions to the study of human growth and development made by Arnold Gesell have been highly significant. Current students do not have access to materials which will help them place the life of Gesell into a historical perspective. This project will give students access to important materials.

To professionals in the field of Child Development/Early Childhood Education: As stated in the letters of D. Hewes and M. Lane (Appendix A), professionals feel that a gap exists in the literature relative to the life of Gesell. This manuscript would help to fill that gap.

To the University of Wisconsin/Stevens Point: Arnold Gesell is listed among the most distinguished alumni of this institution. It, therefore, seems appropriate and timely that this project should be completed at the time when UW-SP is celebrating its centennial.

To the proposer: Perhaps the person who will benefit most from this project will be me. The opportunity to hone my skills as a historical researcher will be one benefit that I will gain. Both the process and the product of this project will help me to become a more effective teacher. I am certain that this project will be both challenging and rejuvenating.

Evaluation

The evaluation plan for this project includes both formative and summative components. Two professionals in the field of Child Development/Early Childhood Education have agreed to serve as evaluators and to provide formative evaluation (See letters from Janet Sawyers and Mona Lane in Appendix A). They have agreed to the following tasks:

Review the proposal between the pre-proposal and the final draft to search for any inconsistencies or gaps which they feel should be filled.

Review the framework which will be the basis for the analysis and organization of the data and submit evaluative comments.

Review and provide evaluative comments on drafts of the manuscript as they are completed.

Review the final draft and provide evaluative comments prior to submitting for publication.

Additional formative evaluation will come as proposals for national presentations are accepted (or rejected). Feedback in the form of evaluative comments will be requested from peers in attendance at the presentations.

Summative evaluation will primarily be based upon the response of publishers to the materials. In addition, evaluation materials will be collected from students as the materials are used in classes and from professionals who incorporate the materials in their classes and other professional work.

References Cited

Published materials

Berger, K.S. *The Developing Person Through Childhood and Adolescence.* New York, NY: Worth Publishers, 1991.

Berk, L.E. *Child Development.* Boston, MA: Allyn and Bacon, 1991.

Buehler, T. A tribute to the memory of Dr. Arnold L. Gesell. *Buffalo County Journal:* Alma, WI, June 15, 1961.

Salkind, N. *Child Development.* Fort Worth, TX: Holt, Rinehart, and Winston, 1990.

_____. Educator to Speak at Re-dedication. *Stevens Point Journal,* November 23, 1971.

_____. Will Name Lab School for Arnold Gesell. *Stevens Point Journal,* November 6, 1971a.

Unpublished Materials

Gesell, G.A. Arnold L. Gesell: 1880-1961. Paper presented upon the occasion of the dedication of the portrait of Arnold Gesell, Yale University, November 13, 1986.

Personal Interview

Gesell, G.A. U.S. Court House, Washington, DC, March 27, 1991.

(Author's Note: *Appendices, Vita Summary,* and *Grant Proposal Critique* not included.)

MARQUETTE UNIVERSITY

SABBATICAL PLAN FOR 1990–1991
RICHARD A. ABRAMS

1. Dr. Richard A. Abrams

2. Associate Professor

3. Community Health; School of Dentistry

4. 1977

5. 2620 W. Custer Ave., Apt. 6 Glendale, WI 53209

6. Home: 527-1333 Office: 224-7656

7. One academic year, 1990–1991

8. During the period of my proposed sabbatical, I plan to continue and to expand my work with dental projects relating to salivary diagnostic testing. Most of my activity will be in Scandinavia, primarily Sweden.

   For the past five years, I have been carrying out research with salivary diagnostic products which can be used to measure, predict, and quantify one's future risk for dental caries. (At present, most dentists are unaware that the possibility exists of being able to predict which persons will, in fact, develop dental caries. Through the use of salivary diagnostic testing procedures, it is becoming possible to determine ahead of time who will develop dental caries. This information makes it possible for the dentist to focus his attention on the high risk patient, and make certain that extra preventive efforts are directed at the high risk patient.) The salivary diagnostic research originated in Scandinavia, and much research has been performed since the late 1970s, both in Finland and Sweden.

   In the 1986–87 year, I was the principal investigator on a $42,000 grant from the Swedish Corporation, Orion Diagnostica, AB (located in Trosa, Sweden) to perform a salivary diagnostic project in the Milwaukee area. The project focused on testing children's caries susceptibility in three schools in the Milwaukee area. The overall goal was to see if it would be possible to lower children's dental caries risk, and we were successful in this endeavor. This project, which has culminated in several publications and presentations at scientific meetings, has laid the groundwork for future research in this new and developing field. The research project which we performed at Marquette University was the first of its type in the United States.

   While in Scandinavia, I will be working with Dr. Sune Wikner, who is one of the pioneer researchers working in the salivary diagnostic field. Dr.

Wikner has a joint appointment: he is employed by the Public Health Dentistry Division of the Stockholm County Council, and also is a professor at the Royal Karolinska Institute, in Stockholm. I know Dr. Wikner well, and am confident that we can work together while I am in Sweden. He and I will be carrying out epidemiological investigations using the salivary diagnostic products.

In addition to working on the salivary diagnostics project, I plan to do some guest lecturing in "Dental Public Health," and "Dentistry in the United States" at the Royal Karolinska Institute Dental School in Stockholm, Sweden, as well as some other institutions. During my previous sabbatical in Sweden, in 1983–1984, I was asked to present many guest lectures, and believe that probably I will again during this sabbatical. As with all teaching, when I teach, I also learn. The benefit of this teaching to myself and to Marquette University School of Dentistry is self-evident.

The benefit of salivary diagnostic collaboration with Dr. Wikner is that I will develop more expertise in this new and growing field. Salivary diagnostics have been available for patient use only in the last 5 to 10 years, and still are in the early stages of development. In the United States, it is only within the last year that salivary diagnostic tests have been used, and, today, their use is extremely limited. In the 1983–1984 academic year, I was on a sabbatical to Sweden, which resulted in the personal contacts and background for me to write the grant which was funded. I anticipate that the new knowledge and experience I gain in Scandinavia will assist me in writing new grants and publishing results of projects.

9. At present, I anticipate that the majority of the sabbatical will be in Sweden, with additional time in Finland, Denmark, and Norway. It is quite likely that there will be other countries involved in this project, as Dr. Wikner and Orion Diagnostica, AB have been performing epidemiologic investigations with salivary diagnostics throughout the world.

I am requesting a 12 month, one academic year sabbatical. However, it is entirely possible that these plans will need to be modified, and that this sabbatical could take less time. It is difficult to assess the future status of the School of Dentistry, and changes which may impact on this proposal. If any changes requiring modification of this proposal should surface, I will be in contact with the appropriate individuals at Marquette University and the School of Dentistry.

I will be seeking the financial support for this project from several sources. The National Institutes of Health has limited funds available, and I shall apply for them. The Fulbright Scholarship Program also may be a source of funding; the application and information packets for

1990–1991 are not yet available. When they arrive, I will examine them to determine if this proposal could be within their guidelines. In addition, I have been in contact with the Office of Research Support, and they will be a useful resource in locating potential sources of funding for this sabbatical.

10. Attached to this proposal, as requested, is a list of publications.

VANDERBILT UNIVERSITY

Date: October 18, 1990

To: Gary Jensen, Chair, Sociology Department

From: Dan Cornfield, Associate Professor of Sociology

Subject: Request for a leave of absence

As per your memo of October 16, 1990, I am requesting a leave of absence as described below.

WHERE: Nashville, TN

WHEN: Fall 1991 Semester

PURPOSE: The leave would facilitate the research for two projects. First, I am engaged in a large research project on the development of the legislative agenda of the U.S. labor movement. This project, which extends my earlier work (e.g., see *Becoming a Mighty Voice* and "Union Decline and the Political Demands of Organized Labor" on my cv), entails a time-series statistical analysis of all policy resolutions which were ever passed by conventions of the AFL, CIO and AFL-CIO (i.e., approximately 9,000 resolutions passed since 1881). As I have indicated in my forthcoming article on labor research for the *Annual Review of Sociology*, no such analysis has ever been undertaken. I have compiled this unique data set and will analyze the impact of changes in macroeconomic and political conditions and in the social composition of the labor movement on changes in the kinds of legislative claims organized labor has made on the state.

The second research project is a theoretical article on labor action which was solicited recently by the editors of a special issue of an annual book series. The special issue addresses the link between organizational theory and unions (see attached letters from Bacharach, Seeber and Walsh).

APPLICATIONS FOR EXTERNAL FUNDING: I will apply to the agencies listed below for funding of the first project mentioned above as soon as I have completed some preliminary statistical analyses of the data:

> National Science Foundation
> Ford Foundation
> Rockefeller Foundation
> Guggenheim Memorial Foundation
> Olin Foundation
> RGK Foundation
> Richardson Foundation

TERMS: Full pay and fringe benefits

PREVIOUS LEAVES: Fall, 1986

FINANCIAL TERMS FOR PREVIOUS LEAVE: Full pay and fringe benefits

NORTHERN ILLINOIS UNIVERSITY

REQUEST FOR LEAVE OF ABSENCE

(Submit in triplicate)

(For sabbatical leaves, see Section 1.3652, page 18, of the Constitution and Bylaws.)

Name _Edwin L. Simpson_ Soc. Sec. No _____

Department _Leadership & Educational Policy Studies_ Rank _Professor___

Leave requested: Semester(s) or Dates _Summers: May 16–August 15, 1992_
   & May 16–August 15, 1993

Kind of Leave: Sabbatical __X__   Full pay (4.5 months) _____
   Without pay*_____   Non-sabbatical_____
   Half pay (9 months)   Other*_____

Years service at NIU (include current year)_ 24 years__

Tenured: __X_ yes_____no (see Note:)

Previous leaves (dates) _Spring 1985_ With or without salary __with salary__

Type of leave __Research____(See reverse side for categories)

I.   Brief, nontechnical statement of proposed program:
   See attached

(If additional space is required, please attach sheets.)

*A leave "without pay" or "other" only (1) need be completed.

	Applicant's signature	
	Date	Priority Ranking

Approval:

**Department Chair _____   _9/25/91___   __2 of 3____
(Or Chairperson of Personnel Committee
in the case of a Chair's Application)

**Dean or Division Head _____   _10/28/91___   _____

Vice President and Provost _____   APR 3 1992_   _____

**If not approved for financial reasons, attach explanatory note and forward.

NOTE: "Time spent on a leave of absence or sabbatical leave shall not be counted toward the probationary period of service unless the University and the faculty member agree at the time the leave is granted that the purpose of the leave is such that it should count in the probationary period. Ordinarily, a leave of absence to pursue political activity will not count toward the fulfillment of the probationary period of service." (Board Regulations III.A.12.g.) The agreement as to whether the leave shall count is to be approved by the dean of the college and the faculty member concerned and a written record of the agreement filed with the dean of the college and the Provost's Office.

SABBATICAL PROPOSAL

EDWIN L. SIMPSON
Professor
Leadership & Educational Policy Studies

ABSTRACT

The proposed program is to pursue a branch of research that enhances my study of what influences faculty career renewal within higher education. Little research has been conducted on the nature of university and college faculty career development. The proposed research addresses a national concern for the changing meaning of academic work within higher education institutions and how this affects faculty who are the center of the enterprise. New areas for study, which I plan to pursue, have emerged from the analysis of descriptive data on patterns of career change among 81 professors throughout the U.S., gathered during a previous sabbatical, and subsequent investigation into some related topical areas. Gender and cultural influences related to regenerative learning among faculty, for example, are two areas I plan to study.

A third area for study is renewal among two-year community or technical college faculty. In many ways two-year higher education institutions have become the catalyst for increasing participation in higher education among a broader racial and ethnic representation of society. The move to serve this important role in society has also brought with it the need for, and understanding of, community and technical college faculty career renewal.

NATURE OF THE STUDY

Through a previous study of how faculty members in higher education address renewal in their professional careers, salient variables emerged as contributors to what faculty experience as they approach career renewal (see 1985 sabbatical report). Participants in the previous study were identified by university academic vice-presidents. No faculty were selected necessarily because of gender or ethnic background, and all were members of large four-year comprehensive research universities.

Dramatic changes in demographics during the last quarter century have brought a greater mix of faculty and students to higher education in the U.S. and the development of institutions with orientation toward adult learners (Bowen & Schuster, 1986; Carnegie Foundation for the Advancement of Teaching, February 1989; Clark, 1987). Because of these changes, variables such as gender, race or ethnic origin of faculty and institutional orientation have become significant and viable variables for investigation.

How these variables relate to regenerative learning and thus result in career renewal will be the focus of this investigation (Simpson, 1990).

Types of career expectation, nature of job satisfaction, and bases for academic career decision-making have been investigated and reported in the literature (Dixon, 1983; Shores, 1984; Williams & Johansen, 1985). These studies present questions for further examination. It seems, for example, that women are attracted to the academic profession for different reasons than men, and they expect something different in satisfaction from their academic work than do men. Likewise, it appears that women faculty approach and experience renewal differently than their male counterparts. What are these differences and what do they mean to administrators, mentors, counselors, and colleagues who wish to assist faculty traverse some of the rough roads they may travel to remain vital in their professional lives?

Cultural backgrounds of faculty also seem to play a significant role in how faculty view and progress through periods of academic career renewal. Additionally, the growth of two-year institutions of higher education in North America has brought with it a large group of faculty with different needs and expectations. Professors from four-year colleges and universities have somewhat inappropriately served as models of professional development to two-year college faculty. When one examines the patterns of renewal, it appears that community/technical college faculty develop naturally as professionals quite differently from their colleagues in most four-year institutions.

METHODOLOGY

The ultimate purpose of this research is to better interpret the phenomenon of renewal so that assistance to faculty engaged in academic self-renewal is relevant, timely, and appropriate. However, researchers first must explore the phenomenon by examining first-hand experience of faculty themselves, rather than attempting to apply a "band aid" treatment to the symptoms of disillusionment and eventual burnout that some faculty experience.

This study will be conducted using ethnographic methodology with the technique of constant comparative analysis of data gathered through in-depth interviews of participants selected for the study. To the degree possible, all three variables of gender, cultural background, and type of institution served will be used to select research participants and conduct the study.

A protocol of questions developed from previous research will serve as the means to begin gathering data. Each interview of from one to three hours will be tape recorded and transcribed for analysis. After the completion of approximately five interviews, the first transcriptions will be reviewed in the attempt to identify salient ideas that appear to represent the experiences of faculty as they have engaged in career renewal. The protocol will also be reviewed and modified, based upon the degree of success the researcher has experienced in producing pertinent and quality data at this initial point. As the interviews and analysis progress, categories that emerge will be formed from constructed categories. The actual number of interviews that are conducted will be governed by the degree to which saturation of the data is achieved as the analysis proceeds.

PARTICIPANT SELECTION

Many of the participants will be available within the U.S., but some will be selected from Canadian universities, such as the Universities of Calgary, Saskatchewan, and Montreal. In order to bring more of a cross-cultural comparison to the data analysis, the researcher intends to select some participants from higher education institutions in China, such as Shanghai Second Institute of Education, Tonggi University or East China Normal University; the University of Helsinki; and from Chulalongkorn University, Bangkok, Thailand. Access to these participants will be possible through exchange relationships NIU has with institutions in these countries.

The relevance of this line of research might be cast as an effort to conserve one of the most valuable human resources in higher education—the faculty, who are the center of the enterprise. Although faculty, historically, have been central to the function of colleges and universities, they typically have received very little attention regarding their continuing professional development. The need for being sensitive to what faculty experience in their personal and professional lives is more frequently being documented in current higher education literature. The importance of understanding how faculty remain vital in their work is growing with greater diversity among faculty and student bodies of most colleges and universities.

Between 30 and 40 experienced faculty with 10 or more years teaching in higher education will be participants in the study. The group will consist of approximately equal numbers of men and women and will equally represent two-year community colleges or technical institutes and four-year institutions. Participants will also include a significant number of faculty that are non-white and whose original language is not English.

RELATIONSHIP OF PROPOSED RESEARCH AND PROFESSIONAL WORK

The proposed program of study is pertinent to my previous line of research. Both as Professor of Adult Continuing Education with interest in adult learning and as Director of the University Faculty Development Program I have had an abiding interest in how professionals, particularly academic professionals, renew themselves and remain vital in their roles as professors. My previous sabbatical was used to study over 80 professors from throughout the U.S. who had made career changes, but remained within their universities. Two studies were reported in refereed journals or conference proceedings from that work, "Patterns of Change Among Academic Career Changes in Comprehensive U.S. Universities," *Issues in Higher Education* (1986) and "Patterns of Successful Faculty Career Change: An Investigation of the Career Transition Process," *To Improve the Academy* (1987), both with S. Supapidhayakul who studied this phenomenon in her own dissertation research. These two studies, in addition to my experience interviewing over 150 faculty members in the faculty development position at NIU, became the basis for a book completed in 1990, *Faculty Renewal in Higher Education*, Robert Krieger Publisher, in which the theory of regenerative learning is proposed. Recently, the LEPS Press published a monograph, *Learning Patterns Among Women Professionals: Theory Grounded in the Lives of Nurses* (1991), which I edited, based upon four dissertations completed under my direction. I also gave a refereed paper in April 1991 on the topic of gender differences among faculty related to what enhances and creates barriers to academic career development, which was published in the proceedings of the Adult Education Research Conference at Oklahoma University.

PERSONAL AND INSTITUTIONAL BENEFITS

As stated previously, the line of research proposed is very congruent with my work, both as a professor interested in continuing learning among professionals and as Director of Faculty Development at NIU. I view this as a continuation of studies in quest of the ultimate question: How do professional academics successfully engage in renewal? Knowledge gained from the study will add to my resources in teaching about continuing professional learning and will better inform me in my practice of helping faculty members develop their careers. A number of doctoral students I am working with whose research interests are faculty development should also benefit.

REQUIRED RESOURCES

Requirements for carrying out the proposed project include travel, audiotapes, transcription costs and expenses in arranging to meet some of the participants to be interviewed at sites away from the NIU campus. The estimated total cost is $15,000. I plan to absorb the expenses of conducting interviews conducted during the first summer, 1992. I have begun to prepare an application for a Fulbright Fellowship to cover expenses for the second summer, 1993. However, if outside funds are not forthcoming, I am prepared to satisfy the requirements of what is proposed through contacts in North America and with professionals from China, Finland, and Thailand who will be visiting lecturers in the U.S., or whom I will meet while I am in Shanghai and Bangkok in October/November 1992, while attending a conference. Transcription costs will be covered through a Graduate School research grant, or internally, through the Faculty Development Office. I am prepared to adjust my schedule and to absorb any costs necessary to complete the project proposed.

RELATIONSHIP OF STUDY TO PREVIOUS SABBATICAL

As previously outlined, the rationale for the sabbatical proposed here is an outgrowth of the sabbatical taken in 1985. What is proposed in this request emerged from questions raised as the result of the descriptive analyses of data gathered in 1984-85 and subsequent investigations of related variables by the researcher. This line of research, I feel, is critical to meet the demands of the modern college or university in providing support for their growth as professionals.

REFERENCES

Bowen, H.R., and Schuster, J.H. (1986). *American professors: A national resource imperiled.* New York, NY: Oxford University Press.

Carnegie Foundation for the Advancement of Teaching (1989, February). *Characteristics of college and university faculty members.*

Clark, B.R. (1987). *The academic life: Small worlds, different worlds.* The Carnegie Foundation for the Advancement of Teaching.

Dixon, T. (1983). *Faculty issues: Surviving the stress of the eighties.* (ERIC Document Reproduction Service No. ED 233 622).

Shores, D. (1984). A farewell to the professoriate: The story of an academic refugee. *Bulletin of the AAUP,* 70(1), pp. 33-38.

Simpson, Edwin L. (1990). *Faculty renewal in higher education.* Malabar, FL: Robert E. Krieger Publishing Company.

Williams, J.E. and Johansen, E. (1985). Career disruption in higher education. *Journal of Higher Education,* 56(2), pp. 144–160.

ST. NORBERT COLLEGE

APPLICATION FOR SABBATICAL LEAVE: FALL SEMESTER, 1984

DR. JOHN R. PHYTHYON
Assistant Professor of Biology

A. PROJECT OUTLINE

1. *General Focus* (proposed activities):

I propose to use sabbatical leave to study, and to conduct research, at the Institute of Paper Chemistry in Appleton, Wisconsin. While there, I intend to pursue three kinds of activities as follows:

a) I will audit two courses taught by the graduate faculty at the Paper Institute from among the following five:

A171 Biochemistry
A371 Plant Biochemistry
A373 Forest Genetics
A374 Principles of Forest Management
A378 Plant Tissue Culture

At the time of the submission of this proposal, the Institute had not yet declared which courses would be offered for the 1984-85 academic year during the time frame of my sabbatical. All of the above courses are taught on a quarter system and all would provide pertinent background information to the research proposal to be described below.

The course descriptions of each, taken from the 1982–83 *Academic Catalog*, are as follows:

A171 Biochemistry
The major topics of this discipline are presented in this short course which probes the molecular logic of the living state. To some extent, it is intended to help bridge the gap between the physical sciences and the biological sciences. It is particularly recommended to any student contemplating biological research. Subjects covered include biochemical structures, enzymes, metabolic pathways, the generation and utilization of energy in biological systems, and the storage and transfer of information (molecular biology). Three credits.

A371 Plant Biochemistry
This course considers the molecular functioning of living plant cells. Special consideration is given to organic constituents peculiar to

plant cells and their metabolic interrelationships. To provide the proper setting for the metabolic subjects, some time is devoted to an examination of the chemical and physical nature of complex structural and functional components of plant cells. The regulation of plant metabolism is considered. Prerequisite: A171 or equivalent.

A373 Forest Genetics
Genetic improvement of forest tree species as sources of raw materials for paper-making will be emphasized. The first part of the course reviews basic genetic principles and includes such topics as inbreeding, hybridization, heritability, and genetic gains. Also included are discussions on propagation techniques, pollination procedures, progeny testing, and a review of the procedures employed by several of the most successful U.S. forest genetics programs. Two credits.

A374 Principles of Forest Management
Included in this course will be a discussion of the forest regions of the United States, factors affecting forest growth, silvicultural systems and management of forest lands. Forest genetics, tree physiology, and forest soils are stressed in discussions of factors affecting forest growth, and serve as the scientific basis for considering silvicultural systems and proper forest management. Prerequisite: A163 or equivalent. Three credits.

A378 Plant Tissue Culture
This course is intended to cover most of the aspects of plant tissue and cell culture. Various ways of applying this technology to provide solutions to problems relative to rapid clonal propagation, genetics, and breeding of trees will be discussed. Some background in plant biology or botany will be essential.

b) I have been invited by Dr. Dean Einspahr, Director of The Forest Biology Division, to join a research team directed by Dr. Morris Johnson, Associate Professor of Biochemistry, to investigate the role of polyamines as modulators of plant development. The rationale underlying the research is as follows:

In some plants (for example, the carrot), it is possible to take individual differentiated cells from an adult plant and culture them under sterile conditions in a tissue culture medium. By manipulating the chemical composition of the medium and environmental conditions, individual cells can be induced to clone into entirely new plants. This allows for the replication of a large number of genetically identical organisms.

In most plants, however, manipulations in tissue culture techniques have not as yet succeeded in cloning due to an incomplete understanding of the controls of development. The forest trees, such as Loblolly Pine, are in this group. The ability to take individual cells from a pine tree that has shown superior genetic composition (e.g., rapid growth rate, disease resistance, etc.) and produce multiple copies of this strain would have great advantages in forest management.

The control of differentiation of cells is tied to the controls which prohibit certain genes in the mature cell from being expressed. These genes are influenced by modulating molecules. In Loblolly Pine cells being grown in tissue culture, the process of embryogenesis appears to be tied to "turning on" those genes responsible for producing the enzymatic pathway required to produce the polyamines *putrescine, spermidine*, and *spermine*.

Arthur Galston has reviewed this topic in the June 1983 issue of *Bioscience* (Vol. 33, No. 6: pp. 382–388.) The following figure, taken from that article, summarizes the enzymatic pathway: *(Figure 1 placed here in original proposal.)*

Using the 10-D cotyledonary tissue culture strain of Loblolly Pine, my specific problem will be to investigate the synthesis patterns that begin with the amino acid, methionine. Since this amino acid contains sulfur, a radioactive label (S 35) can be added and its fate determined by liquid scintillation counting techniques.

Also, since the pathway involves ATP utilization, its fate can be traced by a variety of research techniques.

c) I will have the opportunity to associate with faculty and staff, graduate students and others, in scholarly activities associated with research in a field that has held my long-term interest.

2. *Purpose of Leave*:

The overall general purpose is to develop a knowledge of plant tissue culture techniques and of the assay methods for components of the tissue culture medium. This could be used as the basis for laboratory activities at St. Norbert College for both myself and my students in advanced Biology courses. Secondarily, it will restimulate my personal research interests in Botany and provide me with the intellectual stimulation associated with dialogue between scientific colleagues. Additionally, the enrichment of exchanging views and ideas with other scientists will result in a renewed enthusiasm for teaching and in new ways of imparting material to students.

3. *Projected Outcome(s)*:

   a) Through the auditing of courses at the Institute, I will update my knowledge in the areas of Plant Biochemistry, Plant Genetics, and/or Tissue Culture techniques. The courses will also deepen my background so that my courses at St. Norbert College will benefit from the latest thinking in these fields.

   b) By being exposed to new ideas, concepts, and research methodologies, I will be able to continue the research procedures here at St. Norbert by pursuing outside funding for equipment and supplies.

   c) By associating with a research group such as the one at the Institute of Paper Chemistry, I will establish a rapport and continued association that might lead to further joint projects, the identification of qualified St. Norbert College graduates for admission to graduate studies there, and other long-range benefits both to myself and to St. Norbert College.

   d) At the conclusion of my research activities, I will be able to publish the results in appropriate professional journals.

B. RATIONALE FOR PROJECT

1. *Validity* (effectiveness of methods):

   a) The purpose of auditing courses while on sabbatical leave is to help me update my background in the areas of Plant Biochemistry, Plant Genetics, and Tissue Culture techniques. Since my last formal training in these areas was during my graduate training, this aspect of my sabbatical will familiarize me with recent developments in the fields. This will also provide a specific focus for my research activities.

   b) The proposed research activities consist of biochemical analyses by techniques with which I have had previous experience. I have had practical experience in the radioisotopic methodologies of liquid scintillation spectrometry and radioautography. I have utilized the separation methodologies of gas-liquid chromatography (GLC) and thin-layer chromatography (TLC). I will be able to adapt these methodologies, plus new applications with which I will become familiar during the course of the sabbatical, to the problem of identification of components in the tissue culture system.

   c) With respect to interaction with other scientists in the field, the value to me as a teacher-scholar will be in the opportunity to explore a new field with others and obtain the stimulation of their viewpoints.

2. *Viability* (preparation means and resources to reach objective):

   a) I am currently beginning a literature review of the field in order to be at the forefront of research in the field of polyamine biosynthesis in plant cells. In addition to having read Galston's review in *Bioscience*, I am at present reading *Methods in Enzymology*, Volume 94; *Polyamines*, edited by Herbert Tabor and Celia Tabor (Academic Press 1983). This should give me the most up-to-date information on currently accepted methodologies for analysis. I will also conduct a complete literature search between now and the beginning of my research activities in May, 1984.

   b) On October 24, 1983, I will attend a conference sponsored by the Institute of Paper Chemistry on the current status of research in the Forest Biology Section. This will provide an overview of the goals of the tissue culture research group.

   c) I have been given assurances of the willingness of the Forest Biology Section to accept me as a visiting scientist. Included in this application is a copy of a letter from Dr. Dean Einspahr, head of The Forest Biology Section, detailing their commitment.

3. *Applicability*:

   With respect to my growth as a teacher-scholar and for the betterment of the academic life of the College, the results of my sabbatical leave will be as follows:

   a) I will develop a viable research expertise which will make me capable of both engaging in scholarly discourse (published papers), and in imparting to students the current research methodologies and their scientific validity.

   b) I will be able to suggest research activities for science majors which might result in course/research work for which they could receive degree credit.

   c) I will be able to develop in the courses which I offer, an up-to-date knowledge of the status of the field of gene/cell control mechanisms.

   d) The College will benefit from my renewed vigor as a teacher and from my more current knowledge of research activities in this field.

   e) I will establish a rapport and a working relationship with members of the Paper Institute which may provide further research opportunities and/or scientific dialogue which will enhance St. Norbert College's reputation.

APPLICATION FOR FACULTY IMPROVEMENT FUND GRANT

I would like to apply for funds from the Faculty Improvement Fund to support research activities during my proposed sabbatical leave. I intend to associate with the Institute of Paper Chemistry as a visiting scientist for the time period of May, 1984 through January, 1985. I will be commuting on a daily basis.

I would like to request support for the round trip mileage to Appleton during the course of the sabbatical period. The following calendar lists the proposed travel dates and mileage. I have assumed a round trip between Appleton and St. Norbert College to be 60 miles.

One hundred and forty two days at 60 miles per day equals 8,520 total miles. At 20¢ per mile, the total support for which I am asking would be $1,704.

I have contacted Mr. Dennis Day, Director of Development, with regard to finding other sources of funding. We will be attempting to find an alternate source of support. If such support can be found, I will, of course, return the monies you have allocated.

TIMETABLE

Monday to Friday — DATES	TOTAL DAYS
May 21-25, 1984	5
May 28-June 1	4
June 4-8	5
June 11-15	5
June 18-22	5
June 25-29	5
July 2-6	4
July 9-13	6
July 16-20	5
July 23-27	5
July 30-Aug. 3	5
Aug. 6-10	Vacation Days
Aug. 13-17	Vacation Days
Aug. 27-31	5
Sept. 3-7	4
Sept. 10-14	5
Sept. 17-21	5
Sept. 24-28	5
Oct. 1-5	5
Oct. 8-12	5
Oct. 15-19	5
Oct. 22-26	5
Oct. 29-Nov. 2	5
Nov. 5-9	5
Nov. 12-16	5
Nov. 19-20	2
Nov. 26-30	5
Dec. 3-7	5
Dec. 10-14	5
Dec. 17-21	5
Jan. 2-4, 1985	3
Jan. 7-12	5
TOTAL	142 Days

Sabbatical Reports

A JOURNEY INTO RENEWAL:
FACULTY DEVELOPMENT LEAVE 1991

DANIEL W. WHEELER
University of Nebraska-Lincoln

Overall, the faculty development leave for me was what I needed at this point in my professional and personal development. It provided the opportunity to be away from my everyday situation, to have the distance to reflect, to establish new priorities, and to develop new skills and knowledge. I want to express my appreciation to have had such an experience.

In this report, I will examine my proposed leave activities and provide some measures of success, and also point out some disappointments. I should initially indicate that I had hoped to obtain a Fulbright to Australia for research and teaching, but unfortunately I was not selected. I was disappointed but decided there were sufficient activities available to further my career and bring back to IANR.

GOALS, ACTIVITIES, AND ACCOMPLISHMENTS

Beyond a desire to remove myself from the immediate situation and address some symptoms of "burnout," I wanted to engage in some serious reading and writing in faculty and administrative development.

My writing to this point has resulted in the following manuscripts:

(article) "Developmental Strategies: More Than Workshops." *Journal of Dental Education.* Vol. 55, #10, pgs. 659–661. October 1991.

(chapter) "The Department Chair as Junior Faculty Developer." in M.D. Sorcinelli and A.E. Austin (ed), "Developing New and Junior Faculty," *New Directions for Teaching and Learning,* Winter 1992.

(article) "Impact of a College Renewal Program Over Time." *Innovative Higher Education.* 16(2), Winter 1992. (with J.P. Lunde, T.E. Hartung, and B.J. Wheeler).

Presently I am working as a co-author on an additional *New Directions for Teaching and Learning* chapter on "Emerging Roles and Functions of Instructional Development and Faculty Development." I am also a member of the Creswell, Seagren and Wheeler group writing an ASHE-ERIC monograph on the research base for chairing academic departments. My assignment is two chapters—one on faculty evaluation and the other on the future of department chairing.

All of this reading and writing has provided a better knowledge base and useful information to incorporate in my work at IANR. However, I have not progressed as far on my word processing skills as I had expected, but I continue to work at it.

REFLECTIVE PRACTICE

Another goal was to understand and develop some everyday consulting ability in the use of "reflective practice." This concept suggests that practitioners can have "breakthrough learning" by reflecting upon the hard cases in their practice. I am presently, and will continue, working in this area with Dr. Ron Smith of Concordia University in Montreal. Dr. Smith has studied intensively with Drs. Argyris and Schoen, the originators of the concept. In addition to reading and conversation, Ron and I have made one presentation on "Chairs as Reflective Practitioners" at the Professional and Organizational Development Network in Higher Education conference this past fall. We have developed two cases to use in our workshops and will be offering a workshop at the Orlando Department Chairs Conference in February 1992. This work takes considerable skill and insight, but I believe I have the fundamentals to use it in my work.

CONSULTING/ADMINISTRATIVE WORKSHOPS

Another expectation for me was to continue serving as a workshop presenter in chair development. One activity was a workshop for chairs at Maricopa Community College (all eleven campuses) on "Facilitating Faculty Growth and Development." As a result of that presentation, they have invited me to do a pre-conference workshop on the same topic at the first chair conference for community colleges to be held in Phoenix, Arizona in late March of 1992. I have also been a consultant to the American Council on Education's Leadership Center. This work resulted in presentations in Colorado to the semi-annual workshop for the American Council, and an on-campus workshop at Central Arkansas University. I would like to continue to do some work with ACE since it provides a good catalyst to integrate my ideas and learn from other institutions.

One other primary activity was being a consultant to a planning group of the Agricultural Economics Chairs in developing and staging the first workshop on chairing in agricultural economics departments in Denver, Colorado during October 1991. The workshop was judged to be highly successful. Another is being planned for 1993. Highlights will be included in symposium proceedings which should be available in the near future.

FACULTY DEVELOPMENT AND THE AMERICAN PROFESSORIATE

Another important goal was to become better grounded in the literature and background of the American Professoriate. Two activities provided much of the focus.

The first was a study with Dr. Elaine El-Khawas of the American Council on Education's Policy Research Division on various aspects of "faculty shortages" and hiring. Our original intent was to survey VPAAs and deans concerning various aspects of faculty shortages and hiring. I developed an extensive interview protocol to gather information but preliminary interviews indicated that with the cutbacks in many budgets (this was mid-January 1991), we were not going to gain the level and type of planning information we had expected.

Eventually we decided to interview department chairs. Eighty chairs were interviewed through the efforts of an ACE Fellow. Some of the information has direct applicability to personnel and faculty development issues at IANR, but I was disappointed that we did not accomplish more.

The second experience was as a Visiting Scholar at the Claremont Graduate School of Education in California. I was sponsored by Dr. Jack Schuster with whom I co-authored the "Faculty Careers" book. Highlights at Claremont included: (1) giving a seminar on "Faculty Development and Faculty Diversity," (2) serving as guest lecturer in the American Professoriate course, (3) work with graduate students either working on or considering dissertations on faculty development or faculty issues, (4) reading in the area of faculty hiring and diversity, and (5) reading for the upcoming ASHE-ERIC monograph on the research base for department chairing. I particularly enjoyed the stimulation of the work with graduate students and the faculty at Claremont.

PERSONAL DEVELOPMENT

All leave experiences have elements of personal development and mine was no exception. Highlight experiences include keeping a journal during the year, a visit to Niger, Africa to be with my oldest son, daughter-in-law and only grandchild; a two week professional/personal trip to Scotland in which my wife and I traveled considerably; attendance at the Second Midwest Bird Symposium in Chicago; and a number of opportunities to spend some of the fall with my wife B.J. at her new position with the University of South Dakota.

The journaling experience has been particularly helpful to me because of the reflection and insight about new experiences during a time away from the usual rituals and routines. I would recommend this process to others and expect to build an article from my journal.

APPLICATION TO MY WORK AT IANR AND UNL

In the area of administrative development, I see the following as particularly useful to unit administrators:

- Use of "Reflective Practice" in everyday interactions, workshops, and consulting. This concept can raise practice to a higher level through analysis of hard cases.

- Some ideas and strategies about attracting and retaining minority faculty. A resource book by the University of Wisconsin system has a wealth of ideas and strategies which include a combination of organizational flexibility and commitment as well as individual unit commitment and planning.

- Research-based information on department chairing which can be shared in many situations.

- My involvement with ACE's Leadership Center and Policy Research Division has provided a better grounding in the national scene—both information and resources which can be available to unit administrators.

- I do see a number of uses of the publications available. The American Council on Education's Leadership Center is in the process of reorganizing their chair activities which may provide more fruitful activities for chairs and heads.

- In the area of faculty development, I have focused on conceptual frameworks, evaluation of programs, and in-depth experiences for faculty.

- The conceptual work and program evaluation will be useful to my own work in OPOD and with other units. Evaluation schemes work best when they are well conceptualized and grounded. My experience as an evaluator for the State University of Minnesota System's Bush Faculty Development Project has provided insight into what needs to be communicated. Certainly our OPOD process can be enhanced by having others understand what we do.

- Examination of the faculty development literature indicates that intensive, longer-term experiences have the biggest impact on faculty. We are on the right track with NUPROF and we can offer other high impact experiences. Certainly faculty development leaves are often another of these focused, learning experiences.

- Developing a chapter on faculty evaluation is most helpful in providing the grounding that should be useful to both faculty and administrators at IANR. Even though this chapter has been most demanding, the writing certainly organizes what is out there for me.

THE CHALLENGE

Beyond the professional and personal aspects described, I believe my experience of having taken a leave will help me be more effective in helping others consider and plan leaves. Taking a leave is both an art and a science. One is also aware that any experience with significant changes in lifestyle and new learning tests one's assumptions and beliefs. The challenge for me and for others is how to integrate those new learnings into old structures and create new frameworks without just falling into old patterns. I look forward to continuing my work in administrative and faculty development—both practice and theory. My thirst for learning needs both, which suggests the continuing association with higher education scholarship particularly through the new doctoral program in higher education in the Department of Education Administration.

MARQUETTE UNIVERSITY

REPORT ON SABBATICAL ACTIVITIES

Name: Linda Milson

Rank: Associate Professor

School: Program in Medical Technology

Duration of Sabbatical: One Semester, Fall, 1989

BRIEF SUMMARY OF ORIGINAL PLAN

One of the three major objectives of my sabbatical was to compare state-of-the-art laboratory instrumentation used in large diagnostic settings to the type of instruments found in smaller hospitals and/or physician offices and clinics. Another was to assess new technologies and instruments in anticipation of the future market, while the third objective was to update my knowledge of hematology/immunology and the utilization of flow cytometric analysis for diagnosing pathological states in these areas. Benefits of my sabbatical were anticipated to be in the areas of teaching and curriculum development and possible publication of my findings.

WHERE SABBATICAL WAS SPENT

Mayo Clinic, Rochester, MN
Marshfield Clinic, Marshfield, WI
Akron City Hospital, Akron, OH
Cook County Hospital, Chicago, IL
Sacred Heart-St. Mary's Hospital, Inc., Rhinelander, WI
Rhinelander Medical Center, Rhinelander, WI
Redwood Falls Medical Center, Redwood Falls, MN
Hartford Parkview Clinic, Ltd., Hartford, WI
Howard Young Medical Center, Woodruff, WI
Eagle River Memorial Hospital, Inc., Eagle River, WI
Eastman Kodak Company, Rochester, NY

SUMMARY OF SABBATICAL ACTIVITIES

To maximize the benefit of instrument comparison, I chose to spend time on-site (several days to two weeks/site) observing instruments in operation during peak workload demands. This also afforded me the opportunity to evaluate the amount of down-time encountered with specific instruments and to learn troubleshooting techniques. Because the greatest variety is found in instruments manufactured for chemistry and hematology analyses, I spent most of my time in these two areas of the clinical laboratories. I did observe microbiology and urinalysis instruments at institutions where these laboratory departments were automated. Due to my familiarity with instrumentation used in Milwaukee area hospitals, I selected clinical facilities in other geographic locations. Each visit was preceded by independent study preparation and followed by time to evaluate and condense my notes and read pertinent literature and suggested references.

During August and September I visited institutions in northern Wisconsin and southern Minnesota. Instrument set-up calibration along with specimen processing and work flow patterns were observed. I learned about analyzers providing throughput of 300 samples per hour, extensive monitoring of quality control and computer interfacing for patient reporting. Medical technologists shared with me their rationale for instrument selection and freely discussed customer support efforts provided by various manufacturers. Not only was instrument variation dramatically different among the laboratories, but also their managerial practices and scheduling protocols were quite unique to ensure 24-hour service at a time when certified medical technologists are in short supply.

October was spent in the diagnostic immunology laboratory at Cook County Hospital learning principles of flow cytometric technology. Using a Coulter Epic V analyzer I evaluated histograms and correlated pattern recognition with diagnoses of the leukemias, lymphomas, and Immunodeficiency syndromes (AIDS and others). While at Cook County I had the opportunity to observe and compare instruments in the hematology and chemistry laboratories.

My visits to Eastman Kodak and Akron City Hospital occurred in November. The experience at Kodak far exceeded my expectations of learning about instrument manufacturing. Their principle of dry slide technology was not new to me, but observing the entire manufacturing process from research and development to customer delivery and support led me to appreciate the quality of their laboratory products. Meeting with Dr. Margaret Smith-Lewis, senior research chemist, resulted in another unexpected benefit. She explained to me that team effort is what makes it possible for Kodak to produce quality products with superior performance and encouraged me to try experiential team-based learning in my college classroom. As a result, the emphasis in my instrumentation class this semester focuses on a team approach to troubleshooting and problem solving. Students work together in small groups to share knowledge and experiences. Feedback from them has been positive. Medical technologists with problem solving skills and experience in group dynamics will be valuable assets to clinical laboratories in tomorrow's marketplace.

In December I returned to northern Wisconsin for a visit to the large medical clinic and spent a few days at Hartford Parkview Clinic. Workload demands and testing patterns differ from those found in acute care facilities, but I found these laboratories to be highly automated only on a smaller scale. All of the instrumentation I viewed is based on principles and theory identical to those taught in my course. It is merely an application of these principles that differs with advanced technology in the most sophisticated instruments.

DEPARTURE FROM ORIGINAL PLAN

I did not delete any of the activities outlined in my original proposal but did alter the time spent at each institution. This afforded me the opportunity to expand the number of laboratories I visited providing me more data for comparison. When making the arrangements with the Eastman Kodak Company, I realized that manufacturers were not going to share proprietary information with me regarding new products, thus limiting my experience to only one company.

While in Chicago I met with the medical technology program directors and faculty at Rush University and the University of Illinois. We discussed curriculum as well as recruitment activities and lamented about the problems anticipated in health care delivery due to the shortage of qualified medical technologists.

In December I served on the University Promotion and Tenure Committee as the representative for medical technology and physical therapy. I had accepted this committee assignment in June, 1989, knowing that it would not jeopardize my sabbatical activities.

APPRAISAL OF SATISFACTION/DISSATISFACTION

I was extremely satisfied with my sabbatical and my original expectations were exceeded.

BENEFITS OF SABBATICAL

This sabbatical updated my knowledge in hematology/immunology and flow cytometric technology used in evaluation states. Being immersed in the clinical laboratory environment of acute care facilities helped me appreciate the problems management faces in providing reliable results with minimal resources. As a result of my meeting with faculty from the University of Illinois, I was asked to author a chapter in an instrumentation book scheduled for publication in late 1990. Offers for collaboration on continuing education and research were made by the staff of Cook County Hospital.

The people I met were very impressed with Marquette University for giving the faculty release time to update their knowledge. Many more institutions outside the Milwaukee area now know that the medical technology program at Marquette still graduates a relatively large number of students compared to other colleges and universities, and I have contacts at these facilities for placement of our graduates. Because of my positive interchange with the Eastman Kodak Company, Marquette University will be remembered for paving the way for other medical technology faculty to have a similar experience with their Clinical Products Division.

The benefits of the change in teaching strategy for my instrumentations course were discussed previously. Medical technologists at every institution I visited verified for me that we are using valid teaching methodologies in our program. They encouraged me to continue teaching instrumentation based on theory and principles because if a person understands these, application to state-of-the-art instrumentation is easily made.

As a result of my visit to Eastman Kodak, they donated a clinical chemistry analyzer to us. This instrument is different from many of our other "gifts" because it is a functional unit that has been calibrated and is capable of producing reliable results. With this instrument in our possession, there is a possibility that we can use it for research as well as teaching purposes.

SUGGESTIONS FOR MODIFICATIONS

The only modification that I can identify would be to schedule my next sabbatical for an entire year in order to visit more facilities.

SUPPORTING AGENCIES

Due to the fact that my sabbatical involved multiple facilities, I did not seek external funding for expenses. Additional dollars were not required for the salary of the medical technologist who carried my teaching load during the Fall semester. She was paid the exact amount of my salary reduction.

ST. NORBERT COLLEGE

REPORT ON SABBATICAL LEAVE

ROBERT H. BOYER
Department of English
Spring, 1983

During the spring semester of 1983 I gathered material for and began writing a historical fantasy novel. I was able to do so through the generous support of St. Norbert College which granted me sabbatical leave and a faculty development grant for travel. I trust that the following report of my activities during and since my sabbatical leave will justify that support. The report consists of some prefatory generalizations on sabbaticals and their residual benefits, followed by two major sections dealing with my two central activities while on sabbatical: research and travel in Spain; the writing of the novel.

I have two prefatory comments that are of some interest. First, it is important to have professional contacts outside of St. Norbert that extend beyond the conventional ones. I offer the following two examples. When I corresponded with the English Department at the University of Pennsylvania, my alma mater, I rediscovered some of the kinds of intellectual excitement generated by the larger, research oriented university. The English faculty at Penn kindly offered me the use of their facilities and a semester position as Scholar in Residence. I was unable to accept the offer, but they have suggested that I apply again. My alternate plan, the one I pursued ultimately, also brought me some important professional contact, the most important occurring while I was doing research at the University of Seville in Spain. I met and consulted with the Chair of Medieval Spanish History, Manuel Gonzalez Jimenez, who is also the Vice Chancellor of the University. He opened up a number of doors for me both literally and figuratively. Other important professional contacts I made include individuals connected with such funding organizations as the Guggenheim and Rockefeller Foundations and the National Endowment for the Humanities, as well as editors of several publishing houses. The importance of such contacts for the future of my sabbatical proposal, as well as for myself professionally, are readily apparent.

The second prefatory observation is a comparison of two fairly standard kinds of sabbaticals—those that involve a significant, albeit temporary, break from the SNC community and those that don't involve such a break. I have experienced both types. In 1974-75 I stayed in De Pere, except for monthly trips to Madison for tutorial sessions in Russian Literature with Zenia Gasiorowska. The rest of the time I read, studied, and wrote in an office on campus. Last year, I was outside the country for two months and away from the community for virtually the entire semester. In both cases I feel that I accomplished the purpose of my sabbatical leave, so that one type cannot be said to be necessarily preferable to the other. The sabbatical involving the complete break, however, had one significant advantage that I think would be the case regardless of the nature of the study. It was a more intense experience. Naturally, I spent much more time—including evenings and weekends—since I was away from family and other social contacts. More important was the more efficient use of time since it was relatively free of distraction. I cannot claim that my case would apply in every instance, but, given the circumstances of most of my colleagues, I believe it would apply in most.

If the complete-break sabbatical is a more intense experience—a total immersion rather than a splash on the head—it is, however, also a more traumatic one. The separation from the familiar, perhaps, gets one out of a rut, but it involves a wrenching tug to do so. The tug and the continued separation require significant sacrifice on the part of the faculty member, family and community. Also the re-entry process takes much longer when the break has been more complete. I was genuinely discontented for more than a semester after resuming my normal duties, frustrated that I had to put aside my writing for a time.

The reason I offer this comparison of sabbaticals based on leaving or remaining in the community is twofold. First, I know that the Personnel Committee wrestles annually with the question of which is better. Secondly, I wish to offer a suggestion. If the Personnel Committee, including the academic dean, view the total-break sabbatical as preferable, then I believe it is important that there be opportunities for those faculty who would use them to be away more often than once every eight or ten years. My point is that an intensive experience away from the community doing research or writing would not entail traumatic departures and re-entries if it were more frequent. I am suggesting—and this is in line with the new Faculty Development Program—that leaves become more common, leaves for writing, research, or faculty exchange.

The above observations have perhaps exceeded in length what are usually considered prefatory comments. They are, however, important and relate, moreover, to our sabbatical program in general. The two major activities of my particular sabbatical were the writing of a novel and research in Spain. The latter started out simply as a means to the former, but it became of at least equal if not of greater importance to my future professional development; thus I will treat it last.

I have thus far succeeded in following the time frame mapped out for my novel: spring and summer of 1983, complete the novel; fall of 1984, actively market the manuscript; time in between, revision. I completed a typed draft in July, 1983 and submitted it for editorial comment and possible publication. While I did not get an acceptance, I received an extensive critique from the senior editor at Avon, John Douglas, who invited me to resubmit after revising. I have gotten feedback also from several colleagues and am currently well into what should be the final revision. I should thus be ready to market the manuscript this fall.

More importantly, however, by writing a novel, I have better equipped myself to teach. As I stated in my proposal, "My major goal is to become more familiar with literature." In fact, the results have exceeded my expectations. I had hoped to enhance my teaching of DH 224 (Science Fiction and Fantasy), but the effects of my extended bout with writing the novel have reached out to practically every course I teach. To offer one example, I discovered how necessary keeping a daily journal is to a writer; I will use this technique in En 250 (Advanced Expository Writing). In fact, I submitted a journal entry to *Alps*, the campus literary magazine; it appeared in the spring, 1984 edition. *Alps* also published an excerpt of the novel (fall '83).

My future plans include two, and possibly three, more novels that will form a trilogy or tetralogy. Since the present as well as the projected novels are set in medieval Spain, Spanish history and language have become important in my present and future professional plans. I was amazed and embarrassed by my reading in medieval history in Spain, amazed to discover the central importance of Spain in the spread of learning form East to West; embarrassed as a medievalist that I was ignorant of facts of such importance. I can only conclude at this point that Western historians, certainly French, English, and American, have diminished the Spanish contribution to the Middle Ages and the Renaissance either through ignorance or, more often, through political biases. I intend to pursue the study of medieval Spain for its historical importance to me as a medievalist as well as for its rich background for me as a novelist.

In order to pursue these studies, I have begun the systematic study of the Spanish language. I sat in on Sn 101 and then audited Sn 102 from Dr. Buchanan this past year (1983–84), taking all tests and exams. She is writing a letter to this effect for my permanent file. This coming year I plan to take Sn 201 and 225.

One of the opportunities I hope to take advantage of in about two years time is the American-Spanish Exchange Program, administered by the Fulbright Fellowship Program. I would teach a light course load of English and American literature for eight weeks apiece at three different Spanish universities. Doing so would afford me ample opportunities and time for firsthand research in some of the marvelous medieval collections, many in illuminated manuscripts, in Spain.

My interests in Spain and in Spanish resulted in a corollary interest in Latin America, the people, culture, and history. Father Fresno has recommended that I contact an organization that is already preparing for the

500th anniversary of Columbus's discovery. They will be commissioning historical and fictional works commemorating the event.

This last possibility is so far in the future as to be hardly worth mentioning. I include it, however, primarily to further illustrate the intensive and extensive impact on me of my sabbatical in Spain. The experience has focused my previous interests in the Middle Ages, in fantasy literature, and in creative writing on the study of the Spanish language, history, and culture for their own sake and as a source of material for my creative writing.

It should be clear from the foregoing that, despite the fact that more than a year has passed since the sabbatical leave ended, this report is not late. If anything, it is a bit premature, since the results of the project are mostly yet to be. I thank those who have read this for their time and forbearance.

Respectfully submitted,
Robert Boyer
Associate professor
July, 1984

WHITMAN COLLEGE

MEMORANDUM

Date: December 20, 1989

To: David Deal, Dean of Faculty
             Whitman College

From: John Winter, Department of Geology

Subject: Sabbatical Leave Report

My sabbatical leave was spent in Copenhagen, Denmark from mid August, 1988 to March, 1989 and in Eugene, Oregon from March, 1989 to June, 1989. In Copenhagen I had an office at the Geological Museum with a working relationship there and at the Institute for Petrology across the street. During that time I finished the writing of an article: "Deformation and Mass Transfer in the Nordrestromfjord Shear Zone, Central West Greenland" by Sorensen and Winter, published in a book by Reidel this year. I also continued the analytical work on samples collected in East Greenland on an expedition in 1986. I am collaborating on this study with scientists from Copenhagen, St. John's, and Oslo. I have been analyzing the minerals in the felsic gneisses and determining the conditions of metamorphism during events that occurred 1.8 to 2.8 billion years ago along the East Greenland coast. The collaborative effort deals with the metamorphism, deformation, and timing of events during this time period. We are still at the data analysis stage of this project. A further project concerned the analysis of some very strange corundum-bearing rocks from East Greenland. Such rocks have not been described in the literature before. I have analyzed the samples and am beginning to draft a report for publication.

A major portion of my time, besides the rather laborious analysis itself, entailed the creation of a computerized data-handling routine and a program that would calculate temperatures and pressures from the mineral analyses. This project became rather large, but proved quite successful. In fact, a colleague and I expect to publish and distribute the package in the coming year. I also rewrote a large thermodynamic data base and calculating program to operate on the IBM PC which I have had a number of requests for.

In addition to the research that I conducted at Copenhagen, I taught a graduate seminar on Fluids in Metamorphic Processes. I also spent a week at the University at Oslo where I performed some analyses and assisted on computer automation of the data there. And I served as the outside examiner for the PhD committee of a student at the Institute.

In Eugene I worked at the Department of Geology at the University of Oregon. I continued work on the geothermometry/geobarometry program and analytical work. I also became familiarized with several new petrologic programs that will be of use in my research and teaching.

I spent the period from July 24–August 23 doing field work in NE Labrador. This is an extension of the Greenland work across the Davis Straight onto the North American continent. Our small party made a number of original observations that should contribute to the understanding of that rather poorly explored area.

UNIVERSITY OF RHODE ISLAND

MEMORANDUM

TO: Dean Richard Gelles
        College of Arts and Sciences

FROM: Robert Rohm
        Professor of Art

RE: SABBATICAL REPORT

DATE: September 30, 1987

I am pleased to report on a very successful sabbatical leave during the Spring term of 1987. I accomplished all of the goals as stated in my request. My extensive travels through Asia and Europe have certainly enhanced the visual vocabulary that forms the basis of my art-making process.

I spent the month of February traveling through India, March in Thailand and Burma, April in Indonesia, May in Japan, and June, July and August in Europe and Africa (Kenya). During these travels I made extensive notes and notational drawings as well as taking close to 2,000 35mm color slides. These visual materials are the "core" from which I will work. A "sabbatical" exhibition is scheduled to open February 22, 1988, in the Main Gallery of the Fine Arts Center. In this exhibition, I will present new work which has been developed and made since the sabbatical semester. In April of 1988, I will have a solo exhibition of new work at the O.K. Harris Gallery in New York City.

In his book, *The Quality of Mercy*, William Shawcross writes: "The flood of instant information in the world today—at least in the Western industrialized world—sometimes seems not to further, but to retard education; not to excite, but to dampen curiosity; not to enlighten, but merely to dismay." Archibald MacLeish once noted, "We are deluged with facts but we have lost or are losing our human ability to feel them. We all know with the head now, by the facts, by the abstractions." MacLeish believed that the endless accumulation of mere facts about the world was no way for men to master their experience of "this darkling earth."

Having physically experienced in their cultural milieu some of the monuments, religious sites, vernacular architecture and market places of twelve countries around the world, I return to the university and my studio with renewed spirit and feeling. It will serve my students and my art-making well.

Index